OXFORD HISTORICAL MONOGRAPHS

Editors

N. GIBBS   R. W. SOUTHERN   R. B. WERNHAM

NOTE

Oxford Historical Monographs will consist of books which would formerly have been published in the Oxford Historical Series. As with the previous series, they will be carefully selected studies which have been submitted, or are based upon theses submitted, for higher degrees in this University. The works listed below are those still in print in the Oxford Historical Series.

The Medieval Administration of the Channel Islands, 1199–1399.
By J. H. LE PATOUREL. 1937.

The Corporation of Leicester, 1689–1836. By R. W. GREAVES. 1939.

Durham Jurisdictional Peculiars. By FRANK BARLOW. 1950.

English Monasteries and their Patrons in the Thirteenth Century.
By SUSAN WOOD. 1955.

The Estates of the Percy Family, 1416–1537. By J. M. W. BEAN. 1958.

The Radical Duke. Career and Correspondence of Charles Lennox, third Duke of Richmond. By ALISON GILBERT OLSON. 1961.

The Norman Monasteries and their English Possessions.
By DONALD MATTHEW. 1962.

Edward III and the Scots. The Formative Years of a Military Career, 1327–1335. By RANALD NICHOLSON. 1965.

A Medieval Oxfordshire Village: Cuxham: 1240 to 1400.
By P. D. A. HARVEY. 1965.

Cardinal Bainbridge in the Court of Rome 1509–14.
By D. S. CHAMBERS. 1965.

The Later Lollards 1414–1520. By JOHN A. F. THOMSON. 1965.

The Impeachment of Warren Hastings. By P. J. MARSHALL. 1965.

The Passing of the Irish Act of Union. By G. C. BOLTON 1966.

THE ORIGINS OF
MILITARY POWER
IN SPAIN
1800–1854

BY

E. CHRISTIANSEN

OXFORD UNIVERSITY PRESS

1967

Oxford University Press, Ely House, London W.1

GLASGOW NEW YORK TORONTO MELBOURNE WELLINGTON
CAPE TOWN SALISBURY IBADAN NAIROBI LUSAKA ADDIS ABABA
BOMBAY CALCUTTA MADRAS KARACHI LAHORE DACCA
KUALA LUMPUR HONG KONG TOKYO

PRINTED IN GREAT BRITAIN

TO PAMELA

PREFACE

THIS sesquipedal essay contains neither the military history of Spain nor the social history of the Spanish army; it merely covers the political activities of the army in the period before 1854 and is meant as an introduction to Professor S. Payne's forthcoming account of more recent military politics. The want of published information on this subject, either in English or Spanish, is my justification for writing it.

I should like to thank Mr. A. R. Carr, my tutor and supervisor, whose advice and encouragement enabled me to undertake this work, and the Warden and Fellows of New College for giving me the Stone-Platt studentship, which allowed me to complete it. Through the offices of the Marquess of Santa Cruz I received the courteous assistance of Major Arias in the Servicio Histórico Militar of Madrid, and the hospitality of the Consejo Superior de Investigaciones Científicas. Lord Clarendon has given me his kind permission to include extracts from his papers in the Bodleian Library, and I am indebted to the Librarian of All Souls for access to the Vaughan collection. Professor N. H. Gibbs has helped me greatly in preparing this book for publication.

CONTENTS

LIST OF ABBREVIATIONS

NOTE: the place of publication for Spanish books is always Madrid unless otherwise stated; for English books, London, and for French, Paris.

Archivo Nacional	Papers in the Sección de Estado of the Archivo Nacional (Madrid) relating to army estimates under Ferdinand VII; in particular Legajo 217.46.
BAE	Biblioteca de Autores Españoles.
Clarendon MSS.	The Clarendon Papers on loan to the Bodleian Library, Oxford, for Lord Clarendon's correspondence, etc., from 1833 to 1839.
Clonard MSS.	The Colección del Conde de Clonard at the library of the Servicio Histórico Militar in Madrid; this contains correspondence between the Count and his friends relating to war and politics from 1835 to 1840, and includes pamphlets and other documents connected with military history.
Decretos Fern. VII	*Decretos del Rey Nuestro Señor Don Fernando VII*, 18 vols. (edited successively by F. M. de Balmaseda and S. M. de Nieva, 1818–34).
Diario, Congreso Procuradores Senado	
F.O.	Foreign Office records in the Public Record Office, consisting of Ambassadors' Reports in the series F.O. 72 (vols. 367 to 847). These provide a commentary on Spanish affairs as well as miscellaneous information about the army and finances.
S.H.M.	Servicio Histórico Militar.
Vaughan MSS.	The Spanish sections of the Vaughan Papers in the library of All Souls, Oxford, which provide miscellaneous and diplomatic correspondence for 1808 to 1824.

MONEY VALUES *c.* 1840

$8\frac{1}{2}$ *cuartos* (copper) = 1 *real* (silver)

20 *reales* = 1 *duro* (silver)

16 *duros* = 1 *onza* (gold)

A *real* was worth about $2\frac{1}{2}d.$, a *duro* about 4*s.* 2*d.*, an *onza* about 3 guineas. A hundred *reales* made one pound sterling

Military map of Spain 1800-1854

- - - - - Boundaries of the Captaincies-General known as 'Military Districts' from 1821 to 1823 and from 1841.

◉ Headquarters of the Captains General, or in the case of Navarre of the Viceroy. These and other named places are also capitals of the new provinces established in 1833, and all have Military Governors presiding over 'Commandancies' as well as Civil Governors or 'Jefes Políticos'.

■ Fortresses, forts, and villages classified as 'Plazas', all constituting military commands.

Miles
0   50   100   150   200

GALICIA
CORUNNA
Lugo
Pontevedra
Orense
Oviedo

LEON
LEON
Zamora
Salamanca

OLD CASTILE
BASQUE PROV.
Bilbao
Tolosa
VITTORIA
Logroño
BURGOS
Palencia
Valladolid
Soria
Segovia
Avila

NAVARRE
PAMPLONA

ARAGON
Huesca
SARAGOSSA
Teruel

CATALONIA
Gerona
BARCELONA
Lerida
Tarragona

VALENCIA
Castellon
VALENCIA
Alicante

NEW CASTILE
Guadalajara
MADRID
Cuenca
Toledo
Ciudad Real

MURCIA
Albacete
MURCIA

ESTREMADURA
Caceres
BADAJOZ

ANDALUSIA
Cordova
SEVILLE
Jaen
Granada
Malaga
Almeria
Huelva
Cadiz
(Ceuta)

BALEARIC ISLES
PALMA

I

THE EMERGENCE OF THE POLITICAL ARMY

1800–1832

DURING the present and the last centuries, the Spanish army has often made decisions which in other countries have been left to cabinets, parliaments, and popular revolutions. While military intervention in politics has taken many shapes, from the general seeking office in a civilian régime, to the emergency dictatorship, the praetorian palace-coup, and the strike of officers, in Spain the ambitious soldier has tended to adopt an idiosyncratic expedient, the *pronunciamiento*, which may involve all these things and follow a not unvarying but formalized procedure. There, he has been able to appeal from established authority to military insurrection as from one established institution to another, and the predominance of one has never extinguished the other.

The Golden Age of the *pronunciamientos*, 1814 to 1874, was also the period of social, political, and economic revolution which converted an imperial sea power and its hierarchical society into an insignificant parliamentary state run by an *élite* of politicians, capitalists, and landowners who accepted the values of contemporary Europe and had excluded from power all who did not. The influence of the army was therefore a subtle element, remarkable for its ability to harmonize with other forces in society, and not to be explained in terms of social and political 'backwardness'. It existed as part of the transition from a closed to a more open society, and reflected the various reactions which this provoked; thus the attitudes of the various groups of officers who decided what was known as the *opinion of the army* were never consistently radical or conservative, but altered according to the role of their profession in contemporary events. This versatility is evidence of the army's internal tensions, which have been too little explored; for in these, as well as in the changing relationship between the military and civilian worlds, lie the motives that impelled the soldiers to assume the political initiative which had not been theirs in the eighteenth century, and then construct a political system which included a formal appeal to arms.

I. THE OLD ARMY

The eighteenth-century monarchs, besides encouraging the revival of Spain as a naval power, had tried to keep up a respectable land force, and under Charles IV (1789–1808) this consisted of about 50,000 men: a corps of Guards regiments supported by infantry and cavalry of the line, and separate units of artillery and sappers. In wartime the regulars could be reinforced by about 30,000 militiamen, and along the coasts they were backed by a species of home guard called the Urban Militia. (The Basque provinces, Navarre, and Catalonia were exempt from normal military obligations and provided their own volunteer regiments of a more or less irregular kind.) From the peninsular army detachments were made available for overseas service as required; normally the Guards stayed at Madrid and the Royal residences, and the line were deployed in separate provincial 'armies' of which the regiments relieved each other every three years, moving round the kingdom in an anti-clockwise circuit. The Bourbons had built up this system on the French and Prussian models, with the assistance of imported military experts such as General O'Reilly; but it had features that were peculiar.

For example, there were fewer mercenaries—a seventh of the Spanish to a quarter of the pre-revolutionary French army were foreigners—since, although the Irish and Swiss were the best soldiers, they were too expensive and unpopular to be maintained by the impecunious government of Charles IV. Also there were comparatively few volunteers, perhaps less than half the rank and file, and the native regiments had to be recruited by conscription, which in France was used only for the militia; many regulars, therefore, had homes other than the regiment. And since in Spain the nobility was too diffuse and divided a class to imitate the *esprit de corps* of the French *noblesse*, the *hidalgos* were unable to monopolize the officers' commissions. About a third of these went to promoted rankers or N.C.O.s, even if they seldom rose above field rank; only the Guards, the artillery, and certain cavalry regiments were able to exclude commoners from their vacant places for ensigns, and thus, within the conventions of a somewhat static society, the army offered a career open to talent, or at least to longevity. Obstacles of privilege existed, as elsewhere under the *ancien régime*; promotion often went by influence at Court, the Guards were kept above the line by humiliating distinctions, and the *jeunesse dorée* of Madrid were given the rewards for which antiquated and unfashionable lieutenants had soldiered in vain;[1] but the situation was not explosive.

The great defect was inefficiency. Thanks to the increasing emptiness of the Treasury and the vested interests of the bureaucrats and generals at the War Office, there was a want of attention to every detail unconnected with the flow of patronage. Nothing was uniform,[2] training was neglected in the interests of economy, the pay of all but the highest ranks was insufficient, the condition of the men was deplorable, and the whole cost was enormous.[3] In common with the other institutions of old Spain, the army attracted the disparaging criticism of those enlightened intellectuals who hoped, with the assistance of the King, to modernize society. They disliked its costing so much, doing so little, and offering so many occasions of unjust influence to the Court nobility. The political economist Cabarrús proposed in the nineties that the regular soldiers should be employed in digging canals, and leave the fighting to militiamen;[4] and

---

[1] In 1808 the average age of a lieutenant was 50, and most guardees were commissioned at 16 (see J. Moya and C. Rey Joly: *El ejército y la marina en las Cortes de Cádiz* (Cadiz, 1912), 12–28). Yet, before 1808, the only vocal military malcontents were privileged guardees and gunners.

[2] Moya and Rey, op. cit. 37: there were three current systems of drill and no annual manœuvres.

[3] In 1799 half the total expenditure of the State and three times the cost of the navy (see H. Baumgarten, *Geschichte Spaniens*, 3 vols. (Leipzig, 1865), i. 111). In 1778 the army was estimated to have cost 42 per cent. of the whole expenditure: public works accounted for only 2 per cent.

[4] *Cartas* (BAE, 1870), 566, 567. In 1786, Townsend found 2,000 infantrymen navvying on the Canal of Aragon (*A Journey through Spain in the Years 1786 and 1787*, 3 vols. (1792), i. 215).

Jovellanos, in his pamphlet *Pan y Toros*, made a joke of the 'body of general officers numerous enough to command all the armies of the world', and the 'multitude of regiments which although deficient in men are skilled in the military fatigues of curling their hair, bleaching their uniform, regulating their paces to the tune of a country dance, expending powder in salutes in the meadows, and oppressing their fellow citizens'. And the system by which this soldiery was lodged and fed gave rise to general resentment. Since 1719 every unprivileged householder had been obliged to pay taxes[1] and offer transport and accommodation for the convenience of regiments on the march; and the job of collecting other taxes was sometimes delegated to army paymasters, who were authorized to pay their men out of sums owed to the Treasury by the municipalities: 'and should there be any demur on the part of any of the inhabitants, which often happens, the soldiers live at full quarters on his house and he is besides obliged to pay to each soldier a certain sum daily, sometimes more, sometimes less, until he has paid his entire contribution'.[2]

But the 'blood-tax' by which the army was recruited was the most vexatious, for in the *quinta* and the *leva* the needs of the State conflicted most painfully with the interests of the people.

Periodically the King would order a general levy, for which municipalities were empowered to take up the idle, the vagrant, the mendicant, and the morally suspect of every category, imprison them, measure them, and draft the fit men directly into the army.[3] The licence to victimize which was thus conceded to the leaders of village life no doubt accounts for the relative popularity of this method, but it was unproductive and had to be supplemented by a wider form

---

[1] The *contribuciones de alojamientos, bagajes, paja y utensilios*, originally levied as compensation for the householders who had supported the troops, later became a regular imposition. In the period 1830 to 1840 it produced about 40 million *reales* a year: see P. Pita Pizarro: *Examen Económico, Histórico-Crítico de la Hacienda* (1840), 208.

[2] F.O., Wellesley to Castlereagh, 7 Apr. 1815. The other expenses of the army were met by the customs, the poll tax, and the *frutos civiles*, a levy on food and wine producers according to the average price of their products.

[3] *Instruccion que ha de observarse en la ejecucion de la leva general*, issued by the Audience of Catalonia in 1828.

of conscription in which the State chose the recruits. This was the *quinta* (introduced from France in 1704, and regulated by the Ordinance of 1800), by which a fixed number of single laymen, not of noble birth, but over 16 years old and 4 ft. 10½ in. high—with certain exceptions—were chosen by lot for eight years' service. The King would decree that so many be raised from each province; the Provincial Deputations would apportion quotas to each municipality; these would then make out the *alistamiento* (enrolment) of liable youths, by hearing pleas for exemption, and from this roll the quota would be chosen in the presence of the *alcalde* (mayor) and an army officer. The *sorteo* (draw) was the climax—a dramatic ceremony in front of the town hall, in which children drew out names and lots from two urns and a herald announced each combination to the crowd. The eyewitness of such a draw in the 1820s recalled the 'distress, the sorrow, or the joy, which was depicted on the faces of the people, or broke out in shouts, tears or transports of delight. In that sea of emotions I heard my brother's name amid the hubbub, but I could not hear the number, until a person who stood near me said *soldier*. My blood froze. . . .'[1]

Well-to-do families could still keep their sons out of the army by purchasing a volunteer from a substitution-agency, which kept a fund of broken and desperate men for the purpose, but the price was high, and if the *re-emplazo* (substitute) deserted, the original *quinto* was re-enlisted.[2] The exemptions were capricious—novices, but not choristers or sacristans; graduates, but not students; town councillors over 25, but not under; one apothecary per town, but not village apothecaries; postillions, but not barber-surgeons; married men, but not widowers with children.[3] And to add unfairness to illogicality, the Provincial Deputation might be subject to the influence of deputies from certain towns, who would ensure that their native places had to send smaller quotas than the rest; or the municipality might flood their roll with undesirables, if they could not tamper with the *sorteo*.

[1] *Revista del Ateneo Militar*, i. (1872), 435: the author, Colonel Casamayor, was an advocate of voluntary enlistment.

[2] *Diario*, Senado, 1850, ii. 213: Valgornera's speech. A substitute cost 3,000–6,000 *reales* by then.

[3] *Ordenanza* of 1800, amended 1819 (*Decretos Fern. VII*, vi. 50 and x. 115).

However, what made the *quinta* a cause of popular commotion were not such defects as these, but the whole imposition of military service on an agricultural existence, so that a man's best years had to be spent in unskilled idleness with the risk of being drafted on an overseas service that was practically a death sentence. Eighteenth-century governments therefore raised few *quintas*, and in 1802 Godoy attempted to introduce the old French system of reinforcing the regulars with drafts from the militia; but with the war of 1808–14, and the colonial campaigns of 1815–24, the need for men became too pressing to be met in any other way. Catalonia was allowed to compound for its quota of recruits by enlisting volunteers out of a charge on the rates, and the Basques contributed no *quintas*, for they were liable to serve in their own army of *tercios*; but other exemptions were diminished, and by 1833 the Navarrese were being recruited, under protest, and *hidalgos* were having to pay money for their exemptions.

So the army was neither loved nor efficient; but the mechanism existed by which its defects could be remedied. While in England supreme military command was shared among a confusing number of authorities, the unitary tradition of the Spanish monarchy ensured that its forces should be supervised by a meticulously graded bureaucracy, dependent in all its parts on the King's generalissimo, Manuel Godoy; and if, in practice, the military reforms[1] by which he hoped to be remembered nearly all miscarried, so that the army of 1808 was not an impressive one to foreign observers, the fault lies less with the system than with the generals who ran it. There were far more than was necessary, but all were liable to be employed, since there was no retired list, and about half actually were. This congestion resulted in the end from the smallness of the junior officer's pay and the practice of making mass promotions at times of crisis or public rejoicing: the favourites of the War Office could hardly be fobbed off with subalterns' brevets, and had therefore to be accommodated with regimental commands, from which the existing colonels had to be promoted; they were thus kicked upstairs for the convenience of their successors.[2]

---

[1] See *Cuenta dada de su vida política*, 6 vols. (1836–42), iii.
[2] See S. Miñano y Bedoya, *Cartas* (BAE. ii, 1870), 613, for a sketch of the courtier-

It was not therefore surprising that the system appeared by the end of the century to be falling into decay. While the prizes of a military career were shared between aged administrators and infantine guardees, the fortresses of the coast and the colonies enclosed detachments of 'dirty melancholy dwarfs' in a routine of verminous lethargy which the efforts of a few capable generals at Madrid were unable to dissipate. After 1795, when Godoy withdrew from the war with revolutionary France, no money could be found for the reforms which this adventure had shown to be necessary, and there was no future for an inferior and antiquated army in the field of Napoleonic warfare; nevertheless Godoy began to pursue a policy of furtive aggrandizement which was bound to involve him in conflict either with England or France. By invading Portugal in 1801 he adopted an attitude of military ostentation which only emphasized the inadequacy of his resources; but if his confidence was vain, it was shared by many of his subordinates, whose morale was by no means as deficient as their training and equipment. The position of the officer in society was a respectable one, whatever the state of the men, and there was no lack of aspirants for the epaulette; in fact, writers such as Alcalá Galiano, who remembered the old régime, later maintained that under it the military enjoyed a prestige which was never to be regained.[1]

This paradoxical situation is explained by a fact which historians have been apt to overlook: that the role of the soldier in eighteenth-century Spain was as important in administration as it later became in politics. To assume that the social importance of the military was a consequence of their active intervention in public affairs after 1808 is to forget how the old monarchy had been run. For officers of the army —the captains-general[2] of provinces, and the Viceroy of Navarre—had governed the country in peace as in war from

general, promoted to captain at the age of eight. The sons of grandees were entitled to a captaincy at birth.

Charles III began the accumulation of generals by creating over 30 brigadiers at once in 1779 to get rid of peacetime colonels in preparation for war with England. In 1788 a quarter of the generals were titled nobles, fifty years later only 7 per cent.

[1] A. Alcalá Galiano, *Memorias*, i, gives a good account of a cadet's life *c*. 1800.

[2] Captains-general of provinces were always major- or lieutenant-generals holding the title as an appointment, and must not be confused with 'Captains-General of the Army' who held it as a rank equivalent to our field-marshal.

the thirteen local capitals through a network of military governors and King's lieutenants who were responsible for the smaller towns. All civilian officials—except in fiscal matters the Intendant—were subordinate to the captain-general, and the provincial high courts known as Audiences, which had originally served as a kind of constitutional check to this authority, had all, by 1805, accepted him as president. In emergency the military governors could declare a 'state of siege' and take over all the powers of the civil; after 1784 they were given private jurisdiction over bandits, and in the following century this was to be expanded into powers over all political suspects. As early as 1718 a French observer had noted that while the provincial governors of France concerned themselves with police and military duties alone, the captains-general of Spain 'se mêlent de ces deux choses, et de l'administration de la justice contentieuse, ce qui leur donne une puissance incomparablement plus grande . . . on peut dire qu'ils exercent presque toute l'autorité Royale'.[1]

This was no less true in a prospering and self-confident city such as Barcelona than in the obscurer garrison towns of the interior. There, civic affairs were administered by a board of self-perpetuating aldermen and elected deputies, but this was answerable to plenary sessions of the civil and criminal sections of the Audience, and these could only be called by the Captain-General of Catalonia. When the rule of subordination was broken the guns of the fortress of Monjuich could enforce his authority; but this was seldom necessary.[2] A general such as the Marqués de Mina could govern the principality 'more like an independent sovereign than like a subject invested with a delegated authority'.[3] On his own initiative he modernized the harbour, laid out the promenade, drained the streets, encouraged industries, and built the village of Barceloneta; it was part of his duties to cope with unemployment, bread prices, and flooding as well as public order and local defence. Elsewhere, the picture was similar: captains-general were the chief managers of the improvements by which the Bourbon régime was distinguished,

---

[1] Vayrac, État présent de l'Espagne (1718), iii. 291.
[2] Townsend, A Journey through Spain, i. 128–30.
[3] H. Swinburne, Travels through Spain, in the Years 1775 and 1776 (1779), 17.

and it was their officers and men who levelled and constructed the new roads and canals, who enforced quarantine
and the payment of taxes, who expelled the Jesuits (1767),
and harried the gipsies (1784).[1] The soldier-administrator
thus occupied in fact as well as in form the leading position
in provincial society, and his privileges, coveted by every
officer, reflected glory on the profession as a whole.

Nor was the self-consciousness of the military class something peculiar to the nineteenth century, since both officers
and men had long enjoyed a privileged status (the *fuero militar*) comparable to that of the nobility and clergy. This en-
tailed permanent military courts, to which, in 1793, Charles
IV finally granted 'exclusive and absolute jurisdiction over
all criminal and civil cases in which members of my army are
cited . . . excepting only entail cases . . . and the partition of
inheritances', thus, as Bentham later observed, 'making
military men, in so far as it shall please them to come into
conflict with non-military men, judges in their own cause'.[2]
If this was not much advantage to the private, it was a
valuable privilege for the officer, who was also, with his wife,
children, and servants, exempt by virtue of the *fuero* from
the police powers of *alcaldes*, the performance of onerous
civic duties, and the payment of *bagajes* and *alojamientos*.[3] As
well as his own law, he had his own lawyers and his own law-
book—the *Ordenanzas Reales*[4]—a combined drill-manual
and Queen's Regulations which was to win the admiration of
the Duke of Wellington and provide texts both for disciplinarians and mutineers.

These, therefore, were the foundations of a military interest
which under Charles III had been protected at court by the
faction of the Count of Aranda against the lawyers and

---

[1] See G. Desdevizes du Dézert, *L'Espagne de l'ancien régime*, ii. 133–9; and
J. Mercader, *Els Capitans Generals* (Barcelona, 1957).

[2] J. Bentham, *Works* (Edinburgh, 1843), viii. 528, in *Letter to Count Toreno on
the proposed penal code*.

[3] See *Ordenanzas*, viii, *passim*: the *fuero* was maintained by a corporation of military lawyers and judges, and was so widely claimed that the census of 1787 put the
number of *aforados* at 77,884, that is, twice the size of the effective army. The most
thorough account of this system in the nineteenth century is to be found in J.
Vicente y Caravantes, *Tratado de los procedimientos en los juzgados militares* (1853).

[4] First published as a canon in 1768, after preparations begun in 1749. The
edition used here is A. Vallecillo's, 3 vols. (1850–2).

bureaucrats who were inclined to look on it with disfavour. When Floridablanca attempted to get the highest civilian functionaries awarded the same salutes as captains-general (1788), he aroused such a bombardment of lampoons and protest that he was almost compelled to resign;[1] and five years later, under the lifeguardsman Godoy, the State was subjected to the rule of a would-be Caesar. Thus by 1808 a façade of militarism had already been erected, but on an infrastructure of incompetence and dereliction that was ill adapted to meet the challenge of actual warfare.

2. THE WAR OF INDEPENDENCE AND THE POST-WAR ARMY, 1808–1820

In 1806 Godoy had let Napoleon confiscate the best troops in his army for service abroad, and among those who remained to participate in running the government there were few who could preserve their authority in any situation where correct conduct—according to the *Ordenanzas* —was not enough. Such a situation was precipitated by the events of 1808, when the Emperor decided to annex the monarchy of Spain and secure the resources of central and southern America. Charles IV and his son Ferdinand were persuaded to abdicate after admitting an occupying force to the capital, and the crown was handed to Joseph Bonaparte.

Ostensibly, the officer owed allegiance to the Crown, not the country, and the facility of this transfer invited his acquiescence. The popular risings that broke out against the French assumed so closely the lineaments of mob-violence— matters of police—that the urge to suppress them was felt by all in authority; yet there were few who were not aware that to do so was to surrender national independence and self-respect.

Therefore, during the Madrid rising of 2 May, the garrison remained inert or gave that assistance to the French authorities for which Murat publicly thanked them, and the artillery officers who refused to hand over their guns to the

[1] See A. Ferrer del Río, *Historia del reinado de Carlos III de España*, 4 vols. (1856), 228–44.

occupying forces did so on the pretext that the order in question had not come through the proper channel.[1] The generals who were summoned to confer with the usurper at Bayonne obeyed, and on 8 July the Duke del Parque congratulated him on their behalf. Joseph replied: 'You may assure in my name all those who have served the state under my predecessors that they will continue to enjoy their pensions, titles, and emoluments', or, as he put it to his brother three days later: 'Toutes les troupes espagnoles se réunissent à ceux qui les payent.'[2] The captains-general and governors, most of them nominees of Godoy (and thus unpopular), succumbed to a kind of moral paralysis in the face of provincial tumults.[3] They appealed for tranquillity and were ignored, but neither would, nor could, use the army against the mobs—yet none declared openly for Ferdinand until compelled to. They might be Francophobes, but like Cuesta, Captain-General of Old Castille, they were 'accustomed to blind obedience, and saw with disgust that the populace were venturing to deliberate on matters which, in their opinion, were not their concern'.[4] In the serving armies, the Marquess of Ayerbe confessed, 'the privates deserted [from Joseph] . . . but the officers who imitated them were few and far between'.[5] It was the men, and groups of junior officers, particularly gunners, in liaison with civilian *meneurs*, who made the decisions which brought the army over to the national cause. This was emphasized by the collaborationist *Madrid Gazette*: 'A few individuals of the lowest rank abandon themselves to unbridled licence on religious or political pretexts. . . . All those who compose the upper classes will never forget that their interests are inseparable from those of authority.' But an army without privates was no use to anyone, and by

---

[1] Galiano, *Memorias*, i. 169–71, also M. Artola, *Orígines de la España contemporánea*, i. 123.

[2] *Gaceta de Madrid*, 12 July 1808: and Du Casse, *Mémoires et correspondance politique et militaire du Roi Joseph*, 10 vols. (1854), iv. 340.

[3] Toreno's *Historia del levantamiento, guerra y revolucion de España* (BAE. lxiv, 1953), 58–78, gives the most accessible account of their conduct: the Prussian Schepeler describes them as 'ohne Hülfsmittel des Geistes in solcher Epoche' (*Geschichte der Revolution Spaniens*, 2 vols. (Berlin, 1826–7), i. 77).

[4] Toreno, op. cit. 63.

[5] *Memorias del Marques de Ayerbe sobre la estancia de Fernando VII en Valencay y el principio de la guerra de la Independencia* (BAE. xcvii,), i. 241.

the end of July King Joseph found he had no officers either
—'moins cinq ou six personnes'.[1]

The old system of government was thus exposed as too in-
flexible to provide leadership in an emergency; but the army
was not destroyed by the hesitations of its generals, because
the patriots needed an army where they could do without a
bureaucracy. A few officers were murdered for their
imagined treason to the cause, but the rest, even if they had
their minds made up for them, emerged with their authority
unchallenged, even enhanced. When the sapper regiment at
Alcalá decided to join the rebels of Valencia they marched
from their Colonel's house to the town gates *en bloc*, the
officers mingled with the men, the orders given by a senior
sergeant: once outside, they formed up in the usual way and
marched on as if the system of officer control had been re-
juvenated by a moment of Antaean solidarity.[2] This was the
military equivalent of the popular election of juntas and
governors, and by it the 'spirit of the *Ordenanzas*' was preserved despite the fact that the army had made a political
decision opposed to that spirit. In theory the soldiers had
simply renewed the military oath which they had sworn to
Ferdinand VII in March: in practice they 'pronounced'[3] for
the pseudo-democratic federation of provincial juntas which
had been erected against the unitary monarchy at Madrid,
and were carried to the head of the movement.

There was a brief honeymoon between the civilian insurgents and the generals, but the disasters of 1809–10 produced a reaction, and since the *levantamiento* was a movement
of decentralization it was not long before conflicts arose between civil and military authorities who both claimed
autonomous powers as representatives of the absent monarch.
Castaños was provoked into shouting at the Seville junta
that he was General of Spain, not of Seville, and in return

---

[1] *Mémoires*, iv. 393: the *afrancesados*—collaborators—never became a problem
for the army as for the civil service, for despite his efforts to raise Spanish regiments
he was accompanied back to France in 1813 by only 830 military men, as compared
with 2,252 civilians (*Cien años en la vida del ejército español* (1956), 163).

[2] Ayerbe, *Memorias*, 245.

[3] Hence *pronunciamiento*—the act of making an overt or implicit declaration,
with the assistance of troops, civilians, or both against the government or its policy.
Toreno uses the word only of General Castaños' decision to support the Seville junta.

Seville refused to supply him when he reached Madrid.[1] In Old Castille and Leon, General Cuesta organized 'une sorte de proconsulat militaire' through the various juntas which he controlled, and repudiated the authority of the old Royal council and the new Central Junta alike.[2] In Aragon the 'whole administration civil and military . . . rested with General Palafox—the only Junta in the place consisted of officers appointed by himself',[3] but in the Asturias relations between the junta and their General, the Count of La Romana, became so inharmonious that in May 1809 he sent fifty grenadiers to secure his share of the English subsidy and dissolved the session.[4]

In answer to these encroachments the juntas put on the uniforms of generals and surrounded themselves with military pomp, distributing commissions and promotions by the hundred; and the Central Junta, set up in September 1808 as a provisional national government, went so far as to send representatives as 'ginger-men' to the serving armies[5] and dismiss their generals for incompetence and political unreliability.

Thus, while in 1808 Castaños admitted that if he had opposed the juntas, 'he would be disobeyed by the army and by his own Division', two years later Ayerbe could write that the Central Junta 'desire neither the return of the King, nor to expel the French from Spain . . . because in the first place their power would be ended, and in the second they fear that the General who achieves this Glory will remove it from them'.[6] They certainly took care not to appoint a supreme

---

[1] C. Oman, *A History of the Peninsular War* (Oxford, 1902), i. 346.

[2] Desdevizes du Dézert: 'Le conseil de Castille en 1808' in *Revue Hispanique*, xvii (1907), 261.   [3] Vaughan MSS.: Tour in Spain, i. 258.

[4] *Cartas de Jovellanos y Lord Vassall Holland sobre la Guerra de Independencia (1808–1811)*, ed. J. Somoza Garcia-Sala, 169–74. Jovellanos found the news ominous, but Romana was acting almost in self-defence: in Feb. 1810, at Ferrol, General Vargas was murdered with a carpenter's compass for his inability to pay his men.

[5] Notably Tomas de Veri, to the army of Catalonia, who urged General Reding on to his defeat and death at Valls in Feb. 1809: and Francisco de Palafox, to the headquarters of Castaños, whom he got removed from command of the Army of the Centre in Dec. 1808.

[6] *Memorias*, 259. The Central Junta included three serving officers (Brigadier J. Palafox, Generals the Marquess of Campo Sagrado and the Count of La Romana), but was dominated by civilian bureaucrats.

commander, and the want of one contributed to the military collapse that reduced the area controlled by the patriots to the walls of Cadiz.

This situation provoked a public protest[1] by La Romana (December 1809) in which he demanded a more vigorous executive power and a Cortes to represent the nation. He was careful to state that only because he was a member of the Central Junta himself did he presume to challenge its authority, but it was clear that only because of his prestige as a general was the manifesto effective: administrative responsibility under the old system had developed into political initiative under the new.

The *Centralistas* were superseded by an 'executive commission' and a regency dominated by the conservative General Castaños (January 1810). The conduct of the war was resigned to the very old-fashioned War Minister Eguía and an attempt was made to subordinate the provincial juntas to the captains-general,[2] but the authoritarian trend was checked by the assembly of the Cortes which, although including sixty-six military and naval officers (of whom fifteen were generals and fifteen colonels),[3] showed from the first a determination to remove the government from the hands of ambitious soldiers—especially since the administration of the regency had produced neither victories nor money.

The opponents of military power were now able to build their objections into the framework of constitutional and social reform on which the '*Liberales*' took their stand, and the conflict between soldiers and lawyers entered a new phase. The reformers wanted to turn the army out of administration and put an end to its peculiar relationship with the Crown by making it the instrument of the sovereign—the nation represented in Cortes—thus reducing at the same time the chances of a military dictatorship and of a restored Royal absolutism. In return they offered a New Model Army and a military profession enhanced with civic rights; but since, in the event, the Cortes could provide neither the men nor the money which were needed first, the exchange was hardly a fair one.

---

[1] See R. Southey, *History of the Peninsular War*, 3 vols. (1823–32), ii. 492–7, for the best account.

[2] M. Artola, *Orígines*, i. 373.   [3] Moya and Rey, *el Ejército y la marina*, 41.

For example, the Asturian *juntero* Alvaro Flórez Estrada presented schemes of politico-military reform[1] both to the Central Junta and to the Cortes in which his concern that the powers of the executive should be strictly limited led him to dismiss the accepted military values as subversive; he insisted at first that King, Cortes, and provincial juntas should each be provided with their own armies in order to maintain an internal balance of power—the soldiers to drill on feast-days and at other times be employed as factory hands by the State. He later abandoned this plan, and when the Cortes appointed a committee of officers to prepare a new set of military laws—the *Constitución militar*—he suggested that the King be left in the position of commander-in-chief for the time being: but his designs were to be held in check by an overwhelming citizen militia, and the conduct of regular officers guided by standing orders against un-civic activities. They must never 'act against the people' and their men must disobey them if they did, on pain of four years' suspension from the army;[2] they were no longer to be 'vile automata', oppressors of the nation, the pawns of ambitious generals; 'blind obedience' and absolutism were to be destroyed together as mutually sustained abuses; the chain of command to be less important than the national will, and discipline to be reconciled with liberty.

He was echoed by the Liberal orator Arguelles in Cortes, who conceded that 'the soldier cannot and must not examine the objectives of his commander, lest he destroy the basis of subordination', but 'he must not ignore the Justice of the cause he defends; on the contrary, he would then be a vile mercenary, whom ambitious men would use for their sinister ends',[3] and on the eve of the Restoration a radical pamphlet insisted that if the King acted against the Constitution the soldier's duty lay with the people, not with the Crown: 'no tenemos dueño ni señor', a private is made to affirm, 'somos soldados nacionales'.[4]

[1] *Constitución para la nación española. Presentada a S.M. la Junta Suprema Gubernativa de España è Indias en 1 de noviembre de 1809* (Birmingham, 1810), and *Constitución política de la nación española por lo tocante à la parte militar* (Cadiz, 1813).

[2] *Constitución . . . militar*, 17–25. This was intended as a punishment at a time when men were shooting off their fingers rather than begin serving.

[3] Gómez de Arteche y Moro, *Guerra de la Independencia*, xi. (1899), 33.

[4] *Mi Asistente y yo*, published in Catalonia in 1814 and in Cadiz in 1822.

Such thinking, hatched behind the walls of Cadiz while the territory won back from the French was being surrendered to the dictatorships of successful generals, was both unrealistic and provocative. It was answered by conspiracy after conspiracy against the Cortes, by the beating of journalists for articles offensive to the military, and by a theory of civilian ingratitude which finds expression in the writings of Miguel Capabon:

The only way of preserving our Liberty . . . is not by isolating the soldier or diminishing his well-being, because in the army are to be found men of enterprise whom it is not easy to placate or deceive . . . there will come a time when . . . they will issue forth from their barracks like raging lions—breathing Vengeance . . . if this does not happen we will approach a constitutional King or a general who has earned the goodwill of the soldiers while the ungrateful nation has 'emancipated' them. What security will their wise Constitution offer them then? He who commands force subjects all to his will. Pacts, laws, and the most sacred oaths are broken when it comes to Fix Bayonets. What use will their Urban Militia be then?[1]

This kind of resentment accumulated because the material advantages which were supposed to endear the Constitution to the soldier could never be realized for want of money;[2] provincial captains-general were the only effective paymasters, wringing taxes directly out of the municipalities, and it was they who most resented the authority of the Cortes.

Later it was to be remembered that from 1811 to 1814 corporal punishment, distinctions of birth, exclusive corps privileges, and exemptions from military service had been abolished, that officer-cadets had all been given a respectable education in the military school of La Isla, that a scale of pensions for retired officers and wounded men had been published, if not paid, that the capable generals had been organized into a staff corps, and that a party of military deputies had tried to speak for the interests of the army in Cortes

---

[1] *Exposicion que hace un oficial subalterno D. Tomas Fenestra á sus compañeros de armas sobre la decadencia de los exércitos españoles* (La Palma, 1813), see also *El Exército español destruido por las leyes* (Cadiz, 1812, and Majorca, 1813).

[2] On 26 Jan. 1811 a deputy complained: 'While the men only get a contemptible bread-ration, what use are other reforms?'

and humanize the *Ordenanzas*,[1] but at the time the senior officers who disapproved of this legislation had the stronger hold on military opinion. The guardees and the artillery officers resented the loss of their privileges, but the generals feared for their power: wherever the Constitution of 1812 was proclaimed, the captains-general were supplanted by civilian *jefes políticos* who became 'the first agents of the government in the provinces', and civilian authorities were relieved of their wartime obligation to find the salaries of military administrators.[2] There were other slights to remember, such as the censure of Liberal newspapers, the favour shown to politically sympathetic soldiers by the governments of 1813–14, and the clandestine influence at the War Office of hostile deputies; but what gave these disgruntled *caudillos* strength was the knowledge that the loyalty of the mass of the army, as of the nation, remained emotionally engaged in the person of the absent King.

Thus on Ferdinand's return a rite was performed at Valencia which inverted the significance of that enacted by the engineers of Alcala in 1808. At the head of his officers, General Elío[3] bade Ferdinand welcome and handed him the baton which he had received from 'the Nation represented in Cortes' as token of his command. Ferdinand, who was probably still undecided whether or no he should swear allegiance to the Constitution, demurred, but Elío insisted: 'Grasp it, Sire! If your Majesty grasp it but a single moment, it will acquire new virtue, new power.'

The King did so and handed the thing back; the General, who had saluted the constitutional monarch, then kissed the hand of a master.[4] In a month the Cortes had been dissolved, the Constitution abrogated, and the Liberals proscribed.

Therefore it might have been assumed that the events of 1808–14 had confirmed the role of the officer as the servant

---

[1] See Moya and Rey: *El Ejército y la Marina, passim*.

[2] *Instrucción para los ayuntamientos constitucionales, juntas provinciales y gefes políticos superiores*, 1813: and *Gaceta de Madrid*, 10 Sept. 1813.

[3] Francisco Javier Elío (1767–1822), a Navarrese nobleman, celebrated for his American exploits 1807–11, governed Valencia and Murcia as Captain-General with great efficiency from 1814 to 1820.

[4] See Miraflores, *Apuntes histórico-críticos para escribir la historia de la revolución de España*, 3 vols. (London, 1834), *Documentos*, 30. This incident occurred on 15 April, the *pronunciamiento* for the absolute King on 4 May 1814.

of absolute monarchy, and joined him to the group of high Tories, called *serviles,* who had taken a stand against all the innovations and reforms of the Cortes, and against the very idea of a limited Prerogative. But the ceremony at Valencia was delusive, since the King had not, as Elío pretended, re-surrected the army, but the army had resuscitated the monarchy; and *Vox exercitus vox dei* was no formula for abso-lutism on the traditional pattern. Nevertheless, Ferdinand VII had no intention of ruling in partnership with an am-bitious military; he had inherited his father's dislike of uniforms with a determination to 'be a king' that was his own, and might have succeeded in keeping the army in its place had not the outlook of many officers been radically changed by the war.

While it lasted, promotion and prestige had been better than ever before; the regular army had been enlarged to in-clude 150 regiments—no Guards—and about 160,000 men, three times the pre-war total, and the heavy incidence of casualties had helped send the more ambitious officers to the top with unusual speed.[1] Commissions had been granted to hundreds of amateur patriots by local juntas in the ebullition of 1808, and the Central Junta had allowed them to join the regulars; thus the army list of 1814 was crowded with mili-tary enthusiasts for whom there was no future. Peace meant redundancy—a life sentence of provincial picquet-duty, or retirement without a pension—but there were many as un-willing to suffer in silence under Ferdinand as under the Cortes. They had been exposed irretrievably to the influence of a freer society than that of the Restoration; they had read newspapers, attended parliamentary debates, and joined masonic lodges. Some five hundred were graduates of the military academy of La Isla, and had been taught to reason, and many more were former *guerrilleros,*[2] who had not been

[1] See Clonard, *Historia orgánica,* vi. 259–78, for a summary of changes brought about by the war. The best example of quick promotion is that of Pablo Morillo, a former naval N.C.O. who rose from lieutenant to lieutenant-general in the war. The casualties included 56,000 captives sent to France.

[2] Francisco Espoz y Mina (1781–1836), for example, who organized his bands into the army of Navarre, where the future Generals Oráa, Santos Ladron, and Irribarren learned their trade. Another, Francisco Longa, was able to buy his general's sash on the profits of war and later founded a company to supply the government with armed sloops on a monthly basis.

taught to obey the War Office. Had it not been for the determined action of Elío and a few Royalists in 1814,[1] they would have continued, perhaps grudgingly, to accept the Constitution, but now they had abandoned it they looked to the King for redress of their grievances and refused to be silenced.

Unfortunately their situation was hopeless. The army had to be reduced, and there was too little money to pay the units which were retained. What made things worse was the attitude of the War Minister, General Eguia (in office 1814–15 and 1817–19), whose violent Basque conservatism led him to destroy everything that was foreign to the 'System of 1808'; from the staff corps, the military academy, the better pay and pensions, and the masonic lodges,[2] down to moustaches, whiskers, daggers, ear-rings, and mufti; he reintroduced caning and running the gauntlet for the men, and subjected the officers to a process of discrimination which they were quick to resent. He was determined that whoever drew full pay it was not to be Liberals, war heroes, or *guerrilleros*, and thus, when the reductions of 1814–18 and the return of the French prisoners of war left a surplus of over 10,000 unemployable officers, they were able to blame their relegation (which meant in many cases a block to their only hope of social advancement) on a deliberate policy of political victimization. Their leaders, the war heroes and *guerrillero* chiefs, thus began to side with the Liberals, and the process was accelerated after the failure of the War Minister Ballesteros to keep up full employment had convinced them that the men of the new army could acquire no influence at the palace.[3] The redundant officers were given

[1] Of the four armies in being in May 1814 only Elío's was thoroughly Royalist, at least among the officers; La Bisbal waited on events, and the corps of Generals Freyre and the Prince of Anglona were persuaded to accept the revival of absolutism by the Duke of Wellington, to whom they were attached in the south of France (see Wellington, *The Dispatches*, xii. 17, and J. Arzadún, *Fernando VII y su tiempo* (1942), 62, 65).

[2] The society was banned in Jan. 1815, as the officers who had returned from captivity in France had 'imbibed the most dangerous principles' with the new rites (F.O., Wellesley to Castlereagh, 5 Aug. 1814). It had been introduced to the army by Aranda in the 1760's, and the propaganda of English and French officers in the war had produced lodges in each corps, if not regiment. For the initiation rite see L. Jullian, *Précis historique des principaux événements politiques et militaires qu'ont amené la révolution d'Espagne* (1821), 25–28.

[3] Francisco Ballesteros (1770–1833) rose from excise officer to general in 1808–9,

penurious commissions in the provincial and urban militias, and a few vacancies in the customs police—and even these were threatened by the reforms of the Finance Minister Garay (1816–18), who referred to the army in a Royal decree as 'useless and even harmful in the state of peace which fortunately we enjoy'.[1]

This was the situation which produced the earliest military *pronunciamientos*[2] against the monarchy, led without exception by men of the new army who preferred a gesture, however futile, to impotence and redundancy. Their failure betrayed the reluctance of most officers to carry discontent to the pitch of rebellion, but in the event the work of 'revolutionizing' the army, which a few military agonists might never have achieved, was carried out by the government itself; which, by demanding the great military effort necessary for the reconquest of the lost provinces of America, gave officers and men a common grievance—their hatred of foreign service—which had previously been wanting.

Moreover, the sailing of General Morillo's armada in 1815 (combined with the mobilization of forces against Napoleon in the same year, for which England refused to pay) had plunged the monarchy into a state of bankruptcy which made the recovery of imperial revenues the more vital, but until this could be achieved, the army had to postpone hopes of regular payment; while the new expedition waited to sail, money could only be raised by terrorizing the municipalities, and when this failed the soldiers begged, starved, or accepted tips from bandits and smugglers.

The need for men compelled the government to crown its exactions with an extraordinary *quinta*; the King demanded a total of 71,800 youths in annual contributions of 18,000

made his name as an Anglophobe fire-eater, and as War Minister (Mar.–Aug. 1815) produced a plan by which the army was to take over the entire administration through a series of 'military commandancies' (see *Decretos Fern. VII*, ii. 461, and an account in the *Ensayo imparcial sobre el gobierno del Rey Fernando VII* (Paris, 1824), 96).

[1] In his master-plan for economic reform of 30 May 1817, Garay included a 4 per cent. income-tax on officer's salaries (a mistake Mendizábal was to repeat in 1836) and a reduction of the army estimates from 75 per cent. of the whole budget to 41 per cent. (see *Decretos Fern. VII*, v. 262).

[2] See J. L. Comellas (Garcia-Llera), *Los primeros pronunciamientos en España 1814–20* (1958), for a study and analysis.

from 1818 to 1821;[1] and it was the reaction of these recruits to life in Eguia's army and the prospect of death in America which the disaffected officers were able to exploit. For the upper ranks they had the network of masonic lodges as a means of indoctrination and conspiracy,[2] and, since the army collected in Andalusia from 1818 onwards was the one serviceable corps in Spain, they had only to secure a leader who could command its obedience and the government would be defenceless against them. However, although from 1808 to 1819 a succession of ambitious generals had contemplated using their troops against government, and Elío's venture had succeeded, the execution of General Lacy in 1817 had established the death penalty for failure, and the commander-in-chief of the expeditionary army, the Count of La Bisbal,[3] was a careerist with Liberal sympathies but no appetite for the heroic gesture. When he had joined the conspiracy he discovered that his lieutenant, Pedro Sarsfield, was unsympathetic to the cause, and decided to double-cross the conspirators by arresting all the senior officers involved (June 1819); with which the episode might have closed had not an outbreak of yellow fever prevented the army from sailing.

The task of rebellion thus devolved on junior officers; they were compelled to promote themselves into generals after they had 'pronounced' in order to secure the loyalty of their men,[4] and instead of marching directly on Madrid, to publish their aims and appeal to the rest of the country for support. Major Riego of the Asturias regiment proclaimed the Constitution of 1812 at San Juan de las Cabezas on 1 January 1820, but the rest of the rising was so badly managed that after a month's inaction 3,000 of the rebels had to barricade themselves into their camp at La Isla and wait while Riego struck inland to gain allies with a dwindling 'mobile column' of 1,500 men, singing choruses as they defiled past apathetic peasants. No one joined Riego, but the gesture succeeded: a number of captains-general in the north

---

[1] See F. O., Wellesley to Castlereagh, 29 Dec. 1817.

[2] See A. Alcalá Galiano, *Memorias*, 29.   [3] Enrique O'Donnell (1769–1834).

[4] Like the municipalities in the national rising of 1808 they set up a junta which became a 'promotion-factory' (A. Alcalá Galiano, *op. cit.*, i. 429). How the men were persuaded to move may be read in Arzadún, *Fernando VII y su tiempo*, 123.

were molested by agitators demanding the Constitution, and succumbed or fled, and on 7 March the King himself was persuaded by the attitude of his Guards to accept it. There was no fight left in the absolute monarchy.[1]

3. THE CONSTITUTIONAL ARMY, 1820-1823

The *pronunciamiento* of 1820 was the work of a small group of disaffected officers assisted by a few civilian Liberals: its success depended on the widely diffused opinion, held by generals and shopkeepers alike, that a change of political system was necessary and that the Constitution of Cadiz (which in 1812-14 had been ignored by most Spaniards) was the means by which this could be ensured. The conspirators of La Isla had agreed to proclaim this Constitution only two days before the rising,[2] to give their movement respectability in the eyes of the citizens of Cadiz, and held their men together not so much by the rhetoric of liberty as by promises of reduced service, cash bounties, retirement grants, and no America. On this disparity between a military mutiny and the 'Second Birth of Freedom' which resulted from it depends the history of the army under the Liberal régime of 1820-3.

For the return of the Constitution meant the reinstalment of the Liberals of 1812, who had accepted as one of their principles the reduction of the power of the army in the State, and had not forgiven the part played by the military in the Restoration of 1814. When Galicia went over to the rising in March 1820 the Royalist military commandant warned his troops 'that the Constitutionals hate you much more than they hate the King and his government, that they call you vile mercenaries . . . and have conceived the iniquity of treating you like public enemies, forming certain National Corps to use against you . . . ',[3] and the first economy of the

---

[1] General Freyre, sent to suppress the rebellion, spent weeks firing proclamations at the *pronunciados* 'because we did not really know what the other provinces of Spain desired' (see his *Manifiesto* (Seville, 1820)).

[2] A. Alcalá Galiano, *Memorias*, i. 479-80. As in 1854 the first object of the conspiracy seems to have been a change of king rather than a political revolution.

[3] See the proclamation of the Count of San Roman in appendix to *Manifiesto que la Junta de Gobierno de Galicia . . . hace a la nación* (Corunna, 1820). The

Pérez de Castro ministry (March 1820–March 1821) was to decree the dissolution of the army of Andalusia which had made the revolution. Arguelles, now Minister of the Interior, considered this force a threat to public order and bad publicity for the cause;[1] by the end of 1820 he had restored the régime of civilian *jefes políticos*, authorized the formation of National Militia corps all over Spain, and sent General Riego packing home to Asturias.

In reply the men of La Isla[2] asserted that it was they who had made the revolution, and only by the promotion of their interests and aspirations could it be maintained. They were backed by a large class of new Liberals who found themselves excluded from employment by the men of 1812 (the *Doceañistas*), and by abetting the radical demonstrations of 1821–2 they were able to compel successive governments to meet their pretensions by compromise appointments. In 1821 Riego was made Governor of Saragossa, in 1822 he entered Cortes and was elected President, and after the fall of Martínez de la Rosa's ministry in August of that year his associates were invited to form a cabinet: General Evaristo San Miguel became Premier and Foreign Secretary, and by 1823 almost every important administrative post, and every command in the field, was held by his kinsmen, friends, and adherents.

Thus the army got its interests attended to, and the problem of how its loyalty could be secured to the Liberal State became a central one. The mismanagement of 1814–20 had been so disastrous that soldiers of every political persuasion were anxious for changes, and the new ministers expected to win over all ranks by Liberal reforms. The revival of the constitutional administrative system might offend the older generals, but Riego's friends were promoted regimental

Count of San Roman, a disciplinarian who was later to provoke the La Granja mutiny of 1836, must not be confused with the military journalist Eduardo Fernández de San Roman.

[1] A. Alcalá Galiano, *Memorias*, ii. 108; and Quintana's *Cartas a Lord Holland*, 547.

[2] The most important were Rafael del Riego Núñez (1785–1823) and E. San Miguel (1785–1862), both of Oviedo and the Asturias regiment, both ex-prisoners of war; also Antonio Quiroga (1784–1841), a Galician ex-naval officer; Miguel López de Baños and Facundo Infante (1790–1873) of the engineers; José María Torrijos (1791–1831); Felipe Arco Aguero, and Demetrio O'Daly.

officers who represented the depressed subaltern class. They wanted more pay (and were given an immediate rise of 100 *reales* a month in 1820) and resented the way in which their lives were run by their seniors. They had been forbidden to marry below the rank of captain; they had been subject to arbitrary judicial proceedings in which their depositions had to be on oath, and during which their pay was cut by two-thirds; sometimes their careers had been ruined by 'secret notes' against their characters on their service sheets, or by an order of suspension from the War Office, and their appeals to the *Ordenanza* had been set aside by the inter-pretative power of captains-general. All resented being held back by the unmerited promotion of War Office favourites and, in the case of the infantry officer, relegated to a second-rate status beside the privileges and superior education of the Guards, artillery, and engineers.[1]

These grievances were redressed in the Constituent Law of the army of 1821, and its framers[2] included more ambitious provisions. They ordered the staff corps to be revived, mili-tary schools to be established in every branch, and the *Ordenanzas* to be revised; the *quinta* was to become an annual conscription drawn from all classes for a five-year engagement, and the State took on the responsibility of look-ing after the retired officer, the disabled soldier, and their de-pendants. It was an attempt to 'identify wholly the interests of the armed forces with those of the general mass of the nation', and there was a tacit agreement that the *fuero militar*, although an abuse, should not be touched. The cases in which a man might disobey his officer were specified (if or-dered to interfere with elections, debates, or assemblies of Cortes), and there were to be no more foreign regiments to deface the image of the national army.

But the attempt failed because, in creating the institutions which would restore military self-respect, the government

---

[1] For these grievances see *Proyecto de ley constitutiva del ejército* (1820); *Ex-posición dirijida a S. M. por los oficiales que la firman en Pamplona* (Pamplona, 1820); *Declamación de un militar*, and *Clamores de un militar subalterno* (both Mexico, 1820).

[2] On the committee were Flórez Estrada, the radical legislator mentioned above (p. 15), Romero Alpuente, the Jacobin (both civilians), General Quiroga of La Isla, the Count of Ezpeleta, a Liberal aristocrat, and Brigadier Palarea, an ex-*guerrillero*.

had to act 'the great impresario',[1] and in 1822 there was already a deficit of 18 millions in the army budget, which increased until all ranks were kept months in arrears and sent into action against Royalist *guerrilleros* and French invasion corps in a state of apathetic nudity. The conscripts deserted, and the Liberal optimism of 1820 evaporated into rhetoric: as in 1812, nothing could be done for want of money.

Moreover, by the time the army was called on to defend the Constitution against its enemies, the most dedicated Liberal soldiers, associates of Riego and Mina, had lost their hold on army opinion. They had naturally antagonized the high Royalists, men so closely implicated with the previous régime or so intimately attached to the King that they found all Liberalism intolerable. These came into the open by engineering the Guards mutiny of July 1822, then took to the hills as partisan fighters,[2] or fled abroad; the judicial murder of General Elío at Valencia was notice to quit. This was inevitable; but there were other enemies on the Right who might have been friends—the moderate, rather old-fashioned professionals,[3] whom the governments of Pérez de Castro, Bardají (March 1821–January 1822), and Martínez de la Rosa (February–August 1822) had tried to keep in control of the army. These were soldiers of a reformist stamp but 'liberals by Royal Command', instinctively opposed to the flash radical militarism of the men of La Isla, and when the San Miguel cabinet came to power they were turned out of office with vindictive haste.

These last had a purchase on the loyalty of other officers which made their enmity dangerous, but it was a split in the ranks of the men who had made or placed their hopes in the revolution which did the more harm. When Quiroga first paraded in his self-bestowed general's sash, he was warned

---

[1] See *Opinión de la junta auxiliar del arma de infantería, sobre el proyecto de ley constitutiva* (1821), 123.

[2] By Sept. 1822 about a dozen generals had joined the Royalist resistance movement, the most important being Eguía (see p. 19), the Baron de Eroles (1785–1825) a Catalan war hero, Vicente Quesada (1782–1836), and Carlos O'Donnell (1772–1830).

[3] e.g. Generals the marqués de las Amarillas and Zarco del Valle, who modernized the War Office in 1820; Morillo, returned from America to the command of Madrid in 1821; Álava, President of Cortes in 1822 and friend of the Duke of Wellington; and Blake, a liberal of 1812—when he surrendered to Suchet at Valencia—and a devoted Director of Engineers from 1815 to 1820.

by a fellow officer: 'Ahora veo que comienza la guerra en España!'[1] He meant the fight for jobs and promotions: in which, by means of the network of masonic lodges, the original *pronunciados* attempted to keep the best jobs in their own or friendly hands,[2] and 'formèrent une nouvelle aristocratie, que l'on pouvait appeler *fille ainée de la révolution*'.[3] In retaliation the excluded officers, led by the former War Minister Ballesteros, joined the rival secret society of *Comuneros*,[4] and enlisted the support of N.C.O.s and extreme civilian radicals, so that by 1823 it was estimated that one quarter of serving officers belonged to clandestine organizations. The hatred which *Comuneros* and masons felt for each other (alternating with moments of reconciliation against Royalists and moderates) meant that army patronage was distributed on a purely political basis, and one of the central demands of 1820, a fair promotion ladder, was overlooked.

So was the return to civilian government; there were so many soldiers to appease that the practice was begun of appointing military men to the post of *jefe político*. So was the regulation of the military courts, when it was discovered that they could serve the political purposes of Left as well as Right-wing governments, as shown by the execution of Elío and Goiffieu.[5] In effect the radical soldiers had seized power to find the task of running the government incompatible with retaining their popularity. By the time of the Guards mutiny, the artillery, which had been the most Liberal branch of the army in 1820, was becoming alienated from the cause by radical attacks on its privileges and *esprit de corps*,[6] and only the refusal of the King to side openly with the mutineers prevented the best part of the Madrid line

[1] See S. Rotalde, *La revolución ó hechos sin máscaras* (1823), for an analysis of the split.

[2] The entire Castro cabinet had become masons by Feb. 1821.

[3] S. Miñano, *Histoire de la révolution d'Espagne de 1820 à 1823 par un espagnol témoin oculaire*, 2 vols. (1824), i. 111 (a hostile account).

[4] See A. Alcalá Galiano, *Memorias*, ii. 169–70, and M. Fernández Álvarez, *Los sociedades secretas y los orígenes de la España contemporánea* (1961), for a survey.

[5] Both garrotted by the San Miguel government in 1822 on the unproven accusation of Royalist conspiracy.

[6] A. Alcalá Galiano considered that they 'had turned into partisans of the King by dint of hearing themselves called royalist'.

garrison from pronouncing against the Constitution.[1] The success of San Miguel's government in defeating the first wave of Royalist *guerrilleros* temporarily enhanced their prestige, but the appearance of a major military threat in the French army of invasion of 1823 caused this to evaporate.

Five emaciated armies were assembled to meet the advance of the Duke of Angoulême and his *guerrillero* allies, but the morale of the defenders was low. The Count of La Bisbal, commanding Madrid, stated in an open letter: 'As a General, I must follow the orders of Government . . . but as a Spanish citizen . . . I believe that the majority of the Nation does not want the Constitution of 1812.'[2] General Morillo, in Galicia, agreed and surrendered to Bourke once the Cortes had suspended Ferdinand from the exercise of his powers (borrowing money from the French to pay his men). Mina's soldiers, who showed fight, preferred after their capitulation to be carried prisoners of war into France rather than return to their own villages.[3] The old provincial militia, now enrolled as a 'mobile national guard', went openly Royalist.

No doubt, as Quintana complained, the generals changed sides because 'they believed that thus they would keep their appointments and honours, remaining at the same elevation in both systems'[4] (a mistaken belief; the Royalist reaction swept them into exile or obscurity along with the most committed Liberals)—but this merely emphasizes the disrepute into which the constitutional system had fallen; beginning with the promise of a model army, it had produced neither pay nor justice and had succumbed to the tyranny of a clique.

Events had proved that this clique was too far in advance of military opinion as a whole, and too self-interested, to create a Liberal army. When the King was restored, its members ran for their lives and survived, after a decade of conspiracy, as one among several competing army interest-groups; except Riego, who chose martyrdom,[5] and thus

[1] This appears from Ward's letters to Vaughan in Vaughan MSS., General Correspondence, C.

[2] Miñano, *Histoire de la révolution*, ii. 342–7.

[3] F. Galli, *Mémoires sur la dernière guerre en Catalogne* (1828), 329–30.

[4] *Cartas a Lord Holland*, 581.

[5] See G. Matthewes: *The Last Military Operations of General Riego* (1824), for

ensured that the ideals of 1820 should outlive the failure of 1823. His attitude was to invite the emulation of succeeding *oficialillos*, who accepted the premisses of his career—that army grievances are soonest mended in a freer society; and all Liberals would agree with the committee of Cortes which reported that 'it is no use saying that as the whole nation was prepared . . . the army moved as a part of it. To take the first step towards Liberty under a despotic government is one of the greatest exploits a man can perform.'[1]

4. MILITARY REFORM, 1824–1832

For the time being it appeared as if fifteen years of political activity had destroyed the usefulness of the army for ever. Those units which had supported the Constitution were disbanded and either dissolved or marched captive into France. Whatever the officers had bargained for, they were all provisionally suspended—given *licencia indefinida*—and the privates were discharged without exemption from future service. In February 1824 even the army of Spanish Royalists which had accompanied the French was demobilized, and its officers sent on extended leave as *ilimitados*. The King was left with the French army of occupation,[2] a number of resuscitated guardees, and the First Foot, kept in being as a reward for its loyalty in 1820. Surrounded by his good Swiss and a hysterically Royalist multitude, he might have rested content with a military establishment as exiguous as this, had not Ferdinand been determined to restore the prestige of the monarchy. For this it was necessary first of all to secure himself against the raids of Liberal *emigrés*, who spent ten years in London and the Channel Islands planning a second La Isla rebellion, and then to

a first-hand but highly partisan account by an English volunteer who shared Riego's imprisonment and heard his strangely chosen words: 'O Father, Father, hast thou forgotten thy sons in the time of their trouble? . . . I shall submit to my fate like a man, but Riego shall never die.' According to Miñano, the Andalusian crowds had previously shouted 'Vive saint Riego! vive le très-saint Riego!' Espartero was to carry the self-deification further and fare better.

[1] *Dictamen de la comisión nombrada por el congreso para examinar el expediente relativo al egército de San Fernando, y graduar los premios á que es acreedor* (1820), 1.

[2] From Dec. 1824 this consisted of 22,000 men, including two Swiss regiments at Madrid; all had withdrawn by 1829.

launch a fresh armada at the insurgent Americas, which, after the defeat of the Spaniards at Ayacucho in December 1824, seemed to the rest of the world to have gained their independence, but remained to their repudiated monarch irresistibly attractive.[1]

Therefore a new army was necessary, and was already being recruited in April 1824 by a War Minister—José de la Cruz, in office from December 1823 to August 1824— chosen for his experience of colonial soldiering; but unless the disaster of 1820 was to be repeated, lessons in military organization had to be learnt which hitherto both Monarchists and Liberals had neglected. They had tried to use the army for their own purposes by exploiting the economic weakness of the officers so that promotion went only to the party man, and as a result had defeated their own objects by inducing demoralization and military ineffectiveness. They had demanded political loyalty or death, but had been prepared to undermine the system of officer control on which the political activity of the army depended;[2] if neither was to blame for the national bankruptcy which lay behind bad pay and unemployment, both could expect to become targets for military resentment unless they were able to meet some of the demands of the profession as a whole.

The government of the second restoration, haunted by the continuing fear of sedition,[3] gave signs that it understood these demands, and pursued a policy of military reconstruction that was central to the development of military politics,

[1] F. O., Addington to Aberdeen, 10 Feb. 1830: 'I have no doubt that if money can be found . . . another and much stronger expedition will in due time be sent forth across the Atlantic.'

[2] The radicals by means of their secret societies, the Royalists both in 1820, when the privates in Freyre's army rose against their officers and terrorized Cadiz, and in 1821–2, when they appealed to the Guardsmen to reject their Liberal commanders, and so precipitated the murder of Lieutenant Landáburu. Hence General Morillo's remark, at a meeting at the palace where the chamberlains complained that a crowd had shouted *muera el Rey!*—'*Caracho, es muy malo eso; pero es mucho peor que los soldados maten á sus oficiales!*' (Vaughan MSS.: General correspondence, C: Ward to Vaughan, 5 July 1822).

[3] All parties were attracted by the idea of another army coup; apart from the Liberal raids (Tarifa 1824, Alicant 1826, Mina's 1830, Torrijos' 1831), the fanatical Royalists were to set up the most powerful secret society of the period—the 'Exterminating Angel'—and provoke the Catalan rising of 1827, and the King himself apparently considered ridding himself of these zealots by a 'pronunciamiento from above' (see J. Puyol in BAH, C (1932), 83).

since only a force that possessed a minimum of cohesion and self-respect could play a role in public affairs. Ferdinand saw this achievement as producing a non-political army, by which he meant a disciplined Right-wing army; but what in fact emerged in the last decade of his reign was a military that would support neither party unless on its own terms.

The first problem was to find some kind of correlation between employment and political reliability. The new army had to be small, but the class of unemployed officers was large: in 1822 the government had been paying 6,500 active and 4,000 retired officers, while several thousand more had been disbanded in 1814–18 without pension rights. The Royalists of 1823 contributed another 1,000 to the total, and the mutually exclusive party affiliations of these groups meant that whichever was given employment a pool of discontented half-pay officers would be left whose claims in the event of political change presaged an expropriation of the expropriators. Meanwhile they had to beg or starve, copy for lawyers or join street musicians, while their widows were reduced to laundering or prostitution.

In 1824 the officers with the strongest claims on the patronage of the War Office—those of the 'Army of the Faith'—were, as a whole, the least likely to make a sound professional force. They were mostly irregulars from the north, who had sworn eternal enmity to 'the philosophers, troops of the Line, and militia',[1] and 'if they desired absolute government, it was to be its Janissaries'.[2] Many were being formed into a sort of People's Police, the Royalist Volunteers, clad in celestial blue, who occupied themselves in terrorizing the village Liberals and intellectuals they so much disliked; but the others still expected a monopoly of regular commissions, and although they aroused the dislike of de la Cruz, he could not afford to ignore the pretensions of a victorious faction. After an attempt to avoid the issue by converting the old provincial militia into regulars,[3] he

---

[1] From the proclamation of the Royalist *guerrillero*, *El Trapense*, quoted on p. 611 of E. Blaquière, *An Historical Review of the Spanish Revolution* (1822).

[2] *Ensayo imparcial*, 174.

[3] Clonard: *Historia orgánica*, vi. 453. Cruz was eventually denounced by the Royalist *guerrillero* General Chambon for 'intriguing to re-establish the constitution' dismissed and imprisoned. See Clarendon MSS., c. 457, 'Notes and Information'.

supplied the cadres of the 'miniature army' of 1824 out of the better-trained Royalists. The Guards had the pick, others went to the mere dozen line regiments, and the men were raised by a *quinta*. However, these 'apostolic' officers remained a core, since to employ more meant to bring in strangers to disciplined service; to make a bigger army the proscription of ex-constitutionalist officers decreed on 1 October 1823 would have to be modified.

For this reason, and not, as the Liberals claimed, out of an inherent mania for inquisitional procedure, the system of 'Purification', formerly applied to employees who had collaborated with Joseph Bonaparte, was reinstituted. All officers and civil servants who wished to be employed after having served the government of 1820–3 had to prove their 'Love for my Royal Person, Rights and Government', senior officers before a central committee, the rest before their captains-general, and, during the period of renewed Royalist agitation while General Aymerich held the War Office (August 1824–June 1825), there is evidence that the test was strictly applied and that no more than one appeal was allowed;[1] however, after a few months, when captains-general were no longer interested in upholding legitimist principles, the examination tended to become a formality. 'Purity' could be bought, and second appeals restored the fortunes of those who had been unlucky in 1824–5;[2] only ex-freemasons and *Comuneros* were barred from the service irrevocably, and thus the inspectors-general, who decided whether the purified man actually got the employment for which he was eligible, found at their disposal a fund of experienced professionals who were unwilling to let their Liberalism impede their careers.

The strength of the government lay in the existence of these men, loyal to each other rather than to a political cause, disenchanted with the exclusiveness of extremists both to the Right and Left. They had smarted under the persecution

[1] See *Decretos Fern. VII*, ix. 141. For an illustration of the severity of the Junta of Purification of New Castille in 1824 see A. de Urbina, marques de Rozalejo, *Cheste* (1939), 52.

[2] See *Révélations d'un militaire français sur les agraviados d'Espagne* (1829), 10–11, for the legitimist view of this process, and J. Carrera Pujal, *Historia política de Cataluña en el siglo XIX*, vi. 205–7.

of radical subalterns, and now they winced at the spectacle of Royalist Volunteers executing slovenly drill-movements on disreputable ponies in front of the palace; however, when the Guards were reinforced with units drafted from the provincial regiments (the 'provincial grenadiers') in 1825, when the troops of the line were augmented by another *quinta* in 1827, these were the officers who got the commissions. The Royalists were kept in their own militia, given part-time provincial commissions, or relegated to a penurious retirement in which their pay claims were no longer interesting to the army treasurer, Gaspar Remisa. Neglect drove them to conspiracy and rebellion, and gave the government the opportunity of testing its policy by employing purified officers to suppress the 'aggrieved' Royalists; and the fact that the Catalan rebels of 1827, the forerunners of the Carlists, met with none but a hostile response from the regular army suggested that it had succeeded.[1]

The generals responsible were careerists who, like the men they patronized, put their jobs first. The War Minister Miguel Ibarrola, Marquess of Zambrano (lived 1776–1848, in office June 1825–October 1832), had served the Liberals, but like the Inspector of Provincial Militia, Brigadier Musso, had gone into exile and returned with the Royalist invasion. Manuel Llauder, the Inspector of Infantry from 1825 to 1833, had been refused employment in 1820 on account of his Royalism, but delighted to employ former constitutionalists in his branch; and while among the motives of these men a purely selfish *esprit de corps* and a need to build up the sort of clientage that carried weight in Court politics no doubt came high, they were also co-operating after their fashion in the move towards a modern and rational system of government associated with the Finance Minister Luis López Ballesteros. A fellow Galician protégé of his, General Ramon Rodil, who alone had emerged with credit from the American wars, brought a new party to share the favours of the War Office, in the survivors of the expeditionary army

---

[1] See *Les Agraviados d'Espagne* . . . *par F. C.* (Paris and Leipzig, 1827), and *Révélations d'un militaire français*; according to the latter one regular brigade wore constitutional colours in their shakos and sought out enemies by asking 'Etes-vous libéraux ou serviles ?'

which had surrendered at Ayacucho.[1] Despite the misgivings of the King they were given employment and honours, Rodil himself the highest, and Ballesteros' determination to extinguish the contraband trade by which the State was deprived of considerable revenue led to the establishment in 1829 of an independent force of preventive men—the *Carabineros*—in which Rodil, as Inspector, could employ whom he liked.

The reinvigoration of the finance department also enabled Zambrano to improve on the military policy of his predecessors by actually paying and feeding the troops. He agreed with the British Ambassador and the Liberal exiles in assuming their fidelity to be 'in exact proportion to the punctuality of their pay',[2] and the moral was pointed in 1825 when the garrison of Seville, deprived of their money by a hitch in the contract between the leading merchants and the War Office, were found rioting with the slogan 'Down with Absolute Government!'[3] A year later he established as a general principle that the army's claims on the Treasury must be met before all others,[4] and for the rest of Ferdinand's reign the strength of the establishment was never allowed to outrun the amount bargained for in the estimates. In 1828 this reached at least 56 per cent. of the whole,[5] and was being spent on regular pay, on the addition of a commissariat department to the War Office—the *Cuerpo general administrativo de la hacienda del ejército*—and on a new scale of pensions for officers, less generous than that promised under the Constitution but more within the capacity of the Treasury.

Thus two of the prerequisites of an effective army, fair promotion and adequate pay, were supplied, and each contributed to the third, morale; a commodity which Zambrano also promoted, in a characteristically authoritarian fashion, by using the Guards as a training centre to produce a higher standard of discipline and officer. To this end he converted the old *maison du roi*,[6] which had provided the King with an

[1] 575 officers had surrendered at Ayacucho.
[2] F.O., Addington to Aberdeen, 30 Aug. 1830.
[3] The Annual Register for 1825.
[4] Archivo Nacional, Seccion de Estado, Legajo 217–10.
[5] *Decretos Fern. VII*, xiii. 93.
[6] Consisting of the Interior Guard of halberdiers and lifeguardsmen, gentleman-

entourage of playboy praetorians, into a new model army resembling the Napoleonic Guard, and containing foot, horse,
and artillery. He placed in command such disciplinarians as
the Condes de España and de San Roman, who took in
young members of an otherwise unmartial aristocracy and
put them through a course of rigorous examinations and foot-
drill before admitting them to the privileges of commissioned rank. Under the new regulations of 1824 no one
was allowed to enter as a cadet, the intention being to in-
corporate a supply of already-experienced line officers, but
since at this date all these were politically suspect, boys of
cadet age were given lieutenancies and, after surviving the
ridicule of Madrid,[1] emerged as a generation of proficient
young officers with a pride in their profession and an aptitude
for the regimental commands to which many of them were
later transferred which was certainly novel. Both they and
the men (who got 'Bread, Pay and Stick; the first black,
coarse, and hard; the second, seldom and short; and the last,
abundantly')[2] were kept up to the mark by endless parades
and a close attention to minor points of discipline, but
forty years later Fernando de Córdova could look back on
his life as a Guards subaltern without regret, as an interlude
in which the pleasures of society reached a pitch never
attained thereafter, and where 'no officer occupied himself
. . . with anything to do with politics, knowing no other rule
than the protection of the King'.[3] They were a privileged[4]
but not a closed corporation, 'made up of officers who

rankers who protected the Royal person, and the Exterior, who were regular soldiers.
Zambrano raised their numbers from 4,000 (before they were dissolved in 1822) to
15,000 in 1830, three-eighths of the whole army.
    [1] A wag placed an advertisement for wet-nurses on the doors of the War Office,
and others made out that the grenadiers carried their officers on the march (F. de
Córdova: *Mis memorias íntimas*, 3 vols. (1886), i. 50, 51, 58).
    [2] *Revista del Ateneo Militar*, i. 436.
    [3] F. de Córdova: *Memorias íntimas*, i. 60.
    [4] Promotion went by strict seniority as in the artillery and engineers, but an
effective rank in the Guards could be held with, or exchanged for, a much higher
one in the line. Guards commissions were barred to Guards sergeants, but they could
transfer directly into an ordinary subalterncy or amuse themselves with honorary
ranks up to that of major. Peace-time duties were confined to Madrid or Barcelona,
and pay was 30 per cent. better than that of corresponding ranks in the rest of the
army; until 1835 they were commanded and administered directly by 'the King,
through his commandants of the foot and horse brigades—the latter being Zambrano
himself.

transfer to and from the other corps of the army', as the War Minister was to inform hostile radical critics before their final dissolution in 1841, and the régime of the Conde de España provided many of the officers who were to play a leading role in the politics of the next twenty-five years with a common background.[1] It was in this school that they learnt their *esprit de corps* and the stringent discipline that made most of them conservative politicians; and thus to the work of Zambrano may be attributed the equation of good soldiering with Right-wing government, which although widely recognized in the rest of Europe had been hitherto unsupported by the evidence of Spanish affairs and was only to gain acceptance gradually in the course of the century.

'Crack though the regiment was', the army as a whole was not. General Llauder's infantry, if remarkable for its modest efficiency and its subfusc Liberalism, was 'by no means formidable' in the eyes of foreign observers, one of whom, an English Peninsular veteran, reported in 1832 'that the discipline is generally very lax and that the drilling and military exercizes, although individually good, are not such as to enable the troops to act in mass . . . they would therefore when brought into actual service be probably found altogether deficient in practical military knowledge and wanting in confidence in each other . . . many a Colonel is scarce fit to command a company'.[2] Nor had Zambrano taken pains to restore the prestige of the once famous artillery, whose officers had become receptive to Liberal ideas as a result of their college education;[3] their solidarity had helped to spread the rebellion

[1] In particular, Generals Luis and Fernando de Córdova, the conservative chiefs; Leopoldo O'Donnell, the Liberal Union Premier; Roncali, Prime Minister in 1852, the Count of Clonard, Prime Minister in 1849, Pavía, War Minister in 1847, Joaquin de Ezpeleta, Urbina, and Lara, War Ministers in 1852, and Blaser, who followed them in 1853. Generals Mirasol and De Meer were to carry on the disciplinarian tradition, while the more Liberal Ros de Olano won fame as a poet, war hero, and military reformer in the fifties and sixties; Závala, the only *progresista* of the group, served as Foreign Secretary in 1855, and Minister of Marine in 1859 and 1865.

[2] F.O., Addington to Palmerston, 26 Feb. 1832.

[3] Artillery cadets were given a four-year course including foreign languages and Spanish history and graduated into the 'theoretical' branch of the service, where they were exempted from handling the guns. The N.C.O.s and artisans who did this could also rise to commissioned rank, but on the 'práctico' ladder which stopped at captain, and the two branches kept socially apart from each other. All artillery ranks

of 1820, and the King had not forgiven them. From 1823 to 1830 the college at Segovia was closed, while the new Guards artillery (recruited from those who had deserted the constitutional army in 1822–3) was fostered by the War Office, and in 1828 gunners were ordered to yield seniority to a line regiment, the loyal First Foot. This studied neglect confirmed their Liberalism but reduced their expertise, and brought them, like the infantry and cavalry, ill equipped to meet the challenge of the Carlist war.

Moreover, the conditions of military life were only very slightly improved, enough to keep the troops from actually overthrowing the government but not to the extent of endearing them to their lot. The men were still *quintos* or substitutes, handed over by the municipalities in bewildered droves, and drafted into distant regiments where they were put through a severe and mechanical training. Their pay was two *reales* a day with half a *real* deducted for ration money and another half for expenses.[1] Their food was the *rancho*, a stew or bean soup eaten in regulated mouthfuls out of a communal cauldron with an individual spoon and loaf. Their punishment was a ceremonial caning with the *palo*, up to fifty strokes, but they had also to endure casual blows from the *vara* or pace-stick of the N.C.O.[2] Their pleasures were few, since the lack of regimental schools (which had been planned in the constitutional period, but were not usual until the 1840s) cut them off from books, and marriage was out of the question; surrounded by a hostile civilian world,[3] they had only guitars, *cigarillos*, and brothels to alleviate the dullness of barrack life. Their virtues, in contrast with the soldiery of England and France, were sobriety and gravity;

went by strict seniority on a 'closed ladder' separate from the army list, in which nevertheless artillery officers could hold honorary *grados*. Their numerous other privileges gave them a social and professional superiority which they never allowed themselves to forget (see J. Vigon: *Un personaje español del siglo XIX (el Cuerpo de Artillería)* (1930) and vol. ii of his *Historia de la artillería española* (1947), 420–9).

[1] *Archivo Militar*, 29 Apr. 1841 for details. This was not bad compared with an average labourer's wage of two *reales* a day for all expenses, when he could get it.

[2] Ibid., 25 May 1842. The gauntlet was not formally abolished until 1837, but the men would never submit to flogging in the English manner, as Wellington discovered.

[3] See A. S. Mackenzie, *Spain Revisited* (1836), ii. 128: ' . . . soldiers are looked upon like men-of-war's men about our docks, as a set of outlaws . . . '.

although their duties made them participants at all *funciones* and bullfights, they were seldom found drunk, said prayers before each evening dismissal, presented arms to the Host whenever they met it, and heard Mass with genuflections prescribed by the War Office.[1]

The capable or literate soldiers were promoted to corporal: the next promotion, to sergeant, turned them from conscripts to professionals, with the choice either of forty years' 'perpetual'[2] service as an N.C.O., or an ensign's commission which could lead to the generalate. The sergeants controlled the administration of the company: issued equipment, superintended the messes, kept the order book, and generally managed the men: but they enjoyed power without much privilege. Their pay was double the private's, and they messed apart;[3] but they were forbidden to marry, and could play no part in the social life of the officers. Their only chance of leaving the army lay in further promotion for an officer could retire when he liked. It could be said that 'the corporals and sergeants . . . never think of halting for life in their positions as in England, but still look for their further advancement';[4] however, the gap between sergeant and lieutenant did include a social distinction that was not easily negotiable, and in 1854 a would-be reformer complained that the promoted N.C.O. entered a world that was unfamiliar, for which his education had not prepared him: 'the result being that marked separation between those of the one and the other *procedencia*, by which the friendship and union which should prevail are marred'.[5]

[1] L. Badcock, *Rough Leaves from a Journal Kept in Spain and Portugal during the Years 1832, 1833 and 1834* (1835), 29; and *Decretos Fern. VII*, iii. 430.

[2] The literacy test was made compulsory in 1846. Complaints at perpetual service are printed in *Grito del Ejército* for Oct. 1841.

[3] *Ordenanzas*, i. 433–44.

[4] See *The Times* 22 Dec. 1841—Madrid 11 Dec. Desdevises du Dézert, *L'Espagne de l'ancien régime*, ii. 226: and cf. Foy: *Histoire de la guerre de la Péninsule*, i. 221. In 1828 sergeants of the peninsular army were given the formal right to half the ensigns' places in the overseas army (*Decretos Fern. VII*, xiii. 192): and in the August promotions of 1842, during Espartero's regency, of 219 newly made subalterns, 83 had been sergeants and 39 of these were already honorary subalterns (*Archivo Militar*, 6 Sept. 1842).

[5] R. Madina y Orbeita, 'Reflexiones sobre la actual organización del Ejército: Memoria' (1854), MS., S.H.M. 4–2–2–21, 29. This may account for the comparatively small numbers of ranker-officers who became generals. In the period 1824–54,

The political importance of the sergeant lay therefore not so much in the fact that he represented the feelings and grievances of an oppressed people, but that while he shared the language of the private and controlled his behaviour, he was also concerned with precisely the same promotion anxieties as the officer: so that, were the officer disposed to act against government, the sergeant was able to sympathize and assist. When sergeants came out, it was in response to an impulse from above: either by arrangement with officers, or with the agents of political parties who covered themselves with the authority of subversive generals. In 1824, therefore, Ferdinand was careful to exclude from the new army all sergeants unable to show positive proof of Royalism, lest 'revolutionary ideas and principles be introduced in any way among the men',[1] but with the officers he could not afford to be so exacting.

These remained the most unreliable element in his army, from both the military and political points of view. Those who were not ex-sergeants were usually the sons of officers who had been chosen by the colonel and trained within the regiment as cadets; until 1837 they were expected to be of *hidalgo* status, but this was not essential. Candidates for whom there were no vacant cadetships, gentlemen volunteers, and *hidalgos* picked up as vagabonds in the *leva* or unable to pay their exemption money, served with the men as *soldados distinguidos*, a rank that let them off the dirtiest work of the barracks and gave them the right to live in their own lodgings and rise to an ensign's place without becoming corporals or sergeants.[2] This meant that, except in the privileged corps, there could be no uniform or scientific instruction, and that consequently the general standard of proficiency was shamefully low.[3] For the most part, men who did not want to serve were led by men who did not know how to serve.

out of a sample of 125 of the most notable generals promoted, only four had been privates: of these Alaix, Lorenzo, and Linage rose on the N.C.O.s' ladder while Espartero merely served for a short period as a volunteer in the War of Independence.   [1] *Decretos Fern. VII*, ix. 191.

    [2] See *Ordenanzas*, ii, xviii, for the regulations governing cadets and *soldados distinguidos*.

    [3] 'The officers, from the highest to the lowest (with exceptions necessarily) are

Besides, the officer had more pressing concerns than the drill-manual. He was not a gentleman, as English observers noted with surprise, but then the tradition of country life to which the English officer was wedded had no counterpart in Spain, where the best-bred people were accustomed to an in-door existence, and went out not for sport but for spectacle; he was a member of the military class, a professional living on his pay,[1] whose daily occupation up to the rank of major was making ends meet without hope of comfort, marriage, or smartness. Poverty and the want of a common mess[2] kept the officers apart, and when, during the Carlist war, clubs were started in which the subalterns could learn more about the usages of society and of their own profession,[3] they were discouraged by commanding officers as politically suspect, so that an evening party (or *tertulia*) at the colonel's house, the café, and the gaming-table remained the only common meet-ing-places. Play, gallantry, and gossip were the junior officer's portion in a style that was shabby-genteel; he could not afford novels, newspapers were almost unknown before 1834, and even if the opera acted as a stimulus on the Madrid and Barcelona garrisons, there must have been many who, like Espartero, 'never had to open a book to pass the time'[4] in their lives, and could boast, like the Royalist Colonel Arizabalo, that they 'knew nothing more than the general Ordinances of the army . . . nothing about logics, legislations, or politics', nor 'spoke any other language than the Spanish their mothers taught them, or ever wanted to'.[5]

Yet, in this condition of penurious vegetation, they were afforded the lugubrious pleasure of the elect in watching the torments of the damned—the 'passive army' of unemployed officers, whose lot Zambrano did something to improve,[6] but

painfully and disgracefully ignorant of their profession . . . ' (F.O., Addington to Palmerston, 26 Feb. 1832). 'In a review I witnessed at Madrid, I was assured that the only man capable of putting a thousand men through the common manœuvres was the minister of war himself' (Cook, *Sketches in Spain* (1834), ii. 250).

[1] See F.O., Addington to Aberdeen, 5 Nov. 1830. Ensigns got 325 *reales* a month, lieutenants, 423; the increase of 100 a month voted in 1820 was abolished in 1824.   [2] Badcock, *Rough Leaves*, 29, and *The Times*, 11 Sept. 1834.

[3] José Ferrer: *La moral del Ejército* (1844), 31-36.

[4] S. H. M. Clonard MSS.: Historia de los sucesos . . . Notas.

[5] See appendix to J. Flinter, *Consideraciones sobre España y las colonias . . .* (1834).

[6] He classified the unemployed into degrees of inactivity, and kept a third of the

who still, for want of any provision at all or delay in its payment, dragged out an occluded existence by menial services
or furtive begging. From this example the serving officer obtained an interest in politics which his formal education had
not implanted; if a partial demobilization, or an economy
drive, or a political purge, might at any time reduce him to
such a state, how much the more necessary was it to escape
from the lower ranks, and if this were prevented by a stag-
nant or unjust promotion system, he was the readier to *pronounce* for a new political order that included a new set of men
at the War Office.

In the unemployed, the dismissed, and the underpromo-
ted officer, therefore, the cause of rebellion continued to find
recruits; as Narváez complained in 1866, 'there is no revolutionary, however worthless he be, that does not boast of
having seduced an officer or a soldier', and the wide exten-
sion of the military class ensured that liaison between
civilian and military malcontents was easy to maintain.
Commissariat officials, such as Richart in 1817, Mendizábal
and Beltran de Lys in 1819, and ex-officers turned journalist
—Carsy, for example, leader of the Barcelona rebellion of
1842—or even a lexicographer like Domínguez, one of the
managers of the 1848 mutiny in Madrid, found it easy to engage the sympathy of serving regulars, whether by touting
disaffection round the wine-shops with free cigars and
paternal advice, or buttonholing old comrades at the café and
the assembly. Once the *trabajos* had got under way, the sus-
ceptible officers and sergeants could be organized into lodges
and initiated into the conspiracy; after this, 'pledges' of par-
ticipation would be exacted by a central committee, and
everything was ready for the *grito* or starting-signal. Before
it could be given, those outside the plot had to be arrested or
kept out of harm's way; thus, the La Granja mutineers of
1836 ensured that their officers would be at the theatre on
the night, and Brigadier Hore, who rose at Saragossa in
1854, confined all his subordinates who had served in the
Carlist army to barracks: but when the officers of the España

available active commissions open for them; thus, by 1828 he could claim he had
placed nearly half of them, but this did not include officers who had not been
purified (*Decretos Fern. VII*, xiii. 184).

regiment refused to assist the mutineers of 1848, they were persuaded 'not to disgrace themselves by assassinating innocent men' although it meant the failure of their attempt. When the moment came, the men were got on parade and subjected to a crescendo of speeches; whether crude, as when the conspirators of 1820 read out accounts of the atrocities committed by American rebels, to deter their men from overseas service, or derived from such handbooks as Colonel Paniagua's *Elocuencia militar, o arte de entusiasmar las tropas*. The senior officer present then gave the *lema* or slogan of the movement, and appealed for *vivas*; if all went well the other officers responded and carried the troops with them, if not, as when in 1860 General Ortega's *elocución* was received in puzzled silence and his horse bolted, the rebellion miscarried. It was a clumsy form of political referendum, and no *pronunciamiento* ever went according to plan: once the gesture had been made, however, the reluctance of all troops to shoot each other tended to work in the rebels' favour, and no régime could feel quite secure against it.

Thus, although Zambrano's reconstruction was partly successful in producing a recognizable army and a nucleus of capable young officers out of the debris to which the events of 1814–23 had reduced the military profession, and in averting the threat of military insurrection for the remainder of Ferdinand's reign, it was clear that only as long as his system of regular pay and secure employment was kept up could the truce to military politics be prolonged. Fortunately the duties of the army were confined to the suppression of internal disorder, and the generals, by dissuading their master from another reconquest of America,[1] put off the exposure of their military incompetence until the civil war; however, in the struggle with the ultra-Royalists which occupied the last years of his reign he could not dispense with their assistance, nor could their own political convictions remain undeclared.

[1] F.O., Addington to Aberdeen, 19 Feb. 1830.

II

THE RISE AND FALL OF THE PASHAS
1832–1836

I. THE ELIMINATION OF THE CARLISTS FROM THE ARMY, 1832–1833

IN his second reign (1823–33) Ferdinand VII tried to break the deadlock between Liberals and ultra-Royalists and impose a form of absolute monarchy which would be accepted by all subjects alike. This was the 'enlightened despotism' which meant, ideally, balancing the budget, developing the economy, cutting unproductive expenses, and employing moderate men while allowing no invasion of the Royal Prerogative; but the Enlightenment was tempered by periods in which the threat from the Left or the Right was met by a vigorous and often cruel repression. He adopted a middle policy because the Royalists who had triumphed in 1823 were mostly too primitive in their outlook and too provincial in their interests to administer a modern State; in the words of a moderate, 'among civilian, military, and ecclesiastical functionaries those who reason cannot . . . uphold a system with principles they find particularly shameful, and those who do not reason are of very little account'.[1] By 1827 it was clear that the régime was becoming more congenial to the reasoners, and those who were more Royalist than the King, the *Apostólicos*, took refuge in the theory that his mind had been captured by freemasons. They caballed round his brother and heir, Don Carlos, and in retaliation Ferdinand took a fourth wife, Maria Cristina of Naples (1829), begot a daughter Isabella (1830), and altered the succession in her favour, so as to ensure that the new system would survive his death.

After once restoring the succession to Don Carlos, then returning it to Isabella (September 1832), he devoted the last

---

[1] *Ensayo imparcial*, 209.

year of his life to the destruction of the legitimist faction which was now preparing to seize power in support of her disinherited uncle. The civil war of 1833–40 was thus preceded by an undeclared war in which *Fernandistas* and *Carlistas* competed for the loyalty of State employees, particularly army officers. In this struggle the role of the provincial captains-general was crucial, since after having been restored to their old powers in 1823 they had been given the right to proceed against all forms of political disaffection by *ad hoc* courts martial (the 'executive military commissions') and were able to establish whatever régime they chose in their respective commands: Catalonia, for example, was subjected to an authoritarian terror by the Conde de España, while Valencia enjoyed the moderate Liberalism of General Longa. Despite the policy of the War Office, their co-operation with Ferdinand's policy was not a foregone conclusion, since many servants of absolutism naturally preferred a Divine Right system of politics and this the Carlists claimed to defend. The opportunists had no such illusions, but if Ferdinand saw the Carlists as the strongest party in September 1832, why should not they? The danger from the Left—the chance of a complete Liberal restoration, with proscription and exile for its enemies—dismayed the moderate officers who had implicated themselves in the reaction of 1823–4 and helped repel the subsequent raids of the *emigrés*;[1] so that if among the generals the Conde de España[2] was unusual for his frank legitimism, Generals Sarsfield, Quesada, Zambrano, and Llauder all had reason to fear the consequences of a more Liberal government. And España controlled the Guards, which meant the most effective portion of the army.

[1] The Liberals were encouraged by the July revolution of 1830 in France to launch a concerted attack on Spain; Mina, Méndez Vigo, and 'Chapalángara' penetrated the northern frontier in a series of futile *razzias*, and in 1831 the several attempts of Torrijos on Cadiz ended in the execution of himself and his companions.

[2] Cárlos, Conde de España (1775–1839), younger brother of the Marquess, son of a Gascon nobleman and general (d'Espagnac) who entered the Spanish service after the revolution; fought with distinction in the War of Independence and governed Catalonia in 1818 and 1827–33. He was a talented and honest authoritarian, who believed that 'l'ordre du souverain est la suprême loi du soldat, qu'il soit sergent ou maréchal' and acted accordingly, winning for himself the reputation of an ogre-martinet among Liberals, and the devotion of his men (see F. Lichnowsky, *Souvenirs de la guerre civile* (1844), ii. 115).

He had his personal following among both officers and men (for it was these regiments which still contained former members of the Army of the Faith), and the rigid fanaticism of Don Carlos himself had a certain appeal for the military men who lived in contact with him; if his cause was a lost one among officers of the line, it had proved the only political movement capable of engaging the emotions of the masses, and was thus liable to affect the conscripted peasants who made up the rank and file:[1] besides, regiments were known to be influenced by the politics of the towns they garrisoned.[2] Much had to be done before military opinion was firmly wedded to the female succession.

First the generals had to be won over by an exceptional distribution of favours. At the Royal marriage, birth, and oath of allegiance scores of neglected noblemen and officers were brought back into the King's service and showered with stars and promotions: landowners such as the Dukes of Hijar and Castroterreño, and the Marquess of San José, whose influence over provincial municipalities and militia regiments was one of the enduring factors of Spanish politics, were made generals, and generals who had won local and national celebrity in the War of Independence, such as Palafox, Morillo, Freyre, Castañon, and Castaños, were purified, where necessary, and given titles, commands, and jobs. Their subordinates got earnest of their service by a series of mass promotions that culminated in the raising of two Princesa regiments of horse and foot in March 1833 to provide vacancies for 'the deserving officers of other corps', and in 1831 an attempt was made to focus the loyalty of all ranks on the young Consort by a ceremonial distribution of colours to every regiment from her hands. The King found all this nauseating but necessary;[3] Cristina fancied herself as a soldier's pin-up.

[1] Especially the *quintos* of 1827, enlisted for eight years with a two-year reduction which some of them feared they might not get.

[2] e.g. in 1832 Colonel Espartero complained that officers of his Soria regiment, in garrison at La Palma, were in contact with Majorcan Carlists. In Galicia, Colonel Zumalacárregui's regiment was involved in an obscure disturbance for which he was suspended.

[3] At the review after the oath of allegiance in 1833 he 'passed down the line in a close carriage at a trot, without speaking to or scarcely appearing to notice one single officer, which created great disgust' (F.O., Addington to Palmerston, 20 June 1833).

This policy of 'attraction', designed solely to keep the army loyal to the King whatever the political opinions of its officers, might have succeeded better had it not been interrupted by the events of September 1832, the illness, recantation, and recovery, which put the generals and Guards round the palace of La Granja in the position of having to choose sides prematurely. The infantry of the line, represented by their Inspector, Llauder, supported Cristina, but most of the *Guardias de Corps*, and many of the officers of the exterior Guard, pronounced openly for Don Carlos; so that when Ferdinand, resuscitated, appointed his wife Regent and the Moderate Zea Bermúdez Prime Minister, they took their revenge by means of a thorough political purge of the kind familiar in 1820-4. Some 200 Guards officers were suspended, all the Guards commands were given to new men, all the more conservative generals were turned out of the provincial administration and the War Office, and regimental commanders were instructed to send in reports on the political reliability of their subordinates. It was this action of Zea's which ensured that the bulk of the army would resist the invitations of Carlist agitators, but it also provided the Carlists with the nucleus of their officer corps,[1] and the issue was not decided simply by the redistribution of patronage.

For the reaction of 1823-4 had shown that Carlism was potentially a movement of the masses; Don Carlos stood for the good old times envisaged by a backwoods clergy and peasantry whom the exploitation of the towns—the anticlerical mayor, the bailiffs and the tax-collector—had deprived of hope and denied redress, and his real strength was proportional to the extent of his proletarian following, not to the alignments of the respectable classes. The mechanism of a 'white terror' still existed in the Royalist Volunteers,

[1] The only important generals to desert the Queen's government were victims of this purge—Nazario Eguía, Moreno, Guergué, Santos Ladron, Latorre, Maroto, and the Conde de España (dismissed from the commands of Galicia, Granada, Avila, Cartagena, the police, Guipuzcoa, and Catalonia respectively)—and it gave the Carlists their greatest military genius, Tomas Zumalacárregui, and their one trained artillery officer, Tomas Reina (dismissed from the Guards artillery). For a good account of these events see *Fastos españoles o ephemérides de la guerra civil desde octubre de 1832* (Anon., 1839), and for the Carlist view, Ch. I of the Baron de los Valles' *The Career of Don Carlos since the Death of Ferdinand the Seventh . . .* (1835), and Arzadún: *Fernando VII y su tiempo*, 325-43, for contemporary letters.

who were recruited from 'the refuse of the population' since 'there was in most instances an invincible repugnance in the respectable part of the community to belong to such a corps'.[1] But they were 'better armed, better clothed, and better disciplined than militia usually are',[2] the King feared them for their resemblance to the Liberal militia of 1820–3 —'Same dogs, different collars', and the British Ambassador agreed—'the institution of all others most dangerous to the Spanish Crown, much more dangerous than the wild and disjointed fancies and efforts of the Constitutionalists'.[3]

Although their numbers and influence had declined since 1824, they still aroused the hostility of the army. The captains-general were affronted by their independent powers of police (for which they were answerable only to their own Inspector-General), officers resented their pretensions to social equality, and there were inevitable clashes between a force designed to carry out the will of the government and one which could claim to represent that of the populace; besides, *realista* officers were often former members of the Army of the Faith who had competed with ex-constitutionalists for vacancies in the regular army and lost. Thus a dislike of these volunteers was the one interest shared wholeheartedly by both government and the military;[4] in December 1832 Zea reappointed General de la Cruz, who had objected to them in his former tenure of office, to the post of War Minister, and after abolishing the independent inspectorate and subjecting all Royalist Volunteers to the rule of captains-general, he let them be systematically disbanded.

Reports would be sent to the War Office complaining of their disorderly conduct or political unreliability, and the government would authorize preventive measures; these

---

[1] Cook, *Sketches in Spain*, 250–2.

[2] A. S. Mackenzie, *A Year in Spain*, 323.

[3] F.O., Addington to Aberdeen, 30 Aug. 1830; but cf. V. Boix, *Historia de la ciudad y reino de Valencia*, iii. 221, of 1830: 'los voluntarios realistas eran ya un cuerpo gastado y insignificante'.

[4] In 1830 the Madrid *realistas* had conspired to attack the palace and compel the King to 'throw himself into the hands of the apostolical faction' while they massacred his ministers, but the plot was discovered and only the threat of Liberal raids prevented measures being taken against the *realistas* then (F.O., Addington to Aberdeen, 25 and 30 Sept. 1830).

would provoke a more or less serious *émeute*, regular troops would be sent in, and, having surrounded the slogan-painted barracks of the demonstrators, would disarm and send them home. The better organized and disciplined they were, the more readily they obeyed government orders—the less disciplined, the easier suppressed. Thus the exemplary volunteers of Almeria were paraded in front of an unarmed body of newly raised 'Urban Militia', and on the word of command handed over all their arms and equipment and dispersed to their homes unprotestingly.[1] But the battalions of Leon, which captured General Castañon and demonstrated openly for Don Carlos in the cathedral, were soon overwhelmed by superior numbers; incidents which were repeated all over Spain in 1833, and in a few months reduced the military potential of Carlism to apparent insignificance.[2]

2. THE GENERALS AND THE CONSTITUTIONAL REVIVAL, 1833–1834

As a result, when the King died on 29 September 1833, and the Crown passed with the overt approval of almost the entire civil and military establishments to the Princess Isabella and her Regent mother, the government remained deeply committed to the group of generals and courtiers who had made the succession safe. In his determination to rescue the enlightened despotism from theocracy and mob-rule, Ferdinand had been compelled to set up what he disliked almost as much, a military régime of which civilians had nominal control; and where he had hoped for a prolongation of absolutism on his own terms, the struggle for power between soldiers and bureaucrats was to compel Cristina to make concessions which destroyed it in a few months.

The soldiers fell into groups according to their antecedents. One, reflecting the new policy of aligning the titled nobility behind the throne, was that associated with Javier

---

[1] See P. Chamorro y Baquerizo, *Estado mayor general del ejército Español*, 3 vols. (1851), ii, *José Gavarre*.

[2] At the end of 1833 Don Carlos found himself in Portugal with 150 officers and no money (los Valles, *The Career of Don Carlos*, 105).

Castaños, the veteran war hero and ally of the house of Osuna, who, since 1829, had been raised from disgrace to the Order of the Golden Fleece, the command of Madrid, the Presidency of the Council of Regency, and the Duchy of Baylen. He had always been a courtier, and his inveterate lobbying at the War Office, which he conducted in eighteenth-century regimentals, had brought power and places to his friends and well-connected kinsmen. At his behest the ex-ranker Morillo had been preferred to the government of Galicia in 1832, and General Zarco del Valle, the War Office reformer of 1820 who succeeded de la Cruz as War Minister in November 1833, was also his friend. The Marquess de las Amarillas (later Duke of Ahumada) and the Baron de Carondelet were his nephews, and resumed their interrupted military careers under his patronage; through Amarillas he was connected with the military dynasty of Ezpeleta, and through Carondelet with the Puñonrostros, courtier soldiers who were to acquire considerable influence in the new reign; and, most important, the Prince of Anglona, brother of the tenth Duke of Osuna, was able to return from exile and in December 1833 accepted the government of Granada. These were the *crème de la crème* of the 652 generals listed in 1833, but they shared the commands of the provinces with soldiers of fortune—American veterans such as Canterac (New Castille), Jeronimo Valdés (Cartagena), and Rodil (Estremadura), experienced in the exercise of unlimited authority, or, like Llauder, Sarsfield, and Quesada, survivors of domestic warfare. All made use of the powers granted them in February 1833 to 'take appropriate measures in good time' and 'remove all opposition' to the female succession, and so effective was the political invigilation they imposed with their newly raised urban militia that they won the nickname of 'Pashas' or 'Satraps'.

Between such men as these and the cabinet of Zea Bermúdez there was an instinctive antipathy which made the alliance of 1832 one of convenience alone. Zea and his colleague Javier de Burgos were civilian bureaucrats who had inherited from the reformers of the eighteenth century the same tendency to reduce the role of the military in administration which had led to the régime of civilian *jefes políticos* in

1812–14 and 1820–3. The wide powers of the captains-general had only been necessary because under the traditional system the King had to rely on judicial officers—*alcaldes*, *corregidores*, members of Audience—to carry out the details of administration, and except for the Intendant there had been no authority other than the military directly responsible to Madrid for its proper functioning. The new ministers sought to end this situation by expanding the Royal secretariats into true ministries and sending subordinates into the provinces who would be responsible to the department alone without the intervention of the captains-general. The experiment had been tried by the constitutionalists in 1810 and 1820, but in 1832 Zea followed their example from within the absolutist camp and set up the Ministry of Economic Development (*Fomento*), which was to exercise its own provincial jurisdiction through sub-delegates. This was the beginning of the end for the generals, but in the conditions of 1832–3 the cabinet had too many enemies to attempt the innovation with impunity. It was not long before it was being opposed by a combined front of military men and Liberal activists, the *Cristinos* or 'party of movement', who hoped for a return to some kind of constitutional régime.

This opposition was effective not only because of the independent power of the captains-general—although the hold which General Llauder secured over Catalonia was crucial to its success—but also because Ferdinand's will divided the conduct of affairs between Zea's cabinet and the Council of Regency under Castaños. He and the Marquess of Amarillas were able to make this body an instrument of military opinion, and when the King died (September 1833) the Queen Regent was unable to ignore it. When General Quesada[1] appealed to her privately she refused to dismiss her ministers, but when he got the chief of police, General Latre, and Castaños on his side, she had to make the concession of appointing their nominee, General Zarco del Valle, to replace Zea's, General de la Cruz, as Minister of War. And since the Carlists had now taken up arms in the north, the

---

[1] Vicente Quesada, 1782–1836, a well-born Creole who fought with the Royalist *guerrilleros* in 1823 and in 1833 became Inspector of Infantry, Commandant of the Foot Guards, and Captain-General of Old Castille.

government depended more than ever on the loyalty of its generals; a dependence exploited by Manuel Llauder, who was emboldened by Quesada's intrigues to make an open demand for new ministers and a constitutional system.

As the first native Captain-General of Catalonia he enjoyed a popularity among the commercial population which he had made use of to equip himself with a volunteer militia that was at this date almost his private army.[1] The guilds and manufacturers' association of Barcelona, representing the better-off employers of labour, had welcomed his destruction of the Conde de España's Royalist régime and placed their funds at his disposal; he was thus able to count on their support when he saw his jurisdiction invaded by the new sub-delegates[2] and by the new division of provinces decreed by the Minister of the Interior. He hoped to postpone the new order by his protest, and was supported by Quesada and the Council of Regency; Cristina was only anxious to remain popular, and Zea went.[3]

However, that was not the end of the 'ministerial despotism', because the cabinet which took office on 15 January 1834 was led by the former Liberal Premier of 1822, Martínez de la Rosa, who advocated strong constitutional government on the French model and could count on the support of a large section of educated opinion in Madrid from which Zea, as a solitary bureaucrat, had been cut off. In accordance with what he thought to be the needs of this group, he produced his 'Royal Statute' by which a bicameral Parliament of Estates, representing not the national will but the dominant social interests, was grafted on to the framework of the monarchy; but by giving this body the power to withhold money from the Crown, he furnished a weapon to those who wanted a return to the democratic Liberalism of 1820–3 and precipitated a struggle for office among civilian

[1] In Mar. 1833 some Catalans wrote to the Queen: 'Madam, he is a Napoleon, a Robespierre, in short he is a malcontent who wishes to place the crown on his own head . . .' (*Fastos españoles*, 1833, 192).

[2] See Pujal, *Historia política de Cataluña*, iii. 9–11, and Llauder's own *Memorias documentadas*, 70. When the sub-delegate reached Barcelona in Jan. 1834 he was mobbed and his installation postponed (*The Times*, 28 Jan. 1834).

[3] For these events see *The Times*, henceforward invaluable, and F. J. de Burgos, *Anales del reinado de D.ª Isabel II* (1850, 6 pts.), i. 151–2 and 179–82.

politicians and placemen which was bound to conflict with the military interest. The Council of Regency could only oppose Martínez de la Rosa by amending his first draft of the new Constitution to allow the Parliament to meet more often;[1] but they soon had cause to regret that in their anxiety to secure larger circles of action for themselves they had emancipated so many competitors for power. Too few had foreseen, with General Zarco, 'the danger which would befall the state by the unrestrained use of the political initiative by military chiefs'.[2]

3. MILITARY AND CIVILIAN LIBERALISM, 1834–1835

By this time an unexpectedly successful Carlist rising in the north was presenting the generals with an embarrassing challenge, and while Martínez de la Rosa continued to patronize the nominees of the Council of Regency,[3] neither he nor they could survive in the face of continual defeat. The first legitimist risings had been suppressed in 1833 without much difficulty by General Sarsfield, and Don Carlos himself remained stationary in the camp of his Portuguese ally, Dom Miguel, to which he had been exiled well before King Ferdinand's death; and when the Miguelite cause[4] was overthrown by a month's combined operations in May 1834 (in which an almost unblooded Spanish detachment under General Rodil co-operated with the English and French volunteers in the army of the Liberal prince, Dom Pedro), the military potential of Carlism appeared to be exhausted. In fact, it was untapped. Don Carlos had still hoped for the support of the regular army on his brother's death, and was nonplussed by its unanimous declaration for Isabella: but the attitude of the Basque and Navarrese peasantry indicated the

---

[1] See Clarendon MSS., c. 451: Villiers to Palmerston, 29 Mar., 15 Apr., 5 May 1834. [2] De Burgos, *Anales*, i. 208.

[3] Zarco remained his War Minister until succeeded by Llauder in Nov. 1834; the inspectorates of infantry and engineers he gave to brothers of the old military family of Balanzat, the cavalry to the veteran Freyre, and the command of Madrid to San Martin (Zea's chief of police), the Duke of Castroterreño, Quesada, Canterac, and the Count of Ezpeleta successively.

[4] The Portuguese equivalent of Carlism, centred on the popular rowdy who usurped the throne in 1828 and offended the commercial interests of England and France.

possibility of raising an alternate army of partisans, and while the Liberals paraded through the Portuguese campaign this was being recruited and organized by Colonel Zumalacárregui, who had been deprived of his regiment in Zea's purge of 1832. On 11 July 1834 he was promoted to lieutenant-general by the Pretender in person, who had escaped from a brief exile in London, and took the field with a compact and mobile striking force; by April 1835 he had defeated and destroyed every army that had been sent against him, the insurrection had spread to the uplands of Catalonia, Aragon, and Valencia, the road to Madrid lay open, and the Liberals were appealing for foreign help.

It was clear that there had been disastrous mismanagement, and apart from the purely military deficiencies of the Queen's army—the unfamiliarity of most officers with mountain warfare, the small number of trained men left available by the discharge of the *quinta* of 1827, the lack of information about the Basque and Navarrese terrain, the inadequacy of existing supplies of weapons and equipment, and the want of a reliable system of communication—its most obvious defect was the principle by which the changes of supreme command were regulated. Sarsfield[1] had been a man of the Right: Valdés, his successor (November 1833 to February 1834), a concession to the Liberals: Quesada's appointment, in March 1834, rewarded him for his part in the overthrow of Zea: he handed over to Rodil in June because Rodil was the latest political favourite, and Mina's appointment in October 1834 was a calculated invocation of the last-ditch stand of the *exaltados* in 1823. None of these generals was inexperienced, but all were failures, and they were unable to rely on the co-operation either of their own subordinates, who intrigued behind their backs with Madrid politicians,[2] or of the provincial governors to whom they appealed for emergency reinforcements. Among their divisional commanders the ex-*guerrilleros* and the orthodox regulars fought each other, rather than the Carlists, for prestige.

---

[1] Pedro Sarsfield (1779-1837) rose from captain to general in the War of Independence and served under Lacy in Catalonia: he frustrated the Cadiz conspiracy of 1819, and became known as an old-fashioned professional, a popular and irascible gourmet suspected of Carlism by Left-wing civilians, of opium-eating by others.

[2] See *The Times*, 13 Apr. 1834.

Gaspar Jauregui, a labourer's son who had helped raise the Basques against Napoleon and now led a force of Guipuzcoan volunteers called *chapelgorris* ('red bonnets'), was denied the chief command in June 1834 because his colleagues 'don't want a man who can scarcely write, and was never anything but a Guerillero'.[1] When in October Mina arrived at Pamplona it was reported that 'the regular Army is . . . highly discontented with the idea of being placed under the command of a Guerilla chief';[2] and two months later a want of confidence between two able exponents of the rival methods of warfare—Marcelino Oráa[3] and Luis de Córdova —led to a humiliating defeat at Arquijas and the resignation of the latter. But neither the terrorism of the Liberal free corps nor the laborious strategy of Rodil seemed able to produce a victory, and, as Villiers conceded, 'one knows by oneself that one should be monstrously tempted to give up shooting, if every day for five months whenever one came in at the corner of a field one saw all the birds get up at the opposite end'.[4]

Thus the experiment of a moderate Constitution was dogged by military defeat, and in the Parliament of two Estates which met in July 1834, the ministers were driven by a querulous opposition to make concessions first to the men and then to the measures associated with the régime of 1820–3. On Christmas Day 1834 the extreme radical *emigrés* were amnestied and restored to political life; a fresh crop of disasters on the northern front in the spring of 1835 compelled Martínez de la Rosa to resign, and after ten weeks of the Count of Toreno's administration the tradition of insurrectionary politics was reasserted by a series of provincial rebellions that swept him from office. The Regent was obliged to appoint the Jewish financier and radical hero Mendizábal as her Prime Minister, and by 1836 he was exercising

[1] A letter from Quesada in I. Bermejo: *La estafeta de palacio*, 3 vols. (1872), i. 106.

[2] *The Times*, 14 Oct. 1834. See also F.O., Caradoc to Palmerston, 2 Aug. 1834, and Flinter's letter in F. Duncan, *The English in Spain* (1877), 14.

[3] Oráa (1788–1851), a Navarrese law student who joined Mina's *partida* in 1810, had served the constitutionalists in 1823 and was purified in 1828; he alone of the *Cristinos*, according to a hostile source, 'treated the people as if they were human beings, not savages' (M. B. Honan, *The Court and Camp of Don Carlos* (1836), 46).

[4] Clarendon MSS., c. 451; to Palmerston, 1 Mar. 1834.

a dictatorship of the Left. The situation was no longer in the hands of King Ferdinand's generals, and now that the civil war had become a direct conflict between Divine Right and Liberalism there was little chance of the army's remaining outside the party struggle; the question was, could it in these circumstances avoid the internal collapse which had overcome it in 1823?

Already in 1834 the *exaltado* opposition were planning to use sympathetic military elements in order to seize power. Officers were enrolled in the secret *Isabelina* society at Madrid and Barcelona, and after an unsuccessful attempt to provoke a rising 'of the people' at the first opening of the Estates,[1] a *pronunciamiento* on the 1820 model was actually engineered in the heart of Madrid on 18 January 1835. Men of La Isla—Generals Quiroga and Palarea—were behind the attempt, which consisted of getting the key detachment on picquet-duty in the Post Office (the main Guard house on the Puerta del Sol), to declare for liberty and a change of ministers while civilian conspirators raised the people and arrested the cabinet. In the event, the mutineers, led by Lieutenant Cayetano Cardero, who had spent twenty-two years as a subaltern, disgraced themselves by shooting the Captain-General of Madrid, thus alienating the sympathies of the rest of the garrison, and the civilians left them to their fate. This might have been a hard one, had not certain ministers themselves abetted the rising as a means of discrediting their new colleague, the ambitious Llauder, now War Minister; for their double-dealing to end in a pitched battle round the Post Office, where Cardero was blockaded, would have been an embarrassment, so he was allowed to capitulate and march out with drums beating and colours flying. He was promoted, and, like Riego in 1821, left the army and entered Cortes; but he was never able, as he wished, to speak as the representative of army opinion, because his own grievance—retarded promotion—was not generally felt in wartime conditions, and he had sacrificed the life of a brother-officer in the interests of a clique of Madrid radicals. Events had dulled the revolutionary

[1] See A. Pirala, *Guerra civil*, i. 400–4. This plot was attributed by Villiers to Romero Alpuente, an old Jacobin of the 1820–3 variety.

instincts of the officers; Cardero might have brought the *exaltados* to power, but at the time it seemed equally likely that Llauder would use the troops to establish a dictatorship of the Right.[1]

In the Army of the North, where by 1835 some 40,000 men were concentrated, the return of the Liberal soldiers from exile seemed to have produced a more inflammable state of opinion. These officers had lost ten years' seniority for their devotion to the Liberal cause: 'thus were seen mingled the sad with the joyful, and in a certain fashion, the immolators with the victims. . . . Old officers covered in wounds who had already made many campaigns obeyed youths who had risen while they were proscribed. . . . ' Such is the testimony of Evaristo San Miguel, leader of the 'victims' who hoped to exploit their discontent: but the ill feeling caused by this situation seems to have been directed far more at Madrid than at other officers, and San Miguel found no sympathy whatever in the army for the politicians who had forced Martínez de la Rosa to grant a full restitution of the ranks and decorations held in 1823.[2]

There was a certain amount of friction at headquarters between commanders such as Mina, who had attacked the monarchy of Ferdinand VII in 1830, and those who, like Llauder and Quesada, had defended it, but there was little scope for the agitation of failed revolutionaries with hard-luck stories in an army that was fighting for existence.[3] Thanks to the amalgamation of Royalist and Liberal elements that had been fostered since 1825 the prevailing tone of the officer corps was unsympathetic to the party slogans of Madrid, and when the radical newspapers began to accuse the more conservative soldiers of crypto-Carlism, and make demands for a purge of political suspects, they excited only resentment.[4]

[1] See *The Times*, 9 Jan. 1835. For a detailed account of Cardero's *pronunciamiento* see Pirala, *Guerra civil*, i. 584–602.

[2] Evaristo San Miguel, *Breves observaciones sobre los sucesos de agosto de 1836 y sus resultados* (1838), 14–16.

[3] Rodil claimed that: 'I did more important services to the cause of liberty by commanding the army of Aragon than did Mendez Vigo in his ridiculous posture on top of the Pyrenees in 1831.' *Manifiesto del Marques de Rodil* (1838), 31.

[4] See J. F. Bacon, *Six Years in Biscay* (1838), for a statement of radical views at this time.

For the army was uncompromisingly hostile to the Carlists, who humiliated them on the field of battle and treated prisoners of war like rebels. No general officer deserted to them after the war had begun, and the few units that went over *en masse* were captives, acting on pain of death. Respect for the military capacities of the enemy was accompanied by an aggressive anti-clericalism, excited by the spectacle of Navarrese priests assisting their flocks on the march, and the depredations of the clerical *guerrillero* of Castille, Merino; they discovered that monks were manufacturing cartridges for Don Carlos and that nuns were sewing his grey uniforms and banners,[1] and could remember the support given the fractious *Realista* battalions by the clergy in 1832 and 1833.

Thus the first open attack on the Church under the constitutional monarchy of 1834 was made by the Army of the North, on the orders of Rodil: it was he who gave orders to Jauregui to burn the convent of Aránzazu, and initiated a persecution of the monks which was to be continued by his successors and to contribute largely to the savagery with which the war was fought. Caradoc reported from Vittoria on 7 July: 'The Queen's chiefs say . . . that the people do not care a pin about their privileges . . . that they are pushed on by the clergy in the present resistance',[2] and in 1836 the moderate Liberal, General Córdova, boasted to Mendizábal that he had closed more than twenty convents on his own initiative.

However, this was an attitude encouraged by the circumstances of the position in the north, not by the secularism of the political parties of the Left; these made themselves heard by an attack on the running of the war which serving officers found particularly offensive. They had no mind to be told that their leadership was ineffectual, that they employed too many batmen and took too much leave, or that the punishments inflicted on their men were barbarous and unfair;

---

[1] A correspondent of the *Indicateur* who 'had occasion to communicate with several officers of the Regiments of Gerona, Almansa, Estremadura, Africa, and of the Royal Guard', reported on 20 Dec. 1833, 'The hatred of the soldiers to the monks is incredible: they talk of nothing but exterminating them' (*The Times*, 30 Dec. 1833).

[2] F.O. to Palmerston, 7 July 1834: Caradoc, a diplomatic agent, returned to Spain as Lord Howden the Ambassador in 1851.

they were not amused by songs on the incompetence of their generals and 'very clever little pieces produced about this time . . . ridiculing the civil war'.[1] They resented especially the *exaltado* cry for no quarter after Lord Eliot, acting on the instructions of the Duke of Wellington, had arranged a treaty between Zumalacárregui and General Valdés on 28 April 1835 by which the lives of captured regulars (but not militiamen) were to be spared. 'Gracious God!' exclaimed the Bilbao radical Bacon, 'here is a treaty which carefully excludes the militia, the very pith of the popular cause. . . . The Spanish Generals ought to have spurned the mere idea of bargaining for their own safety at the cost of the families who fed, clothed, and paid them—besides fighting for their cause as well, if not better, than themselves';[2] but when even this hard-won concession was endangered by the massacre of Carlist prisoners, thrown to the revengeful populace by intimidated government authorities at Barcelona and other coastal cities, the regulars suffered for the violence of the *exaltados*. On 19 January 1836 General Córdova expressed to Mendizábal the army's 'profound grief and lively indignation' at such excesses, which jeopardized the lives of 'our unfortunate friends and companions in arms, over whose head the enemy's knife is hanging by a hair in the dungeons of the rebels',[3] but he was protesting to a government that had been brought to power by provincial insurrections and was helpless against the radical clubs which manipulated the instrument by which these were effected, that is, the militia.

This rival army also antagonized many regulars (much as the Royalist Volunteers had turned them against Don Carlos), and in particular the captains-general and military governors responsible for public order behind the lines. Martínez de la Rosa had tentatively continued that demilitarization of the provincial administration which had cost both Liberals and absolutists so dear, by appointing civil governors (who reverted to *jefes políticos* in 1836); however,

[1] See Poco Mas, *Scenes and Adventures in Spain 1835–40* (1845), i. 238. For radical attacks see de Burgos, *Anales*, iii. 5, and *Diario*, Procuradores, 1835, ii. 35. Cf. the parody of Espartero's dispatches in M. Breton de los Herreros' play *Muérete iy veras!* (Clásicos Castellanos: Teatro: 1928: 47–49).

[2] *Six Years in Biscay*, 197.

[3] F.O. Villiers to Palmerston, 13 Feb. 1836.

the war enabled many military authorities to assume emergency powers, and it was only the assault on public order from within presented by the militiamen which undermined the solid structure of captaincies-general as it existed in 1833.

For the organization of this body, which had begun with the generals themselves before the King's death, had got out of hand. The government of Martínez de la Rosa wanted a politically neutral burgher militia, recruited from the same class of substantial householders to which he conceded the franchise in the Royal Statute, but in the first place such people were reluctant to serve,[1] and in the second, the need to relieve regular garrisons sent north against the Carlists made it imperative to enrol anyone who would volunteer— the unemployed, the student, or the 'swell mobsman', classic revolutionary personnel. The town councils paid them and appointed their officers, and it was not long before they had begun to terrorize, on the pretext of political vigilance, all those without friends at the town hall.[2] In Madrid, the 'Urbanos' as they were still called (in memory of the home guard raised by Charles III in 1774) participated in the anti-monastic riots of July 1834, and by September they were already shouting 'Fuera' ('Get out!') at Quesada, now Captain-General of Madrid;[3] they kept up a war of insults throughout 1835 with the regular garrison, particularly the Guards,[4] and showed their feelings about public men by serenades or demonstrations. In the rest of Spain their strength rose to some 130,000, and by lending their aid to the civic rebellions of August 1835 they brought about the

[1] Miguel Tacon, Captain-General of Andalusia, finding that Seville produced only fifty volunteers for the new militia, asked the *Junta de Comercio* why—'They pointed out the danger to which they might be exposed, having besides no guarantee from the Government, by identifying themselves with a body the rolls of which might become, as after 1823, so many rolls for proscription.' Tacon's remedy was forcibly to enrol 'the most noted merchants' and leave them to cover themselves by getting recruits: but Tacon was an exceptionally vigorous public servant (*The Times*, 6 Feb. 1834: Seville 22 Jan.).

[2] See Borrow's account in *The Bible in Spain,* and the complaint in Cortes of the Marquess of Sanfelices, quoted by de Burgos, *Anales,* vii. 189–90.

[3] *The Times*, 1 and 2 Oct. 1834; on 4 Feb. 1835 *The Times* reported that the Isabelina society was able to control the *urbanos*—'who are mere volunteers, and all anxious for places'—by the hope of overthrowing the government.

[4] T. Farr, *A Traveller's Rambling Reminiscences* (1838), 58, and *The Times*, 14 Apr. 1835.

fall of Toreno and the appointment of Mendizábal. For although, as an English observer reported, 'the great body of the people still remain entirely passive, and the whole of this commotion is, as yet, the work of a small minority in the towns', no military authority was anxious to involve his men in a pitched battle with the insurgent militia; the Malaga riots of March 1835 having shown that regulars would join the rebels rather than risk their lives for a political system which meant little to them.[1] Even the government of Toreno, the conservative Minister of June to September 1835, approved of authorities who 'acted more wisely than if they had attempted a vain resistance', and at Barcelona General Bassa, who attempted a 'resistance' to the mob and militiamen who had seized control of the city, was torn to pieces. His murder horrified conscientious officers, all of whom would have been obliged to act as he had, and in 1836, when the government of Istúriz was faced with a similar outbreak of *pronunciamientos*, only one captain-general, Vicente Quesada (again in charge of Madrid), had the courage to take action against the militia—now called 'National Guard' —in the interests of public order.[2] By disarming them, he kept the capital loyal when almost the whole of Spain had rebelled; only when the Regent and her ministers were themselves made to succumb by the mutiny of La Granja did he relinquish his command and flee, in mufti, to a horrible death.[3] Elsewhere the pattern of behaviour was set by men such as General Palarea (see pp. 80, 88), himself an ex-member of the *Isabelina* in 1834-5, but promoted to the command of Valencia by Mendizábal. On 9 August 1836 a Major Antonio Boil entered the city with an insignificant detachment

[1] *The Times*, 18 Apr. 1834, reports that if the *urbanos* attack the government 'it is . . . certain that neither the cuirassiers nor any other regiment of the line will consent to act'.

[2] See *The Bible in Spain*, i. 218-20, for an eye-witness account of his bravery; according to *The Times*, 26 Aug. 1836, 'every person having any mark or token of the National Guard fled at his approach'.

[3] *The Times*, 26 Aug., attempts to scotch the rumour, also found in Borrow, that Quesada's 'ears, nose, and eyes, etc. had been cut off and carried away as trophies' by claiming that his body was rescued from its assassins before it could be stripped; but mutilation may have come first. The movement had begun, at Malaga, on 25 July with the shooting of the military and civil governors, General St. Just and Count Donadio; for an account of the mutiny of La Granja see Appendix II.

and set up a cry for the Constitution of 1812 to which not even the *nacionales* responded, but the fact that they made no attempt to suppress the demonstration was enough; Palarea remained in secure possession of the streets and the citadel alike, but 'loyal to the government, and giving a signal proof of his subordination and respect, he decided to avoid a breach by abandoning the city entirely with the troops of the garrison'.[1] The radicals seized power, Boil was proclaimed a general by his men, and the government was carried on by a provisional junta.

Thus the first impact of popular Liberalism had made government by the Pashas of 1833 impossible; abandoned either by their own garrisons, or by the government they represented, they had lost their nerve. Even the great Llauder fled ignominiously from Catalonia to France, where he was joined by the commander-in-chief of the Army of the North; for the events of previous year had succeeded in bringing the bulk of the serving army, hitherto unconcerned with the party struggle, to declare, with the *exaltados*, for the Constitution of Cadiz.

4. CÓRDOVA AND MENDIZÁBAL, 1835-1836

After the disasters of spring 1835 the troops were thoroughly demoralized, but when Luis de Córdova,[2] the most successful of the divisional commanders yet produced by the war, was given the chief command on 3 July, and shortly afterwards won an indisputable Liberal victory at Mendigorría, confidence was restored. As a lieutenant, Córdova had done his duty by repulsing the rebels of 1820 from Cadiz, and had subsequently made his way as a diplomat and a soldier under the absolute monarchy; this won

---

[1] Boix, *Historia de Valencia*, iii. 379–85. Generals Espinosa and San Miguel, in command of Andalusia and Aragon, went further, and accepted the presidency of the revolutionary juntas set up by the *pronunciados*; yet how factitious was the 'manifestation of the National Will' which they hoped to appease may be deduced from the tariff of agitation printed in de Burgos, *Anales*, iii. 256 n.: 'To Club-members of the frock-coat or tail-coat class, for organization: 70 reales a day; to porters, with jackets and sticks, for special intimidation jobs, 8 reales; to lads, for shouting in mobs, 4 reales.'

[2] *Fernández* de Córdova, properly; born 1798, of a naval family, elder brother of Fernando (see pp. 34, 35 n).

him the dislike of advanced Liberals and their military friends, but his youth, talent, and patrician variety of Liberalism recommended him at the palace. When Toreno fell, he made sure that the contagion of *pronunciamientos* should not infect the army, but he was by no means predisposed against the government of Mendizábal, since, although this meant jobs for the radicals, it might also mean the vigorous war effort which would produce the men and supplies for which he was desperate. Since the death of Zumalacárregui (of an infected leg wound in June 1835) the Carlists had lost some of their *élan*, and stayed entrenched in the northern highlands where they enjoyed an overwhelming strategical superiority. Córdova had too few men to attempt a military occupation of the enemy country, and therefore deployed his forces round it in a series of forts so as to contain the rebels and starve them of supplies until he was in a position to resume offensive warfare; but for the success of this policy[1] he depended on the government's ability to improve the condition of the blockading army and succour him with every kind of reinforcement. This Mendizábal promised; he was determined to mobilize all the resources of the country for the sake of winning the war, and by means of an extraordinary *quinta* of 100,000 men and credit raised on nationalized monastic property he expected to do it in six months. All Liberals, not only the *exaltados*, looked to him with respect; he corresponded amicably with Córdova, and the Minister and the General understood that each was indispensable to the other.

But when Córdova began to demand the promised supplies he was met by empty reassurances and by counter-demands for victories to enhance the government's prestige. These were impossible, because the British Legion, a force of nearly ten thousand which arrived in September 1835 hoping to be paid on the strength of Mendizábal's Stock Exchange reputation, proved unfit for active service until the following spring, and the conscripts of the great *quinta*, who began to arrive in December, were wholly untrained and almost unclad.

---

[1] Which is explained and defended in the best-selling *Memoria justificativa que dirige a sus conciudadanos el General Córdoba en vidicación de los cargos que por la prensa nacional y estranjera se han hecho á su conducta militar* (1837).

Consequently the army had to remain inactive while the Carlists captured a row of forts on the northern coast at the beginning of 1836, and Córdova, despairing, threatened to resign the command; but Mendizábal would not accept his resignation, even when Louis Philippe began to allow his frontier authorities to let in arms and supplies to the enemy, thus frustrating the whole blockade system. The tone of Córdova's dispatches grew resentful,[1] and in the end he complained 'neither you, nor your letters, gave me the least suspicion that mine were ever read'.[2] By May 1836 it was clear that either he or the Prime Minister must go.

Changes at Madrid gave this antagonism a political importance. Mendizábal's hopes of leading the whole Liberal movement had been frustrated by his dependence on the provincial radicals who set up and manned the improvised juntas that were implementing his war drive, after having overthrown the traditional authorities in 1835. On the strength of their support he secured a grant of extraordinary powers from Cortes, and exercised them in a way which other Liberals (in particular the two Cadiz radicals Istúriz and Alcalá Galiano) found intolerable. Thus when Cortes met in 1836 he was confronted by an opposition, and inevitably leaned the more on the deputies who supported him, the *exaltados* under López Caballero, and Olózaga; and it was exactly these men who were the keenest antagonists of the army. Since they saw their own rise to power as a revolution, they tried to equate the efforts of Mendizábal with those of the Jacobin ministries of France, and to his Carnot they wanted a Hoche from Córdova. Their newspapers began to keep up a political censorship of military appointments;[3] the

---

[1] 'They ask me for victories', said Córdova, 'because victories will produce triumphs in Parliament, peace in the country, money in the markets, order and reconciliation among parties, and they don't realize that they put the effect before the cause.' F. Córdova, *Memorias íntimas*, ii. 43.

[2] L. Córdova, *Memoria Justificativa*, 434.

[3] After Juan Van Halen, the radical adventurer, had been appointed military Governor of Catalayud the *Eco del Comercio* of 7 Jan. 1836 noted that 'we desired to see this worthy Spaniard occupying more than the governorship of a subordinate hinterland town', and two weeks later, on 22 Jan.—'we have heard that a certain commander has been put at the head of one of a Corps of Provincial Militia who did not conduct himself as he should have in the defence of Laredo in 1823, and who after that period held important employments under the Government of Calomarde. . . . Therefore . . . we insist that the antecedents both political and military of the

Eco attacked Espartero and the War Office for the deci-
mation of the *Chapelgorris*, and De Meer, the Viceroy of
Navarre, for his control of *ayuntamientos* and repression of
radical demonstrations. On 3 and 4 February it published a
whole programme of military reform, and in May began to
attack Córdova himself. The army is valiant and decided, yet
the war is stationary—'then it can be deduced as a logical
consequence that what has been lacking—and is lacking, is
good leadership from those at the top'.[1] He was accused of
unfairness in his selection of staff officers and promotions
generally: of working in the *Moderado* interest to secure
French intervention and the downfall of Mendizábal: of re-
pressing the urban militia: of being secretly pro-Carlist.

The point of such attacks was to 're-politicize' the army
by getting commands for Left-wing officers. Mendizábal
had begun his administration by giving captaincies-general
to three 'Men of 1820', Quiroga, Espinosa, and San Miguel,
and by putting forward, as a possible successor to Córdova,
the Marquess of Rodil, who had become a devotee of
thorough reform, and sought to permeate the army with
'new men' to give it a more committed character. The
exaltados showed the way to a patronage coup, and were
emboldened by the fact that Córdova's views on the necessity
for getting the assistance of a French army had turned several
of his own subordinates against him.

Ever since August 1834 the question of whether or not to
appeal for foreign aid had divided the officers of the army.
General Valdés (in command from April to June 1835) believed that the Spanish war effort was being nullified by
dissension fomented behind the lines by radicals,[2] and most
of his subordinates agreed; hence the appeal by Martínez de

___

commanders who are appointed to lead the different corps of the army be examined
with the greatest care.'

[1] *Eco*, 3 May 1836: His requests for more supplies provoked a Sr. Varona to ex-
claim in the lower House: 'Let us suppose that rations were wanting for some days, I
believe that if the Generals had been animated with national honour they would have
given the order to forward march! and eat the rations of the enemy.' Almodóvar,
the War Minister, expressed his disapproval of this remark, but Espartero and
Córdova were moved to publish a reply in *El Español* of 4 May, declaring themselves
highly offended. Varona defended himself in the *Eco* of 8 May and apologized to
Espartero alone.

[2] F.O., Eliot to Wellington, Logroño, 28 Apr. 1835.

la Rosa to the governments of England, France, and Portugal which produced three Legions of volunteers. But the more radical generals—San Miguel, Mina, López, and Lorenzo—who had less objection to civil disorder, disagreed: if society were convulsed, the necessary conscripts and money would be released from within the country.[1] Córdova, however, who saw his forces decaying daily from neglect and sickness, was whole-heartedly in favour of getting a regular French army to invade the Carlist territories from across the Pyrenees; an opinion which provoked the opposition of a 'non-interventionist' group of nationalist and radical officers under General Espartero, commander since the beginning of the war of the Queen's forces in Biscay.[2]

While the radicals attempted to exploit this division by buttering Espartero in their newspapers,[3] Córdova made a last effort at reconciliation with the government by going in person to Madrid. However, when he got there he discovered he was too late. The Queen Regent had come to resent the threatening language and revolutionary associates of Mendizábal, and when the *exaltados* got him to press for the take-over of the army by their military allies, she took the opportunity of dismissing him and appointing Istúriz in his place (15 May 1836). She agreed with Córdova that French intervention was the only hope for her cause,[4] and her new ministers, disillusioned radicals who had formed an alliance with the courtiers and conservative followers of Martínez de la Rosa, were anxious to strengthen their position before the elections by getting the public support of the commander-in-chief; thus circumstances placed Cristina, Córdova, and the government in an alignment that the *exaltados* interpreted as a militarist and reactionary alliance.

The ministerialists hoped to cement such an alliance, and although Córdova went out of his way to repudiate any party affiliations, making it clear to the conservatives 'that their principles would find no sympathy with the army, for that the inactive, timid policy of their party offered no

[1] 'Il faudrait faire un appel au patriotisme de la nation', San Miguel to Eliot, 11 May 1835.
[2] See *Galeria militar contemporánea*, i. 110, and Pirala, *Guerra civil*, i. 937.
[3] *Eco*, 14 Mar. 1836.
[4] See F. Córdova, *Memorias íntimas*, ii. 33.

guarantee of order or of improvement'[1] and doing all he could to get a radical officer, General Seoane, appointed War Minister, the idea that he was the chosen dictator of the Right involved him in the downfall of Istúriz; and by a similarly fortuitous association the army was convinced that because they were no better supplied and paid under a Right than under a Left-wing government, they might improve their chances of victory by joining the radical rebellions of August 1836. For Istúriz was bankrupt; no money came from Madrid, and while Córdova could raise morale by his presence, he could not prevent the infiltration of his forces by radical agents who exploited the sense of frustration and defeat.[2]

The men could endure want, but not failure, and when in June and July 1836 the Carlists broke through their lines and routed them in open battle, their discipline gave way. One by one, units joined their protest to that of the *exaltados*, and the more pliant captains-general, such as San Miguel at Saragossa, declared for the Constitution of 1812 without compunction: they 'knew the army too well already'[3] to suppose it would hold out for the government.

With this, Córdova's last hope—French intervention—vanished. Louis Philippe would not succour democratic revolutionaries who affronted his cousin in her own study; as soon as Irribarren's men had gone over, in July, the division which had assembled on the frontier was recalled.[4] In September, Thiers was replaced by the conservative Molé, and French mistrust of the Spanish Liberals was redoubled; Córdova was already an exile composing his written defence.

But if the rule of King Ferdinand's generals was ended, it

---

[1] F.O., Villiers to Palmerston, 29 May 1836. Nevertheless two conservative-Liberal intellectuals, the journalist Borrego and Estévanez, auditor of the Army of the North, had been trying to get him to lead a Right-wing coup since mid 1835; see letters in A. Cánovas del Castillo, '*El Solitario' y su tiempo*, 2 vols. (1883), i. 260.

[2] On 22 April he sent a most confidential circular to his commanders from Vittoria stating that 'I possess information which compels me to believe that agents of several extremist parties are agitating and exciting the men with sinister objects in view and working the Sergeants and Privates as the ranks most open to seduction and surprise.'

[3] San Miguel, *Breves observaciones*, 28.

[4] See the note from Lebon to Clonard, on the back of a wedding invitation, dated Pamplona, 16 July, in Clonard MSS., Legajo 12.

was only with reservations that the army had returned to the tradition of the 1820 rebellion. The dissatisfaction of the soldiers with the Madrid government, which let them fight in rags, unsuccoured, while the newspapers jeered at their inefficiency, had grown irrespective of which party held office, and was unlikely to be assuaged simply by the adoption of a new constitution. One group of generals and officers was tied to the radical cause by historical association and political conviction; but the rest were more anxious to discover whether the new ministers[1] would be able to assist them in winning the war.

[1] The cabinet was complete by 11 Sept. 1836 and included Mendizábal (Finance) and López (Interior) under the presidency of José María Calatrava. For details of the La Granja mutiny see Appendix II.

III

THE GENERALS AND THE PARTIES
1836–1840

DURING the period from the La Granja revolution to the Glorious Revolution of 1840 the ideal of Liberal unity in the face of Carlism was impaired, if not finally superseded, by the emergence of two political groupings opposed to each other within the framework of parliamentary politics. Both accepted the bicameral Cortes, extended franchise, and limited Royal Prerogative contained in the Constitution of 1837; so that the struggle between order and liberty, which had ranged hitherto from the palace to the barricades, could be concentrated on the parliamentary arena.

However, the 'patriots' and *exaltados* of the Left still believed that a radical reform of existing institutions and a victorious war against Don Carlos were two facets of the one political truth; and though the new deputies of 1836 had constructed a more monarchical and less democratic constitution than that of 1812, they remained closely linked with the radical intransigents whom it excluded. 'Enthusiasm' was still vital to their existence; though the strength they derived from small-town demagogues and rogue militia heroes was incompatible with their future as a 'dynastic' party, it gave them a hold on popular emotion which was not always a weakness. For outside this following among the unpropertied classes, traditionally skilled in rebellion, the group which called itself *Progresista* was a rather introverted body[1] —lawyers, journalists, and civil servants to a man, faithful to the rhetoric rather than attentive to the social implications of radicalism, half-ashamed of the tradition of 1820, half-devoted to it.

---

[1] Olózaga, López, and Madoz were the leaders of the post-La Granja movement, although the patriarchs, Argüelles, Calatrava, and Mendizábal, retained their individual authority.

Thus there was an imperfect reconciliation of the parliamentary and revolutionary ideals among the victors of 1836, which produced a drift to the Right embodied in the clubs[1] and deputies known as *Moderado*. No longer a casual alliance between ministerialists and the more Whiggish Liberals, they were now growing roots in the country; all those who saw their possessions—the money, land, and bourgeois civilization that were the prizes of a freer society—threatened by the politics of enthusiasm tended to rally behind those Liberal oligarchs, Toreno, Martínez de la Rosa, and Istúriz, who had rescued public authority from the 'cage' of the 1812 Constitution and enunciated the danger of 'licence' to the Liberal cause. For this the remedy was 'strong government' —the sovereignty of parliament to be enforced, whenever necessary, by the suspension of liberty, and the rule of law to be finally guaranteed by removing the popular element from local government. Thus, in a tranquillized monarchy, established interests would regain confidence in the Liberal cause; the 'Republicans' of Cadiz and Barcelona would be crushed, and the generals, ecclesiastics, and landowners whom they had frightened off would accept a free society through the agency of a Liberal-conservative party.

From this watershed came the Progressive and Moderate parties which were to alternate in power from 1843 to 1858; but in the thirties each remained more of a tendency than an organization, depending on alliances between the bureaucrats and noblemen whom the Queen Regent made ministers, and the recognized party politicians whose chances of office or local standing were able to attract a following. Elections were fought with the assistance of party platforms, but usually decided, except in large towns, by the *jefe político* or captain-general; two party programmes were publicized among the reading classes by the Progressive *Eco del Comercio* and Borrego's *Correo Nacional*, but deputies relied on the patronage-machine to acquire the loyalty of the office-hunters (*pretendientes*) and civil servants (*empleados*) which counted. The alternation of ministries was governed

---

[1] By Jan. 1837 the 'party armed with parchments and money' had infiltrated the hitherto revolutionary militia of Barcelona. (See *Las Bullangas de Barcelona o sacudimientos de un pueblo oprimido por el despotismo ilustrado* (Paris, 1837), 84–5.)

not by election results but by the Regent's will—she, in turn, being guided by her own estimate of public opinion; the elections confirmed her choice by giving the new ministers their majority in Cortes. It remained to be decided whether any group of politicians could achieve the independence and popularity which would enable them to 'force the closet' and inaugurate a more representative system of government.

This was also the period in which the Liberals were able to collect together their overwhelming superiority in men and materials and achieve the victory over the Carlists which had seemed inevitable in 1833; not, however, before many more battles had been lost, and Madrid had been twice threatened (in the autumns of 1836 and 1837) by enemy forces that had broken out of the northern highlands. Military success, as well as the favour of the Queen Regent, decided the fate of governments, and if the parties had succeeded in capturing the loyalty of fortunate generals, public opinion, which was excited by the war as by little else, might have become more closely involved in the competition of civilian politicians; as it happened, the important generals remained uncommitted, and by taking the 'spoils' of government into their own hands, they subordinated the Liberal-conservative debate to the rivalries of military cliques, and fatally hindered the development of parties by getting the Regent to appoint their own nominees to the all-important War Office.

I. RADICALISM AND INDISCIPLINE, 1836–1837

Both radicals and *Moderados* made attempts to capture generals and harness them to their chariots, and in 1836 it certainly appeared as though the army were deeply involved with the Left. General Seoane, the new Captain-General of Madrid, who had risen with the radical cause, informed the British Ambassador that

there is but one experiment left for us to make and from that, however repugnant it may be, we must not and shall not shrink— France in this as in other systems has shewn us the way, and we must have recourse to a reign of terror—A Guillotine must be established in Madrid, and in every capital throughout Spain—the country must be placed under Martial Law, and every man capable of carrying arms declared to be a soldier—death must be inflicted upon all those who are favourable to the cause of Don Carlos—who are lukewarm in that of the Queen, who are even suspected of either—and upon those who do not immediately make over their property of every kind for National uses—General Seoane said, no man could view such measures with greater horror and disgust than himself, but he knew his own countrymen well enough to feel sure they would be effective, for that by terror the services and property of every Spaniard could always be obtained. . . . In short, anything and everything, rather than submit to Don Carlos.[1]

If generals could adopt this language, it is understandable that civilian radicals should have expected them to revolutionize the army and put into practice the military reforms for which they had been agitating in the press.[2] But if, during the Calatrava administration (August 1836 to August 1837) and the life of the Cortes which supported it, something was done to implement these—the staff corps was re-established, a more egalitarian *quinta* law passed, and corporal punishment mitigated—there were aspects of the radical programme which most officers found intolerable. In particular they had no intention of appeasing the ambition of provincial *exaltados* by surrendering the conduct of the war to local juntas of 'Armament and Defence', on which half the seats were held by civilians;[3] and the generals who had done well out of the rebellion of 1836 were not going to subject the army to political purges which would stir up trouble among brother-officers. Rodil, the new War Minister, had no intention of diminishing the authority of the central government in the interests of reform; he appointed ten new departmental chiefs at his office,[4] and gave promotions and jobs to some of the more Liberal generals and those who, like Manuel Gurrea, had been elected president of revolutionary juntas, but on the whole, as the radicals complained,

[1] F.O., Villiers to Palmerston, 12 Oct. 1836.

[2] See *Eco del Comercio*, 29 Sept. 1836, for a summary.

[3] See the *exaltado* pamphlet *La milicia por de dentro* (Cadiz, 1836), which gives an exposé of the military cliques, and *Reflexiones sobre la situación de España y medios para terminar con prontitud la guerra civil, por un ciudadano español* (Nov. 1837).

[4] Who 'didn't know how to put pen to paper for four months', according to Seoane; see *Diario*, Congreso, 9 Apr. 1838.

he patronized his friends rather than theirs. Espartero, García Camba, Alaix, and Seoane, who got the best jobs, had all served with Rodil in Peru, and when the patronage coup of the Left stood revealed as relief for American veterans, his colleagues began to insist that he justify himself by winning a victory over the Carlist army under Gómez which had penetrated to Andalusia.

'Win a battle, they said to me, then there will be money. You want me dead and buried, I said to my colleagues every day':[1] but he was compelled to take the field, and while pursuing the enemy with a systematic incompetence of his own, he fell a victim to one of the loudest *exaltado* demands (which was reinforced by Villiers, who had lost patience with Spanish generals) that incapable commanders should be summarily dismissed. While the British Ambassador and the *Eco del Comercio* got the young Brigadier Ramon María Narváez put in command of the pursuing army, Cortes sent the 1835 mutineer, Cardero, now a deputy, to arrest General Rodil and bring him back to answer for his ill success.[2] His fate was shared by others, but if such dismissals were applauded by radical civilians, they displeased professional soldiers; even though it was necessary that the bad commanders be removed, why should vacancies be given (as after the fall of Rodil) to party nominees such as Brigadier Rodríguez Vera, the new War Minister, appointed on the strength of his having rebelled in 1820 with Riego and voted against Istúriz as a deputy? Why should Sir George Villiers and the newspapers push favourites into senior commands, why should deputies be sent to the front as advisers without bringing money to pay the men, why, above all, should the running of the war be confided once more to the Finance Minister Mendizábal? But what chiefly discredited the Calatrava government in the eyes of most officers was its conduct over matters of supply and discipline.

For while General Córdova had been in command, the War Office Commissariat (*Administración Militar*) had

[1] See *Manifiesto del marqués de Rodil*, 39.

[2] Cardero was turned out of Rodil's headquarters, but the General resigned of his own accord and retired to Lisbon until the next Left-wing rebellion, in 1840, brought him back into favour. In Nov. 1836 a radical deputy went so far as to declare that 'General Rodil ought to answer for his conduct with his head'.

collapsed from the government's inability to pay the contractors, but the wants of the army had been partly met by the system of dealing directly with local authorities, who were indemnified by remittances of their future tax quotas owed to Madrid. Thus basic rations and the men's pay could be found, even if clothing, armaments, and officers' salaries were forgone; but by the end of 1836 it became clear that no further supplies from the municipalities could be expected until government credit improved, and from this period the troops began to suffer from starvation as well as nakedness and disease.[1]

From November 1836 to March 1837 Espartero was supplied with three-quarters of his minimum requirement for bread: with under half the fodder requirement, and with a slight surplus in rice and cod.[2] His chief of staff, General Ceballos Escalera, was therefore able to feed the soldiers, and in fact slightly to increase their basic ration, making up the deficiency in bread with rice, or white beans, or cod: but the emptiness of the Treasury meant that no money could be issued as pay. For this, the men had to give up a portion of their food issue and sell it back to the contractors. The price at which they sold it was estimated by the *Eco del Comercio* at 20 per cent. less than the price the contractors had originally exacted from the government: so that even if the claims of these dealers were not met by the Treasury directly, they were able to make up their losses by reselling what they had bought back from the soldiers, either to the government or private buyers.[3] Thus a penurious government was paying twice for the rations it could afford, while the soldier deducted his *cigarillo* and play-money from his basic issue of food.

Mendizábal claimed that during this period he had sent large quantities of victuals and money to the army,[4] but he

[1] To the eloquent testimony of Espartero's dispatches to the War Office may be added the evidence of the Count of Clonard, provisional commander of the 4th Division of the Army of the North: he writes on 9 Jan. 1837: 'The troops were yesterday without food, and I don't know if they will get anything to eat to-day. It is six months since the officers were paid: all their resources are spent. . . . I have revealed all these facts to the Government but they haven't even answered me.'

[2] *Revista Militar*, viii. 463.

[3] *Eco del Comercio*, 10 Nov. 1837.

[4] De Burgos, *Anales*, iv. 111.

also stated in Cortes that the officers were spending this money in play, or else had their belts filled with gold pieces, since none of it got to the men.[1] Just as the remark of Arguelles in 1813 about 'mercenaries' had not been forgiven, so neither was this; he became the negative pole in the axis of military politics, whatever the officers' other political affiliations might be, and the entourage of General Espartero began to agitate for the removal of him and the government he represented.

Espartero had a private quarrel with the ministry, as he had been appointed to command the Army of the North on the recommendation of Rodil, and had seen both the War Minister and his other comrade-in-arms, General Alaix, ignominiously dismissed; besides, he was dogged by the hostility of Villiers, who, believing that the Queen's cause was endangered not from his 'want of loyalty', but from his incapacity as a General',[1] advocated his dismissal and persuaded ministers 'not to place too much confidence in General Espartero or to leave too much to his discretion', even after he had become a popular hero by his relief of Bilbao on Christmas Day 1836.

Thus an atmosphere of distrust was engendered similar to that of the previous summer. Then the army had assisted the radicals to power, but now there was no alternative clique of politicians to Calatrava's; the *Moderados* were still an inchoate minority, whom Espartero was even less inclined to favour than had been Córdova. Since his differences with the cabinet were not political, they were interpreted by his contemporaries as a war of secret societies; Mendizábal and the 'Scotch Masons' were being attacked either by the 'English Masons' or by the organization of American veterans known as the 'Children of the Sun'.[2] It seems, however, that these societies were civilian hypostatizations of the usual relationship between old soldiers, who, as Balzac says, 'se croient toujours au bivac, obligés de se protéger envers et contre tous'. In this case their enemies were the radicals who were

---

[1] F.O., Villiers to Palmerston, 21 Jan. 1837.

[2] The masonic theory was favoured by the conspirator Aviraneta; for the *Hijos del Sol*, see Dembowski, *Deux Ans en Espagne et En Portugal pendant la guerre civile 1838–40* (1840), 101.

demanding an explanation for the failure of the March offensive of 1837; so that when on top of this Don Carlos was allowed to set out for Madrid at the head of a large expeditionary force, Espartero came behind to protect the capital and punish his enemies—in particular Mendizábal. The government appealed to him in the name of Liberal unity, through General Seoane, but only succeeded in confusing him at a time when other officers at headquarters were determined to go ahead with or without their commander. At Aravacas his guardees went on strike in protest at the ministry, and Calatrava resigned. It was naturally assumed by the Left that the conservatives had infiltrated the army and turned it into an instrument of reaction; but Espartero's ostensible grievance, that, regardless of politics, no commander-in-chief could tolerate the undermining of military discipline by any group of politicians, was speciously justified by events which took place in the north of Spain while he was away.

In the *pronunciamiento* of 1836 only General Irribarren's men had 'committed an act of indiscipline and proclaimed the Constitution of 1812 spontaneously, not by order of their officers',[1] but this act was prophetic of the weakening of officer control. The same men went on to elect their commander General and Knight of St. Ferdinand after he had won a battle at Lodosa, declaring that 'they should like to see the government that would refuse to confirm it';[2] but Generals Alaix and Peón, less fortunate in battle, were deposed by their own divisions shortly afterwards.

Such instances of disorder became more frequent in the following year, and during the summer of 1837 a series of mutinies broke out along the northern front, beginning at Hernani where men of the Princesa foot went on strike for their pay. Their commanding officer, General the Count of Mirasol, had in fact spent his own money and a forced loan from the town council in trying to appease their discontent, but local civilians had been 'sympathizing' with the soldiers, and 'blaming their generals and commanders for the prolongation of the war and the miseries they experience. They say in their own language that if swords were as loyal as

[1] De Burgos, *Anales*, iv. 36. [2] F.O., Wylde to Palmerston, 5 Sept. 1836.

bayonets the war would soon be over';[1] and when the Count instructed his other units to discipline the mutineers, only his dwarfish stature saved him from their bullets. General Escalera, who was larger, and General Sarsfield, who was much less nimble, met a worse fate; both were savagely attacked and killed in the following month of August, at the instigation, it was rumoured, of civilian radicals who had declared that if the men lacked pay, it was because their officers had embezzled it.

There may have been truth in this accusation, since, in the same period, the men of the British Legion were kept 'three or four months pay in arrears, which, they say, should always be the case, because it is a sort of hold it is necessary to have on them',[2] and when, at Madrid, the Reina regiment was paid in full, other commanders disapproved because 'soldiers possessed of so much money would be led to commit lamentable excesses':[3] but the mutineers themselves protested equally at the bad generalship which seemed to be losing them the war. At Hernani they had been navvying at a line of useless entrenchments 'while they were anxious to be led against the enemy', and his troops were first turned against Escalera by his letting Don Carlos escape over the Ebro;[4] but whoever was most to blame, the *exaltado* journalists who had been denigrating the generals were bound to attract the particular enmity of the officers. It was asserted that the whole eruption had been planned by 'a secret society called the Masons of the Scottish Rite' organized by the more radical ministers and directed by General Seoane against commanders who had been protected by Córdova and were politically hostile to the government, so as to create vacancies into which radical colonels could be promoted.[5] This was a far-fetched theory, but it served to

---

[1] *El general conde de Mirasol á la historia* (1843), 20, 21, and 48.

[2] According to Thomas Farr, an ex-guardee don, who visited the Legion in 1837. [3] F. Córdova, *Memorias íntimas*, ii. 295.

[4] F.O., Villiers to Palmerston, 26 Aug. 1837, and *The Times*, 12 July and 6 Sept. 1837.

[5] See de la Fuente, *Sociedades secretas*, ii. 89-95, and Pirala, *Guerra civil*, iv. 664. Aviraneta was a confirmed mystifier, and does not deserve credit: his statement can virtually be disproved by considering the antecedents of the victims of the mutineers. Mirasol alone might be called a political enemy of government, but his own description of the events at Hernani makes no mention of *direct* radical provocation when

heighten the distrust of the officers for the party to which, a year before, they had looked with confidence, and made them not unfriendly spectators of the conservative revival which took place in the winter of 1837. When in October and November Espartero restored the discipline of the northern front with firing squads and penal servitude, his action was associated with the new programme of Order which was the platform of the *Moderado* chiefs; just as the alignment of 1836 between Córdova, the deputies supporting Istúriz, and the Regent led that General to be called *Moderado*, so now the same epithet was applied as fortuitously to Espartero.

He had gone further than his predecessor in using his troops to compel—or, as it happened, to enable—the Regent to change her ministers, but that did not mean that he was more politically minded than Córdova—precisely the reverse. Córdova had been determined to keep the Liberal experiment respectable in the eyes of Europe, and to retrieve the new régime from the stigma of military mutiny which had stuck to that of 1820–3: to Espartero, this was superfluous refinement. His only concerns were to get better conditions for his army and a good press and security of tenure for himself; thus he refused to accept the War Office, which was offered him continuously from July to September 1837, he declined to express any opinion on the stop-gap coalition of Bardají which succeeded the Calatrava government, and when the Regent, confronted in December 1837 by a new and *Moderado* Cortes, appointed a Right-wing cabinet under the Count of Ofalia, he applied the same conditions to the new ministers as to the old—if they could supply him and promote his friends, he would produce victories: if not, he would let them appear a government of defeat.

2. THE RIVALRY OF ESPARTERO AND CÓRDOVA
1837–1838

The armies could only expect supplies from a ministry in control of Congress, and in the winter of 1837 only a

he had every motive for exposing it if it had been applied. Escalera was a returned constitutional exile, Sarsfield was retired and wholly innocuous—O'Donnell, on the other hand, a notorious conservative, was acclaimed by the men who drove Mirasol away as the general of their choice.

Moderado-biased cabinet could hope to secure a majority; but from then onwards the life of this cabinet depended on military success, as a result of either Spanish generalship or French intervention. Louis Philippe had no real intention of sending an army to assist the Liberals, and thus Espartero remained indispensable to Ofalia, although professionally undistinguished and politically suspect. It was an alliance of convenience maintained by a division of patronage; and eventually the commander-in-chief was able to dispose of the military and administrative appointments which fell to him in such a way as to establish a party of friends who prolonged his indispensability by their hold on the working of government. At first, however, the politicians resented this process of strangulation and tried to prevent it; in April 1838, when Espartero began publishing open complaints against the continued failure of the government to supply his men, Ofalia dismissed the radical Van Halen from his post as Espartero's chief of staff and turned his protégé, Major Miranda, out of the War Office. When Espartero remained intractable General Oráa, in command of the Army of the Centre operating against Cabrera, was sent orders from Madrid to secure a victory at Morella at all costs, for the sake of diminishing the importance of the northern front, and only when this attempt collapsed in a bungled and despondent siege were the ministers forced to resign.

It is perhaps surprising that Ofalia allowed his relations with headquarters to deteriorate at all, but he was an experienced (if desiccated) old bureaucrat who was not prepared to surrender to one of his generals without a struggle when he could lean on others; and he was encouraged by the activities of a *tiers parti* in Madrid, a party that owed its origin to the return of Luis de Córdova to politics in December 1837, and its development to a union between all those elements whom the power of Espartero had antagonized. Córdova was still young, able, and ambitious, but his Liberal ideas remained unconnected with the development of party loyalties in Madrid from 1834 to 1836. Some consequences of this have already been noted in his dealings with Mendizábal, and even after the radicals had finally turned on him, he attempted to remain uncommitted. Since both the dynastic parties had abandoned him, he entered into negotiations, from Paris, with the revolutionary extremists who had rejected the Constitution of 1837;[1] and when by the events of the autumn he was enabled to re-enter official political circles in Madrid, he retained a connexion with the underworld which was to do him disservice in the future.

However, for the time being it suited him better to exploit the conservative revival. Ofalia was too dependent on Espartero and the Regent to please the *Moderado* deputies; any political leader with the courage to dismiss the commander-in-chief and espouse a whole-hearted policy of Order would be able to command their loyalty. Córdova might have been the man, and he set up a salon about which his political sympathizers could revolve; the government tried to tempt him north with the command of the army, but he refused[2] (having already promised this post to his ally Narváez), and got himself elected deputy instead. What hindered his rise, however, was his private conviction that only a united Liberal front could command sufficient support in the country for the war effort that would defeat Don Carlos; he was more concerned with a 'fusionist' policy to reconcile Right and Left than to accept the already-made conservative majority which the situation offered. Like Espartero, he would only accept political alliances on his own terms, and since these were not purely military, but the product of his own political outlook, they were more likely to prove distasteful to the party men; however, they, the government, and he, shared a dislike of the commander-in-chief, and the prospect of bringing him down gave them a common interest.

In this task he was given a potentially decisive role by his friendship with Ramon Narváez, a dedicated military careerist who had earlier been prepared to remove Espartero from command of his army with no other backing than a War Office authorization,[3] and now, in the summer of 1838, had built up an 'army of reserve' in the south which could be

[1] Clonard MSS., Legajo 29, loose sheet; 'Montalbo me informo . . .', and F.O., Villiers to Palmerston, 17 Dec. 1837.
[2] In Jan. 1838; Clonard MSS., Legajo 29.
[3] F. Córdova, *Memorias íntimas*, ii. 239.

used effectually to counteract the masses on the northern front which made up his rival's strength. By skilful use of this weapon, it seemed that Córdova might bring the parties to accept his leadership and win control of the whole army; had it not been for the circumstances under which it had been formed, and the rigidly authoritarian régime in the south which admitted of no concessions at all to the Left.

For the government had been compelled to meet the threat of Andalusian insurrection, which had led to the resignation of Toreno in 1835, and of Istúriz in 1836, by entrusting the administration of these provinces to 'Men of Order', military dictators whose disenchantment with the tradition of 1820 committed them wholly to the restoration of public authority. Their methods were those which had been employed by Ramón, Baron de Meer,[1] in Navarre before the 1836 risings; as viceroy he had been in a position where the effects of radical agitation conflicted directly with the needs of the army, and since the proximity of the front line entitled him to govern with extraordinary powers, he was able to suppress newspapers, suspend the *Audiencia*, and apply the legislation of the Cortes only as it pleased him. He rid Pamplona of radicals, so that a *Moderado* deputy was elected for the Congress of 1836 which never met; and even though this made him a bugbear of the Left,[2] his efficiency led Calatrava to send him to Catalonia as captain-general. There, the free-trade policies of Mendizábal had stirred up widespread resentment against Madrid which the radicals were exploiting in preparation for a local *coup d'état*; which he forestalled by disarming and purging the National Guard and thus getting the richer employers on his side—'men's fears have taught them now to appreciate his value'.[3] While intimidating the back streets of Barcelona in the name of Property, he waged war on the highland Carlists with supplies levied on his own initiative independent of contractors

[1] Born 1787, a Catalan of Low Countries ancestry, he had resigned from the Guards in 1822 on being unable to prevent his men joining the mutiny, and was later re-employed under the Conde de España.

[2] See *Eco del Comercio*, 12 and 30 Jan. 1836.

[3] Clarendon MSS., c. 457, Consul Annesley to Villiers, 16 Oct. 1837. See also Pujal, *Historia política de Cataluña*, iii. 146–231, for a narrative of de Meer's tenure of office.

and government commissaries; a system which circumstances made a necessity. The objection that this degree of devolution amounted to an abdication of Madrid from control of the provinces—'establishing *Anarchy* as a principle'[1]—could be met by adducing the hopeless position of the government, unsure of its parliamentary majority and subservient to the wishes of its military chief; as Narváez wrote, 'frankly speaking we haven't got a government'.[2] Order had to begin somewhere.

In November 1837 Serafín María de Sotto y Ab-Ach, Count of Clonard, a cultivated guardee general, the friend both of de Meer and of Córdova, was sent to Cadiz as commandant-general to restore tranquillity after a tumultuous election. He declared a 'state of siege', purged the National Guard, and transported three agitators; the radicals were cowed, and he rose to the Captaincy-General of Andalusia, leaving the city to the American veteran Villalobos. Villalobos was committed to reaction by his former service in the Royalist Volunteers under King Ferdinand,[3] but General Palarea, who took over Granada, was an ex-*guerrillero*, exconspiratorial radical, turned authoritarian after losing control of Valencia in 1836. These three then set to work; first declaring martial law with the approval of all who had been victimized by the radical clubs,[4] and then subjecting the press, the National Guard, and local government to a rigid inspection and control. They excited the fury of the *exaltados*, but kept the support of the propertied classes, who were prepared to sacrifice liberty for security,[5] and consolidated their position by getting 'good', that is, conservative, results at the elections.[6] The opposition was forced back to the

[1] *Eco del Comercio,* 9 May 1836.

[2] To Clonard, 20 Mar. 1838, from Jaen; Clonard MSS., Legajo 29.

[3] Chamorro, *Estado Mayor,* ii, *A. González Villalobos.*

[4] On 22 Jan. 1838 the Provincial Deputation of Seville implored Clonard to do this as 'the only method'. Clonard MSS., Legajo 29.

[5] A Jerez shoemaker 'convinced that the nation will be saved by a military government' asked Clonard to have suspected Carlists impressed out of hand and impound five million *reales* from the legacy of an unpopular citizen to another who was already rich (Clonard MSS., Legajo 29).

[6] After Clonard had reformed the National Guard of Priego he was assured that 'it was a political phenomenon that the elections for Cortes resulted in favour of the *exaltado* candidature . . . it is not surprising that the honourable neighbourhood sacrificed its true political sentiments in order not to offend a powerful Agent which

procedure of conspiracy, grouping into masonic lodges under a *Junta Magna* at Cadiz, tampering with garrisons, and communicating in code;[1] but Clonard was vigilant, and his attitude towards subversion uncompromising.

In these conditions Narváez built up his army, deciding, 'since we have reached the unhappy situation of seeing ourselves reduced in these provinces to our own authority alone',[2] to raise money by direct treaty with the chiefs of administration. After a conference at Ronda (April 1838) they gave him a credit of £20,000 and lent their authority to a campaign of public subscriptions and loans by which he could be subsidized further; reimbursing their own treasuries by borrowing from the *juntas de comercio*, or merchants' associations, which had benefited from the imposition of order and were allowed in compensation to forgo tax payments to Madrid. Arms and uniforms were contributed directly from the manufacturers, and in a few weeks he had raised a force of over 20,000 men which he equipped and trained on regular victuals and a quarter pay.[3]

This was partly owing to his prestige as a typical Andalusian who had already shown his mettle by chasing the Carlists from the south in 1836, and partly because the first objective of his army was a local one—the extirpation of the bandits of La Mancha: but the extent and alacrity of public co-operation was chiefly the result of Clonard's administration. It was he and his subordinates who controlled the Provincial Deputations, enthused the substantial citizens, and kept protest underground; his repression which begot the liberating army. Thus when the collapse of General Oráa's eastern offensive and the fall of Ofalia's government (6 September 1838) left Córdova without sufficient political weight to assume power at Madrid, it seemed that to resist Espartero he must throw in his lot with the

could oppress them as it chose to obtain this contrary vote. From today onwards the citizens of this town will be defenders of legal doctrines.'

[1] For this movement, and its connexion with the radicals in Espartero's army, see Clonard MSS., Legajo 29, Araoz to Clonard, 12 Apr. 1838; Clonard to Latre, 13 July.

[2] To Clonard, Malaga, 31 Mar. 1838; Clonard MSS., Legajo 29.

[3] See *Historia militar y política de Narváez*, 369, 494; Cadiz contributed 900,000 *reales*, and from 66 men and women of Malaga he received the equivalent of 7,000 guineas of that period at once (*Correo Nacional*, 17 Feb. 1838).

Moderados and range himself, like Narváez, with the military dictators of the south; instead of which, true to his pan-Liberal principles, he played a double game and got in touch with the repressors and the revolutionaries at once.[1]

Meanwhile Espartero had begun to make movements towards a seizure of power at Madrid, and the new ministers, under the Duke of Frias, had to appease his military jealousy. Van Halen was put in command of the Army of the Centre, General Alaix was gazetted Minister of War, and on 8 October Narváez was recalled from La Mancha and ordered to accept a subordinate command in the north. The *Progresista* leaders Mendizábal, Infante, and Seoane went over to the Esparterist lobby, and popular unrest, caused by the defeats which the Liberal cause continued to suffer in the field (El Perdón, 19 September, and Maella, 1 October), made the Regent the more inclined to entrust herself wholly to the commander-in-chief. If his enemies were to stop him it had to be before General Alaix, hindered by wounds, reached the capital and organized a thorough Esparterist cabinet.

The *Moderados* acted first, getting their own nominee, Brigadier Francisco Hubert, put in temporary charge of the War Office. Then, when Narváez made use of the respite by marching to Madrid, protesting at his suspension, and demanding a bigger army, they proposed that he take over the capital by armed force and impose a party dictatorship. However, Narváez was no more a party man than Córdova, and much less of a politician; he merely wished to supplant Espartero and win the war his own way, for which he needed more men and a properly authorized command, not a close involvement with the fortunes of a parliamentary party. He was, after all, if anything, a man of the Left. Therefore he refused, and on the night of 28 October the cabinet tried to

[1] Clonard later discovered that one of General Córdova's radical friends in Seville 'wrote to him that he should put himself at the head of the revolution because the revolutionaries feared Espartero at that time lest he should invest himself with a military dictatorship. He went to Andalusia and conferred with Cortina, leader of their efforts there, in Seville. In the beginning it was thought that his antecedents could be an obstacle to his joining them, but by admitting the programme of the *Doceañistas* he tried from then onwards to secure by these means a way of ridding himself of his rival Espartero.'

trap him into a conflict with the National Guard by means of a false alarm; they failed, and he retired, baffled, infuriated, and demoted, leaving the capital to the Esparterists.[1]

Córdova was thus deprived of the army in being which might have sustained his cause, and was thrown back on the radical connexion. While keeping up a show of loyalty and friendship for Clonard, he made approaches to the garrison of Cadiz and laid plans for a general Andalusian rising which was to start at Seville. Such a movement had been anticipated by the radicals to 'spread electrically all over the peninsular monarchy',[2] and would, at least, have thwarted the ambitions of Espartero; whether Córdova would have been able to control it is less certain, but in any case his intrigues had been reported to Clonard, and the attempt miscarried. The cry was given at Seville, and failed to spread; Córdova was publicly compromised, and, having involved Narváez in the affair, had to get out of it as best he could.[3] Espartero was left in control of the country, and published an *Exposición* to the Regent from Logroño in which he condemned both the rebel generals and the conservative politicians for using the methods of conspiracy and sedition to gain their ends; while the *Moderado* journalist Borrego wrote to Narváez that 'Majority, minority, whites and blacks, all condemn you and our best friends say that you have done wrong even if there is no crime in it'.[4]

3. GENERAL ALAIX AT THE WAR OFFICE, 1838–1839

Thus by the end of 1838 both the Right and the Left had attempted to secure the allegiance of conquering generals, and both had failed; the generals had fought out their own rivalries without committing themselves to any set of political principles by which one could be distinguished from the other, and had used the weakness of the government in the face of an undecided war to enforce their demands.

---

[1] *Manifiesto del Mariscal de Campo Don Ramon María Narváez, en contestación á las acusaciones del Capitan General Conde de Luchana* (1839), for Narváez's account of these events, and (p. 52) his plan for ending the war.

[2] Clonard MSS., Legajo 29, C. to Latre, 13 July 1838.

[3] See Appendix III.

[4] 27 Nov., from Madrid; Clonard MSS., Legajo 29.

Espartero had emerged the victor, but the inchoate party system was among the casualties, and the Carlists were entrenched as firmly as ever in the highlands of the north and east: the military could blame the civilians for their inefficiency, the civilians could blame the fractious generals, but the war was not ending. Out of the debris of Madrid politicians and provincial dictatorships the new supreme commander had to construct a victory-compelling government; events had forced him to emerge from his sulky inactivity at Logroño, and assume political responsibility in the same way as Córdova had planned, and the question which had been asked since 1835 was now asked to the exclusion of all others—is he a *Moderado* or an *Exaltado*?

To this the answer was that like all the successful military politicians—Narváez, Serrano, the Conchas, O'Donnell—he was a Liberal, that is a believer in parliamentary government and the spoliation of the Catholic Church, but that he would support any group of politicians who would give him control of War Office patronage, full employment for the officer corps, and protection from 'subversive' newspapers which could damage his reputation in the eyes of the public. However, as he was neither a good enough general nor an astute enough politician to make up his own mind, his sympathies were alternately captured by *Moderado* and *Exaltado* cliques on his staff, and whichever of these was opposed to the Madrid government had the advantage of being able to play on his resentment at the inadequacy of his supplies. In 1836–7 he was influenced by the *Moderado* sympathizers General Oráa and Colonels Mazzarredo, Lavalet, Campuzano, and Roncali; with Ofalia in power, his private secretary Francisco Linaje[1] and chief of staff Antonio Van Halen were able to sway him in the other direction, but the *camarilla* at his wife's whist-table still included uncommitted soldiers like himself, and the snob appeal of Queen Cristina's friendship emasculated his radicalism.

---

[1] 1795–1848; rose from the ranks by serving in America: his Jesuitical appearance gave him the reputation of an intriguant, and he probably composed all Espartero's public manifestoes. His services from 1836 to 1840 raised him from major to major-general.

The 'Esparterists' were therefore not a homogeneous group,[1] but they had in common an identification of their professional success with his political advancement, and when he chose his protégé General Isidro Alaix to take over the War Office and form a government (October 1838) the new Minister's first task was to complete the division of spoils which had been in the making for the past year by placing all important military appointments in their hands. After this he had to select his ministerial colleagues, a task for which he was apparently ill equipped; he had been born at the penal settlement of Ceuta, the son of a private, and had risen from the ranks by volunteering for American service and ingratiating himself first with Rodil and then with Espartero, who had befriended him because he also had fallen foul of Narváez in 1836. He had acquired experience of desk work by managing the secretariat of Rodil's *Carabineros*, but as a divisional commander in the war his record was unimpressive; he was a somewhat discredited *vieux moustache*, a vulgarian messmate of the commander-in-chief, who was expected to lean to the Left in politics and accept the advice of the *Progresista* Olózaga. On his way south he was interviewed by an English volunteer, Richard de la Saussaye, who advised him to militarize the whole administration—'Gefes Políticos, Intendentes, etc. are all *noxious* now, because . . . they necessarily impede the action of the military authority, the sole which can produce results. . . . I want the Minister of War to absorb the other Branches ad interim as the Duke did in England.' Alaix agreed; 'says he, I will speak out to them. I won't be in office with any humbug who pretends to act by routine and palliatives in a monstruous Revolution. If Government persists in hampering the resources and policy and opinion of the country the army should be independent of it. . . .' He was determined to 'discover the faction in the War Office and elsewhere and persecute it to death'; but Saussaye was impressed by him—'a very reserved man, the cut of a *Septembriseur*, of no passions, save that of castigation, not to be come at by intrigue or

[1] They were not all Ayacuchos—neither Espartero, nor Alaix, nor Rodil, nor Seoane had actually surrendered at Ayacucho—or ex-rankers: only Espartero, Alaix, and Linaje had been privates.

flattery. . . . Act, is his favourite principle.'[1] The politicians were in for a surprise.

For the *Progresistas* imagined that they were strong enough to demand office on their own terms; they wanted a party ministry with a party leader, and jobs for their dependants. However, these included men with their own plans for ending the war, whom Espartero abhorred—the *exaltados*, with their policy of extermination, in which the reactionary banditti of the north would fall victims to a national revolution on the French model. They had little time for recalcitrant commanders-in-chief (the Jacobins had guillotined disobedient generals) and they still threatened a political purge of the officer corps;[2] their journalism was uninhibited, and in 1839 Miraflores was able to send Espartero one of their plans for revolution, by which, after the dismissal of Alaix, they would 'discredit the Duke of Victory [as Espartero had then become] by the press and by all possible means until he resigns his command . . . and replace him by another General who will lend himself to be a blind instrument of the revolutionaries'.[3]

It is perhaps more surprising that the old anti-militarism of the Liberal *exaltados* had been so far modified that most *Progresista* deputies agreed with the Count of Las Navas, who declared on 22 January 1838: 'I am the disciple of a man who, on benches such as these, said that while there yet remained a corporal and four soldiers, Liberty would not exist; but I know that is untrue when we are dealing with the Spanish Army: the Spanish army is a repository of civic virtues.' The change of attitude had been deliberately encouraged by a group of soldier-deputies led by General Seoane,[4] who, since the Guards mutiny of 1837, had attacked

---

[1] See Clarendon MSS., c. 463, to Villiers, 29 Oct., 15 and 17 Nov. 1838. De la Saussaye remained in the Spanish service and distinguished himself under O'Donnell in the African war of 1861.

[2] See *Milicianos Nacionales ¡alerta! Que la libertad peligra* (1839), 5: and for a summary of *Progresista* plans for ending the war, *Reflexiones sobre la situación de España, y medios para terminar con prontitud la guerra civil, por un ciudadano español* (1837).

[3] Miraflores, *Memorias para escribir la historia contemporánea de los siete primeros años del reinado de Isabel II* (1843–4), ii. 188.

[4] He had hoped to prevent the Aravacas mutiny, and afterwards made a sensation in Cortes by accusing the Guards officers of cowardice for their part in the La Granja mutiny of 1836 and self-indulgence in lingering about Madrid in 1837; his

the war management of conservative ministers without involving the generalship of Espartero or the efficiency of his officers. They did not form a distinct party, but they usually voted with the *Progresistas*, and as the strength of the government depended on its success in running the war, their technical knowledge—although this was not a monopoly, since many deputies held commissions in the National Guard and had served in previous wars—gave them the lead in attacking government policy. Since the raising of the supplies, men, and money which Espartero demanded meant subjecting the country to unprecedented burdens, they wanted it shown that what had already been levied was being advantageously employed and that future expenditure would be devoted exclusively to the war effort.[1] They wanted not a cheaper, but a more efficient war drive.

Thus, when in February 1838 San Miguel proposed that the problem of the superfluous generals be met by putting a number of them on a half-pay list, this solution was not drastic enough for the more economical radicals and had to be shelved.[2] In April Cortes authorized the government to raise a loan of 500 million *reales*, and Seoane demanded that 'this sum be devoted exclusively . . . to the three armies of operations and the navy actually in service, to be distributed in special consignments without any deductions . . . '; but this would have excluded the payment of the dependants and supporters of the ministry, which was consequently able to command a majority of seventy-one against the amendment.[3] He then took to discrediting these rival pay-claims by exposing the administrative abuses for which the *empleados* were responsible; in May, while the Progressives as a whole were attacking the régime of martial law to which as we have

exordium contains the classic dilemma of the revolutionary officer—'although I became Captain-General of New Castille in consequence of a military insurrection, no one is more hostile to revolutions and military ones in particular'. He was then wounded by a guardee in a duel, and became a *Progresista* hero, and President of Congress, affecting the coarse, minatory style that won him the nickname of 'Thunderclouds' (*Nubarrones*).

He was assisted by Evaristo San Miguel, Fermín Arteta, Facundo Infante, Francisco de Luján, and Sancho.

[1] *Diario de las Sesiones*, Congreso, 4 Apr. 1838: Seoane.
[2] Ibid., I, 1838, iii. 480 et seq.
[3] Ibid., iv. 35 et seq.

seen the provinces had been surrendered, he championed the 'widows of Comares', whose husbands had died in Palarea's jail,[1] and, having collected information on provincial conditions generally during the summer, on 15 November he described to Cortes in detail the extravagance and corruption of the civil service and seconded the opposition demand for new ministers which accompanied the triumph of the Esparterists. By attacking from the Left, he and his friends had done much to recommend the Progressive cause to Espartero and repair the estrangement of 1837.

But the ministers Alaix chose were not *Progresistas*, because he was not interested in forming a party ministry. To his question, whether they were prepared to devote all the resources of the country to winning the war, only two public men were able to give satisfactory answers, and since these were the uncommitted financier Pío Pita Pizarro and the doctrinaire conservative lawyer Arrazola, the radicals discovered on 7 December 1838 to their dismay that after having foiled a *Moderado coup d'état*, having won Espartero's explicit approval, and having been offered a share in the cabinet, they were to be governed by one of the usual quasi-*Moderado* coalitions that had followed each other since the fall of Calatrava, and to counteract the vigorous conservatism of Arrazola and Pita, they could count only on Alaix himself and the un-partisan Liberal diplomat Pérez de Castro, who arrived in 1839 to take over the nominal leadership of the cabinet.[2]

As a result Alaix was confronted by a Cortes in which the majority of deputies distrusted him as a Left-wing militarist, and the minority saw him as a traitor to the Progressive cause; neither comprehending how inessential political allegiances were to the success of his policy. Espartero simply wanted a non-partisan chamber which would vote him supplies without making difficulties; when this one refused, and had to be prorogued, he told the ministers that it was 'contributing to the discredit of representative government' and 'did not represent the will of the country, having

---

[1] Pirala, *Guerra civil*, iii. 168–9.
[2] He remained President of the Council through numerous ministerial reshuffles until July 1840.

been elected under the influence of states of siege'; they must dissolve it. Arrazola, knowing that this might lead to a long period of exclusion for the conservatives, objected, but on 2 June he was overruled by Alaix, and for the first time a general's will dispersed the national representatives.[1] This might have been less easy without the Regent's approval, but two days later she made it plain where her sympathies lay by creating Espartero 'Duke of the Victory' and Grandee of the First Class.

The subsequent election campaign completed the disorganization of political life. The Minister of the Interior, Hompanera, put the resources of his department at the disposal of *Moderado* candidates, as if Arrazola had been at the head of the cabinet; but the Finance Minister, Jiménez, patronized the *Progresistas*.[2] At the same time Espartero issued a public rebuke to the journalists of the Left who had been making personal attacks on himself and the Queen Regent (18 July),[3] and the conservative voters, bewildered by the dissolution of the Congress they had elected in 1837, showed their disapproval by staying away from the polls *en masse*.[1] And when, on 1 September 1839, the House assembled, the large *Progresista* majority discovered that while they had been returned on a platform of 'No Transaction' with the Carlists, Espartero had been doing exactly that, and had ended the war in the north by the most unrevolutionary expedient of placing the whole of General Maroto's officer corps on his own payroll (Treaty of Vergara, 31 August).

This is not the place to describe how the movement of Carlist partisans which Zumalacárregui had led to victory in 1835 had developed into the regular army and official hierarchy which now surrendered to Espartero to preserve its status and pay. As the war dragged on, the rebels had imposed a system of taxation and recruitment on the hill-country of the north which drained the forces of popular enthusiasm faster than victory could kindle them. The fight

---

[1] For these events, see *Historia científica, política y ministerial del excmo. Señor D. Lorenzo Arrazola*, 114–29.

[2] See *The Times*, 25 June, 1839.

[3] See A. Torrija y Carrese, *El Guiriguay, los Ministros, y Espartero* (1839), 48.

[4] *Historia científica . . .*, 131–60.

against the bureaucrats of Madrid saddled the Basques and Navarrese with their own court of Castillian administrators and native careerists, and, just as among the Liberals, the ambition of these men and the successful soldiers became the mainstay of the cause. In 1838 mutinies broke out among the rank and file, and the commander-in-chief, General Rafael Maroto, emulated Espartero's take-over by the more brutal expedient of shooting his rivals out of hand and silencing Don Carlos and the civilians. Espartero and he had soldiered together in Peru, and shared the same professional outlook; Maroto's officers were often 'profoundly ignorant, sprung from the lowest classes of society, hardy peasants, carpenters or shoemakers with *galones* or epaulets',[1] but they had become more concerned for their careers than the Divine Right of their King, and when their remaining granaries and war-chests lay at last within the enemy's reach they took the way out of defeat which seemed consistent with military honour.

This meant that there was no need for a radical crusade, since with the enemy reduced to Cabrera's fortresses in the east the government possessed an overwhelming military superiority. Furthermore, the fact that the *Progresistas* were bound by their Constitution of 1837 to enforce a uniform provincial administration, while the Basques and Navarrese had been guaranteed their old privileges before surrendering,[2] meant that a government of the Left might lead to a renewal of the northern war; thus war-weariness, the only spontaneous reaction to events which the electorate appeared to feel, was harnessed a second time to the *Moderado* cause. Therefore, while Alaix, always inclined to the Left, was prepared to govern with the new Cortes and chose, on 7 October, to embrace the Progressive leader Olózaga amid general rejoicing, his colleague Arrazola was anxious only for a chance to hold fresh elections and send the radicals home. The Queen Regent agreed with him, interpreting the shift in public opinion on her own initiative, and before the end of the year Alaix had resigned and left his conservative colleagues to exchange a hostile for a subservient Congress.

---

[1] Clarendon MSS.: Saussaye to Villiers, 11 May 1838.
[2] The *fueros* which gave them their own legislature, no customs barrier with France, and no military service.

For what, then, had the parties paid the price of this continual humiliation? For even when they sang to Espartero's music their leaders were kept out of office, and their membership remained fluctuating and transitory. The answer lies in the success of General Alaix; even if he had wrecked the parliamentary system, he had carried out his promise of December 1838 'to obtain victory and peace by all imaginable means, and, to this end, to secure all possible resources'. It was the misfortune of the Liberal politicians that their first task was the specialized one of winning a war, and it was their failure to do so which compelled them to accept the expedient of War Office dictatorship, which was fatal to their own interests.

For during his tenure of office Alaix spent only slightly more than a fifth of his revenue on the civil service;[1] as he was not a party leader he could afford to let the *empleado* go hungry, and confine his attentions to his own constituency—the army. After the deputies had voted the last *quinta* of the war, in December 1838, they could do little to help him, and from February 1839 he governed by decree, farming the whole country for the Army of the North as Narváez had farmed the south for the Army of Reserve. He reconnected the chain of command between Madrid and the captaincies-general, and combined the functions of the Intendant—a Treasury official—with those of the *jefe político*, the civil governor, who, under martial law, acted as the agent of the captain-general; thus communities could be taxed and disciplined by the same officer, and the whole process of government accelerated.[2] By this means he was able to collect the money with which he paid the troops, and ensure that wartime production was geared to their actual needs. As the wheeled gun had proved ineffective in highland warfare, he converted the arms factories to making pieces light enough to be carried on mule-back and heavy enough to be of use against town walls; from January to August 1839 the number in service rose from six to nearly a hundred, and when the Carlists were finally defeated in the following year it was this advantage in fire-power that proved decisive. Small-arms

---

[1] *Historia científica . . .* 125.
[2] G. d'Ortasini, *L'Espagne constitutionnelle*, 178–9.

he imported from England, and doubled the native out-
put by founding a new factory at Seville; he increased the
supply of sabres from Toledo, and in six months his requisi-
tions had remounted thirty-seven squadrons of cavalry. His
jefes políticos rounded up the missing recruits from the *quinta*
of 1837, and enforced that of 1838; and these masses were
given form and leadership by five new training-schools
which sent 600 N.C.O.s to the front in one year.

The men were clothed and fed by virtue of his decision to
subordinate all other claims on the Treasury to those of the
war; this attracted bids for the commissariat contracts which
Mendizábal's financial management had made unprofitable,
and enabled him to dismiss the monopolist Orlando from
the head of the supply department.[1] Thus the soldiers whose
misery had been publicized so frequently by their general began to appear a respectable and sometimes ostentatious body.
Espartero's aides fixed imperial eagles to their sabretaches,
and in his campaign of 1839 he won over the hearts of the
Basques by paying for his victuals on the nail; at Vergara, he
gave all the Carlist officers their arrears, and the men a month
in advance. His own troops saw this with 'high good humour
and satisfaction',[2] because their lot was still improving;
regular, if short, wages had buried the resentments of 1837.

Thus Alaix's system of coalitions, although unstable and
unpopular with the parties, was justified by its results.
Espartero could not have fought or negotiated except from
a position of overwhelming strength, and his political activities had made him virtually irreplaceable; it was the man who
supplied him with his strength who won the war. However,
with the retirement of Alaix,[3] and the achievement of total
victory in sight, the situation was changed; it was time for the
civilians to reassert themselves, and before the end of 1839 the
cabinet was dominated by a group of conservative politicians
who were determined, with the help of the Queen Regent, to
rescue the parliamentary régime from its military strait-jacket.

[1] For a summary of these achievements see *Galería militar contemporánea*,
pp. 125-8: and *Historia científica . . .*, 116-25.

[2] Poco Mas, *Scenes and Adventures*, ii. 28 and 101.

[3] He became Count of Vergara, travelled abroad to enjoy his private fortune, and
reappeared, briefly and ingloriously, as a *Progresista* candidate for the premiership
in 1847; the Queen claimed she had never heard his name before.

4. ESPARTERO AGAINST THE COURTIERS, 1839–1840

This attempt, which collapsed in the revolution of 1840, merely emphasized the entanglement of military and political interests which the war had prolonged. On the face of it there was a flat antagonism between the Esparterist system and the view of Arrazola that 'for the Government to abandon the progress of the war as completely as it had to the direction of commanders-in-chief, remaining dependent on their dispatches . . . was an absurdity'. He wanted 'a co-ordinated and general system which would make different armies operate simultaneously, . . . and punish indolent or incapable commanders; a directing and centralizing power like Carnot's',[1] which, with Alaix out of the way, might have been wielded by an ambitious professor of law like himself; but when it came to practical politics, the *Moderados*' fear of the Left dispersed their resolution and enjoined the language of compromise.

For most, led by Martínez de la Rosa and Istúriz, could never renounce their hopes of reconciliation with the army; at the same time as they dissolved Cortes and dismissed hundreds of the *Progresista* placemen whom Alaix had appointed or retained, they appealed to Espartero for his approval in the humblest terms, offering to follow his advice in every way. Even after he had replied from Mas de Matas on 15 December 1839 that 'in his own private opinion he would not have dissolved Cortes, as this house and the cabinet he believes would have been able to reconcile political extremes', they were able to count on his disapproval of the radical press and his veneration for the Royal family; for while he told his wife that 'the trouble makers of the party calling itself *moderado* are those who hate me most',[2] he wrote to the ministers that the army 'and particularly myself, hold as enemies whoever by subversive doctrines or in any other manner, attack or harm the inviolability of Persons as sacred' as Isabella and her mother. It was because he remained sufficiently *bon enfant* to respect the monarchy that the conservatives placed their last hopes on the summer trip of the court to Barcelona in 1840; royalty itself to the rescue.

[1] *Historia científica . . .*, 91.   [2] Romanones, *Espartero*, 384.

By this time the enemies of Espartero had come to depend on the leadership of other military men—especially on an admiralty official, General Montes de Oca. The navy had never recovered from the battle of Trafalgar, but the naval interest, comprising a force of half-pay officers and dockyard officials, was a political factor of some importance; Montes de Oca had therefore abandoned poetry and Espartero's friendship for the sake of nursing this remnant, and from 1834 to 1838 had represented Cadiz in parliament. In November 1839 the Regent's friendship made him Minister of Marine, and he soon discovered that if he was to secure any but a derisory sum for the naval budget, the army's monopoly of power would have to be broken. In April 1840, backed by a new Cortes of ministerialists, he and the War Minister, Francisco Narváez,[1] had tried to limit the number of promotions demanded by Espartero for his army, but the Regent refused to support them and they resigned; after which they planned to re-create the situation of 1838 by building up a rival concentration of forces in the centre and south. The cadres of this existed, because they already relied for their control of the radicals—driven from the polls back to the clubs and back-street presses—on the system of martial law which had prevailed in the provinces since 1837; even in Madrid their nominee the military governor Brigadier Trinidad Balboa had answered an *exaltado* project to withhold unconstitutional taxes by declaring 'that the first man who refused to pay should be shot',[2] and had tranquillized public opinion with a force of 3,000 men. Now that he was dismissed, Montes was still sufficiently influential at the palace to secure the appointment of another enthusiast for order to the War Office; the Count of Clonard. After quelling the Seville *pronunciamiento* of 1838, he had been the victim tossed to the radicals by the Esparterists whose triumph he had ensured; in 1840 he was determined to crush both, to 'venture all for

---

[1] Not to be confused with his kinsman Ramón, the rebel of 1838, now in exile; this Narváez was an American veteran, given the War Office after Alaix as a concession to Espartero, whom he had known in Peru. From 1840 to 1843 he helped the *Moderado* exiles with his Cuban fortune, and after their return, the Progressives: thus rising no higher than Count of Yumuri (Chamorro, *Estado Mayor*, i, F. *Narváez*).

[2] *The Times*, 28 Nov. 1839.

all'.[1] Other conservatives wanted the Queen to go on progress to headquarters and captivate her deluded generalissimo; Clonard and Montes, declining to believe that he could be won from the radicals by further concessions, decided that her first objective should be the Army of the Centre, commanded by Clonard's conservative cousin, Leopoldo O'Donnell, at Valencia, and then that she should negotiate with the Army of the North from a position of strength: if Espartero should still favour the *Progresistas*, it would be possible to secure reinforcements from the conservative municipalities of the south, and he could be met on his own terms. He had antagonized senior officers enough[2] by his rise to power for the *Moderado* generals to feel confident of success.

Thus, the struggle that followed was not simply the result of the misuse of the Royal Prerogative by the Regent, as it is often portrayed. Her enslavement to the *Moderado* cause is supposed to have made her appeal for military assistance in forcing the Municipality Bill[3] on a *Progresista* electorate, and Espartero's refusal, motivated by his respect for the Constitution, only decided her to abdicate in order to lay plans, with the excluded *Moderados*, for the complete destruction of that Constitution which was to be accomplished in 1845; but this view ignores the fact that she consistently preferred Espartero's advice to that of her ministers, who could gain her confidence only by posing as his friends, and as soon as she met him in June 1840 she agreed to dismiss them. If she had made use of her prerogative (in 1835, 1836, 1838, and 1839) to appoint cabinets without choosing them from the majority in Cortes, this was in accordance with the view that a house of deputies unacceptable to public opinion should not govern; an unwritten constitutional maxim which the

---

[1] For an account of these events, see Clonard MSS., Legajo 6, Historia, notas y apuntes.

[2] Notably General Diego de León, his best cavalry commander, whom the Queen hoped would take over the Army of the North in July (see J. Flórez Segundo: *Espartero*, iii. 594), and Brigadier Manuel Pavía, a protégé of de Meer, who kept his men loyal to Cristina to the last stages of the September revolution.

[3] Passed in Congress on 4 June 1840 by 83 to 111 votes; the Regent delayed her consent until she could obtain Espartero's. It provided that the municipalities were no longer to elect their own mayors (alcaldes) but accept nominees of the government-appointed *jefe político*.

Progresistas themselves appealed to in the rebellion of the municipalities against the Cortes which broke out in August and September 1840.

The *Moderados* were trying to end this dual representative system—a Cortes legislating with the check of a national *pronunciamiento* through town councils, a sort of unsolicited plebiscite manipulated by political clubs—which they condemned as 'anarchy', and establish a parliamentary sovereignty on the English model; with the ulterior motive of securing a one-party cabinet backed by their own majority in Cortes. This was also the aim of the *Progresistas*, but if they accepted government-appointed mayors and town councils they cut themselves off from one of their deepest roots—provincial radicalism and the National Guard. Thus while they claimed that the new law was an infraction of the Constitution (and this was by no means certain) they were really concerned with the defence of unwritten political usages; and so was Espartero. His fear was the threat to his monopoly of army patronage implied by the *Moderado* alliance with anti-Esparterist generals; he knew of Clonard's plot through a secret ally in the Regent's employment[1] and was able to frustrate it by insisting that she avoid O'Donnell's army on the way to Catalonia, but his only security lay in getting her to repudiate all but his own nominees to the post of Minister and place her political influence wholly at his disposal.

Thus the motives which brought Espartero and the *Progresistas* together in 1840 were not only dissimilar but conflicting. He abandoned none of his loathing for radical journalism (it was the journalists who changed their tune), nor his suspicion of all civilian politicians as a class—'Toreno, Arguelles, Martínez de la Rosa, or Calatrava, they are all the same to me'—and it was only his wish to exercise the prerogative himself that turned him against Cristina, who showed by signing the Municipality Bill on 18 July at Barcelona without his consent that she still meant to use it. Meanwhile the Progressives simply expected him to put them in power as a party, and the extreme *exaltados* hoped

---

[1] Salvador Valdes, according to the *Historia* in the Clonard MSS., Legajo 6.

that he would abandon the whole parliamentary system, deposing the Regent and summoning a Central Junta on the 1808 model composed of deputies from the rebel town councils, whom he would invest with sovereign powers.

In August negotiations at Barcelona broke down, and the Queen retired to O'Donnell's camp at Valencia; on 1 September the *ayuntamiento* of Madrid pronounced against her latest ministry and the Bill, and when Espartero refused to put an end to the rising, which was joined by almost the whole army and the other municipalities of Spain, it only remained to be decided whether he would let her retain the Regency. On 3 October she accepted him as Prime Minister; he was persuaded by a group of radicals to insist on the election of co-regents, and Cristina, abandoning the struggle, took ship for Marseilles, accompanied by O'Donnell and the leaders of the *Moderado* faction.

Thus by the revolution of 1840 the tradition of insurrectionary politics, exemplified in the *pronunciamientos* of 1835 and 1836, was revived, but with two differences. The war had ended in July 1840 with the expulsion of Cabrera into France, and the army was thus deprived of its natural function; yet it was appealed to both by the *exaltados* and the Queen Regent, and the appeal was made not furtively, but openly and directly to the commander-in-chief as leader and representative of a recognized organ of public opinion. The serving officers and soldiers were not called upon to make a conscious political decision, since the issue was represented to them through the agency of Espartero's private regiment, the Guides of Luchana, as an attack by the Court on their chosen hero, and they were simply asked to avenge the 'horrible ingratitude' with which the Regent had treated him.[1] His officers were also anxious that the post-war demobilization which menaced their careers should be carried out by an Esparterist and not a *Moderado* War Office, and the radical clique at headquarters were eager to occupy it. These

---

[1] However, not all military authorities accepted the rising; notably four ex-American colleagues of Espartero, Generals Aldama, Latre, Sanjuanena, and Rivero, of whom the second died of apoplexy at Valladolid amid popular insult. Old courtiers such as Generals Castaños, Castroterreño, Zarco, Zambrano, and San Román turned their coats quickest.

motives, and a natural reluctance to fire on the people, decided the army, and the army decided the revolution; for it was clear that the events of 1836–40, instead of rescuing the Liberal system from the insurrectionary level, had sophisticated insurrection to a more or less controlled expedient for relieving tensions between the parties, with the army as controller. For its actions, it was answerable to its own political conscience; it remains to be seen how it sustained this responsibility in peacetime.

IV

ESPARTERO'S REGENCY
1841–1843

ESPARTERO was a typical unprivileged line-officer who
had risen, untypically, to the rank of general. Born in
1793, the son of a village craftsman who could afford
him an education, he volunteered for the army in 1809, and
after a month in the ranks he learnt the profession of an infantry subaltern in the Academy of La Isla (see p. 18). Rejected by the rather exclusive engineers, he took the only
way to quick promotion left open at the end of the war, and
accompanied Morillo to America; he returned a brigadier to
marry the daughter of a rich Logroño landowner and be
awarded the command of a regiment by the King. In 1833
he marched from Majorca to Biscay, where his addiction to
well-publicized attack quickly carried him to the top of his
profession. 'If half of what Espartero has told us were true
the existence of the Carlists would be a continual miracle of
providence',[1] wrote his critics, but on the battlefield he
seems to have been anxious to win the approval of his wife,[2]
and while doing so recommended himself to his military
superiors. Although he led the opposition to General
Córdova's policies, it was on Córdova's suggestion that he
received the provisional command of the Army of the North;
his fellow-Ayacucho Rodil confirmed it, possibly because,
with the irruption of the Carlists into central and southern
Spain, the northern front had temporarily ceased to be the
most important.

But if he was not a military genius, and if his policy of
moving only when he had been supplied with an overwhelming superiority in men and *matériel* owed more to
his cyclothymic mental condition[3] than to his conscious

---

[1] *La Milicia por de dentro.*
[2] Romanones, *Espartero*, see appendix, his letters home 1834–5.
[3] His long periods of bed-ridden and querulous torpor, punctuated by phases of

strategical thinking, he knew how to look after his troops
and never disdained the reassurance of popularity. He enacted the ambitions of the obscure in a big-hearted way, and
they accorded him in return an admiration to which he became addicted like a drug, and which survived his political
failures; multiplied on cigarette wrappers, barrack walls, and
broadsheets, his unintelligent features became the embarrassing brand mark of the *Progresista* party, and until the
1860's no insurrection was complete without him. For by
driving out the *Moderados* in 1840 he seemed to have committed himself to their opponents, and to stand forth as the
'Son of the people', a radical leader closer to the soil than the
lawyers and journalists who defended the popular cause in
parliament. He was ready then as always to clasp the toiler's
hand and recall his village background with an ingenuous
nostalgia, but since the army, like the Church, allowed the
poor man's son to achieve the highest honours only as the ex-
ponent of its own mystery, it was a rather artificial gesture.
A strenuous professional career stood between the family
workshop and the distinctions[1] he now delighted in, which
included Godoy's palace, ducal coronets, civic crowns, tiger-
skin saddle cloths, cinnamon mule-teams, and noble aïdes
embellished with imperial eagles; he was the most successful
officer of the army, and it was for this reason, and not as a
result of his democratic propensities, that he had become
the hero of the *Progresistas*.

I. THE NEW OFFICERS AND THE NEW DEPUTIES

Espartero had built up his following among the senior
officers in the same way as Córdova, who had kept open
house at Pamplona in order to entertain promising subordinates and sound the morale of the army as a whole. He lacked

galvanic and hysterical energy, might be taken to indicate either manic-depression
or schizophrenia; his condition was aggravated by a weak bladder.

[1] In 1840 at a commemoration of the relief of Bilbao at San Isidro, Madrid, he
was 'decorated to so preposterous a degree, that I could scarcely discern the colour
of the coat on which the ribbons and baubles hung . . . the Preacher, in a long military sermon, . . . exalted him *by name*, almost to a divinity: nay, he actually alluded
to the circumstance of the final victory at Bilbao and the birth of our Saviour
occurring on the same day of the year, as though he were speaking of events pretty
similar . . . ' (*Spain, Tangier, etc. Visited in 1840 and 1841, by X.Y.Z.* (1845)).

the connexions with good society that gave Córdova's parties their distinction, but managed to receive *en bourgeois* and play whist in his wife's *tertulia* at Logroño, surrounded by a swarm of ambitious colonels.[1] From these he chose his divisional commanders, and by the spectacular ascent of some to the rank of general,[2] the ambition of the whole army was fired; the wartime emergency producing at the same time a situation in which the chances of promotion were generally good. For between 1833 and 1840, in an army that had increased from 40,000 to nearly 200,000 and had lost over 5,000 officers in battle,[3] the depressed subalterns of King Ferdinand's army had become senior regimental officers, and the lower commissioned ranks were flooded with wartime aspirants, many of them recruited from the *quintas*, the National Guard, and the universities. For them, Espartero simply meant promotion; 85 per cent. of the total number of ranks bestowed in the war were conceded after he had been put in command of the Army of the North,[4] and it was his recalcitrance that had sent up the level of employment to a height unprecedented since 1814. These officers, and the sergeants whose claims to vacant commissions he had publicly defended in his *Exposición* against Narváez (see p. 83), were his true proletariat, the *pueblo militar*, which, in deference to the *exaltado* concept of the national will, now begins to be differentiated from the people as a whole; and it was their wishes and opinions of which Espartero was the representative.

Their politics were not predominantly radical. They had applauded without exception the executions of October 1837

[1] For a malicious account see Ortasini's *L'Espagne constitutionnelle*; it is difficult to discover whether the author's unfamiliarity with Spanish habits led him to mistake accepted usage for ill breeding.

[2] In 1837 Diego Leon was made a general at the age of 31; in 1839 Leopold O'Donnell was a lieutenant-general at 30, and in 1840 Manuel Concha and Francisco Serrano were major-generals at 32 and 30, with their contemporaries Shelley, Pezuela (later Count of Cheste), Cotoner, and Lara at the rank of brigadier.

[3] *Revista Militar*, viii. 449. 'Estudios sobre la guerra civil', by F. Luján, Apr. 1851, and xi. 750.

[4] *Archivo Militar*, Nos. 5 and 6 (1841). Fernando Córdova describes how Navarrese girls began to regard soldiers as desirable matches—'the young officers played every day in a lottery whose rewards were gained by valour and heroism and quickly changed the least ambitious subalterns into senior officers and generals' (F. Córdova: *Memorias íntimas*, i. 359).

by which the ghost of the Jacobin armies had finally been
laid,[1] and in 1838, while there was antagonism between the
old-fashioned chiefs and their young subordinates who lived
between cafés and gaming-houses on three days' pay a
month, dressing up in extravagant and eclectic uniforms,
and talking politics over their coffee, the latter were
interested in only one reform—the removal of War Office
patronage from the hands of the 'aristocrats'.[2] Thus once
the last *Moderado* general had been removed from office
by the 'Revolution' of 1840, the radicalism of most officers
was satiated; they had got their chosen hero in power,
and looked to the government only to keep them on the
active list and maintain the newly won prestige of the
profession.

For the victories of 1838-40 and the take-over of all provincial administration by the military had turned the soldier
into a popular idol. By the end of the war, postilions, mayors,
ushers, and clerks began to dress like officers, who became
distinguishable only by their medal ribbons, sheepskin
collars, and martial language;[3] they became nationalist,
eager for a fight with Portugal or Morocco, paranoid up-
holders of military honour, who caned the journalists of the
Left or Right that insulted it,[4] and swaggered about the
streets in threadbare self-assertion. But in 1841 the motive
forces behind this spiritual inflation ceased to operate. The
chance of a war with Portugal over the use of the Douro for
navigation vanished with the agreement of December 1840,
and with it the need for a wartime establishment and hopes
of further promotion. The subalterns who were retained
could look forward to stagnation on the pay-rates of 1824;[5]

---

[1] The extent of their approval may be inferred from the behaviour of Martin
Iriarte, a notably radical officer, who might have been expected to sympathize with
the grievances which the *exaltados* were exploiting: he found himself as military
Governor, in command of a loyal corps at Pamplona after the mutiny, and was instructed by government to secure the city by offering pardon to all who surrendered
without delay: rather than do so he resigned the governorship (Chamorro, *Estado
Mayor*, ii, *Iriarte*).

[2] *L'Espagne constitutionnelle*, 87.   [3] *Grito del Ejército*, June 1841, 18.

[4] In 1840 the offices of the radical *Huracan* and *El Trueno* were raided by officers,
and in 1841 Colonel Prim beat Lafuente, editor of the conservative *Cangrejo*.

[5] By which the second lieutenant got 3,900 *reales* a year when his annual expenditure (including arms, uniform, and subscription to the regimental band) came to
about 6,000 (see *Grito del Ejército*, June 1841, for details).

the officers who were retired could only claim a pension at all after twenty-five years' service (so that all the volunteers who had enlisted after 1833 got nothing), and, what was ominous, the existing body of War Office pensioners were being kept months in arrears. Two army journals were founded for the purpose of expressing the wants and fears of the redundant *pueblo militar* to the government,[1] but by the time the inevitable demobilization was begun, the *rapprochement* between the Progressives and the military had been gravely damaged.

For the Cortes of 1841 was dominated by exactly the type of advanced radical whom the generals had previously found particularly obnoxious. Some of the deputies were openly republican, and many were political *ingénues* open to the influence of internationalist, pacifist, and federalist ideas, which, combined with the Benthamite vogue for cheap government, constituted a platform from which the very existence of the army could be attacked. According to the extremists, Napoleon himself had been defeated by a rising of the people, so there was no need for a costly, luxurious, oppressive, and aristocratic army; national defence could be placed in the hands of an unpaid national militia, and an offensive war had no moral justification. The theory coincided nicely with the alliance of *exaltado* party and *nacionales* which had produced the risings of 1835, 1836, and 1840: it implied the abolition of the *quinta*[2] and a vast reduction in the estimates, and even if it was the chimera of a small group of *exaltados*, many *Progresistas* agreed with Marliani that 'the army will become a terrible embarrassment in the future, unless a superior intelligence . . . manages to convert it into an instrument of labour'.[3] Road-mending apart, they were prepared to economize by dismissing scores of superfluous generals, reducing the salaries of those that remained, and

---

[1] See Appendix IV.

[2] The Progressives had produced the new *quinta* law of 1837, but objected to the unfairness with which it was administered. In August 1841 the town council of Malaga attempted to contract out of the system by raising a fund with which to buy substitutes, a scheme that alarmed the War Office and had to be abandoned; for nearly all Liberals, however much they might dislike the 'Blood tax', had an inherent aversion to 'mercenary' armies.

[3] *Histoire politique de l'Espagne moderne*, 2 vols. (Brussels, 1842), ii. 9.

curtailing the number and expense of governorships, captaincies-general, and commandancies: they even proposed to deny all pension rights to the widows and orphans of officers. They wanted to prise the army out of public administration, prune the War Office of its inspectors-general, and make the military everywhere dependent on the civil authority.

Men who held such views as these were bound sooner or later to detach themselves from the feverish Espartero-worship which prevailed on the Left in 1840.[1] During the elections they were able to exploit a perceptible anti-militarist reaction in the country, and when the Cortes assembled most deputies were determined to reduce the power of their Prime Minister-Generalissimo by setting up a new regency which would include some civilian notabilities as well as the inevitable Espartero.[2] They would then be able to govern the country and the army in their own way, without fear of obstruction by the executive, a prospect the Esparterists themselves were not prepared to contemplate. For the distribution of spoils after the September revolution had turned them into an aristocracy of office particularly unwilling to expose themselves to the policy of reform and retrenchment, and they used General Seoane to save them; by getting Espartero himself to insist on a one-man regency, and by denouncing the three-regent deputies as anarchist assassins, meditating butcheries with imported Genoese daggers,[3] he secured a bare majority for his party in Cortes, and enabled his chief to take office as sole Regent on 10 May 1841. But the victory had only been achieved by setting the Senate against the Congress, so that the defeated deputies could still claim to represent the wishes of the electorate—a

[1] The Democrats of Valencia believed that as a 'son of the people, placed at their head, the Duke would advance towards Federation, accomplishing this political change without having to spill a single drop of blood on the soil of Charles III' (Boix, *Historia de Valencia*, iii. 482). But at the same time, when General San Miguel, who took the alliance with the *exaltados* more seriously, 'proposed to the Duke that a supreme Junta should be appointed at Madrid, his proposal met with an immediate and decided refusal: and that matter dropt' (F.O., Scott to Palmerston, 3 Oct. 1840).

[2] The deputies for Catalonia were given mandates to this effect by their constituents, 'so as to neutralize the military predominance which until now had mastered the Revolution' (Flórez, *Espartero*, iv. 12, 13).

[3] Ibid., 31 et seq.

flaw in the legitimacy of the new régime which it could scarcely afford. To make matters worse, Espartero then appointed a cabinet selected from his own entourage and containing not a single accepted Progressive leader;[1] these got up a ministerial party of about fifty deputies, but were confronted by a large and aggrieved majority of excluded radicals, whose co-operation in passing bills was essential and in whom at the same time the anti-military sentiment was kept alive and aggravated.

Thus the Regent's military policy had to undergo the scrutiny and censure of deputies whom the officers of the army considered basically hostile to their interests. As in 1836-8, a ministry in need of allies had to ensure that its civil list was punctually paid, and this meant that the soldier could be kept in arrears while the *empleado* flourished; as Seoane had complained:

Clouds of employees, some of them collected from the streets of Madrid with no other merit than having gone to the café to hear conversations and relate them to the person with whom they seek to ingratiate themselves, arrive in the Provinces in a pitiful state—a threadbare frock-coat, their beard and moustaches *á la romántica*, exciting public compassion—and after they have been there two months you see them dressed in the finest cloth: in a house costing more than their pay: their family or the person they favour taking precedence over the most substantial people in the neighbourhood—dinners—park—carriages—gentlemen—and all on fifteen reales pay. That is what the people see, that is what discredits the constitutional system.[2]

It was this which lay at the root of the militarist and anti-militarist movements of opinion, not so much, as in Prussia and France, a conflict between authoritarian and libertarian states of mind as a battle for economic survival between two

---

[1] The new ministers were: for war, San Miguel, and for the interior, Facundo Infante, two 'men of La Isla', the latter of whom, having fought with Bolivar and risen in the thirties with Rodil and the radicals, was 'Such an expert at Revolutions that he made an excellent Minister of Police'; another general, García Camba, took the Ministry of Marine, and the lawyer González, who was appointed Premier, was a kinsman of Seoane and an old Peruvian acquaintance of Espartero.

[2] *Diario*, Congreso, 1838, ii. 35. In 1849 it was estimated that the government was paying a combined military and naval force of 171,000 officers and men, and a body of 103,000 retired and active civil servants: over a quarter of a million dependents of government in a population of 15 million (ibid., 1849-50, 139).

branches of the same underpaid and over-staffed bureaucracy, which in 1841 the military seemed to be losing.

First their time-expired conscripts were discharged;
eighty thousand men had been released by June 1841 and
this was only the beginning. The anxiety of the super-
numerary officers reached a climax, and Captain Perrotte,
editor of the *Grito del Ejército*, published a programme of
military demands in which the payment of arrears, increases
in pay and pensions, and provision for the unpensioned
officer are accompanied by 'the presentation to Cortes of a
project of law which will fix the organic bases of the army,
suppress corps privileges and establish the inviolable property
of the rank in a secure and legal manner, also the order of
promotions and the different departments of the army'. He
wanted a fundamental law, like that of 1821, which would
liberate his profession from the arbitrary eviction orders
which were continually presented by economic pressures and
the favouritism of the dispensers of patronage, with whom
a reduction or dismissal often had a political motive. The
cuerpos facultativos were exempted from these injustices by
their closed scales of promotion: if the whole army were put
in their position, the humblest infantry subaltern might
share the prestige of the artillery officer, and if the rank became a property, the disadvantages of meagre pay and slow
promotion would be mitigated.

This was more than most officers wanted, but they still
demanded 'preference over all other claimants on the awards
and attentions of the state',[1] and when it became clear that
the government was not prepared to continue this policy—
in 1842, that is, when pay became chronically short—they
were able to accuse Espartero of betraying them to the
economists. Although his own battle with the *exaltados* was
savage, and although his War Ministers were planning reforms similar to those advocated in the military journals, the
facts of starvation wages and unpaid allowances convicted
him of bad faith; the anti-Jacobinism of the commissioned
ranks became increasingly anti-Ayacucho, and the development was fostered by the exiled *Moderados*, who, by explor-
ing the internal tensions of the régime and associating

[1] *Grito*, Apr. 1841, 15.

themselves with the army interest, were able eventually to provoke the rising of 1843 and expose the nullity of the Regent's power.

2. THE UNDERMINING OF THE AYACUCHOS

For while newspapers and deputies talked of 'military despotism' and the example of Napoleon, betrayer of the revolution, was in everyone's mind, including Espartero's,[1] the conditions of his supremacy were not the same as those which had produced the Consulate and the Empire. No one had actually been guillotined, no foreign invader had been repelled, no war of conquest fought; but, on the other hand, there was a striking parallel with the home situation in 1814. Then, as in 1840, a ruler had been acclaimed by the army and populace alike, and his rise to power had been accompanied by the proscription of an unsuccessful faction; Ferdinand also neglected his troops, and turned them against him, and just as the isolated and abortive *pronunciamientos* of aggrieved war heroes had prepared the way for an effective rising in 1820 by drawing attention to their cause, so the *Moderado* rebellion of 1841 provided the defeated faction of 1840 with the fructifying martyr's blood.

This attempt was planned with the encouragement of Louis Philippe by the civilian advisers of the exiled Cristina, and executed by her military henchman, O'Donnell, who expected a simultaneous movement of the Pamplona and Madrid garrisons to result in the rescue of the infant Queen from Espartero and the collapse of his régime; it miscarried so badly that after a bungled assault on the palace, and a premature insurrection in the north, the conservative sympathizers who were involved had to flee across the Pyrenees in hundreds, leaving a group of unlucky chiefs, and the numerous Guards officers who had assisted them, to the mercy of the government. At first, there was a reaction in favour of the Regent and a demand for 'strict justice' on the guilty conspirators;[2] but just as in 1817 the death sentence passed on General Lacy for a rebellion which they had failed to

---

[1] He modelled his inaugural speech as Regent on Bonaparte's as First Consul.
[2] F.O., Aston to Aberdeen, 14 Oct. 1841.

support aroused so much sympathy among the officers as a whole that the War Minister remonstrated with the King, and each felt obscurely that a greater threat to discipline was contained in his execution than in his treason[1] (agreeing with his own protest to the firing squad, 'Grenadiers, have you the audacity to shoot your General?'), so in 1841 the feeling among the military that their fellow soldiers had not deserved death for repeating what all had done the year before contributed perhaps more than anything else to the decline of Espartero's popularity in the army. For the *pronunciados* knew how to die if not how to rebel: General Montes de Oca (see above, p. 94), who had been betrayed by his own escort, put on 'a splendid costume' and wished to give the command to his own firing squad in the *plaza* at Vergara, but was prevented lest divine casuistry should interpret the gesture as suicide. Three bullets entered his stomach at the first volley: he fell only after the second: he pointed to his ear, where the last shot was fired. The young General León, whose fate was the more lamentable as his complicity with the rebels had been half-hearted, rode in an open carriage out of the Toledo gate of Madrid flaunting the crimson uniform and flamingo plumes of his old Princesa hussars, and distributed to his executioners the cigars which may now be admired in the military museum. As he was 'of so noble a nature that he was beloved both by officers and soldiers, a circumstance the more extraordinary as the Spanish privates seldom attach themselves to their officers',[2] his testament, written in the condemned cell, became the first work of a *Moderado* martyrology; it was published, and widely circulated: his *Vida Militar y Política* by Massa y Sanguinetti came out in 1843, and on 15 October 1842 the *Archivo Militar* had published a black-bordered paragraph commemorating 'The Chevalier of the Age—The Hero of Heroes'.

Espartero's friends were left more exclusively in command of the army than before, but not more firmly. They were rewarded for their loyalty in the crisis by a shower of promotions and jobs,[3] while the Guards were reduced to the status

---

[1] F.O., Wellesley to Castlereagh, 15 Apr., 26 June, and 29 July 1817.
[2] *The Times*, 22 Oct. 1841.
[3] Nearly all the Ayacuchos were advanced a rank, and 115 other promotions

of line regiments (never to be revived) and 2,700 officers suspected of conservative leanings were placed on the retired list; but if, before the rising, the policy of the government had caused 'a section of officers who used not to understand politics, now to talk of *Progresistas* and *Cangrejos*',[1] these reprisals ensured that the talk would continue, and in a tone that was hostile to the Progressives and the Regent himself. His loyal generals became a restricted clique of military monopolists,[2] obnoxious both to the excluded soldiers who aspired to commands and to the radicals, who saw their fears of military despotism confirmed by the conduct of Zurbano and Seoane in the Basque provinces and Catalonia,[3] and insisted when they were at last allowed a party ministry under López in May 1843 that these particular chiefs should be dismissed.

Hopes of gaining by such a move, as well as political conviction, made certain soldiers join the Progressive opposition in Cortes and attack the Ayacuchos from the Left; notably General Serrano and Colonel Prim (of whom the latter, as deputy for Tarragona, condemned the free-trade policies of the government as detrimental to Catalonia). Most officers, however, were unable to forgive such remarks as that of Olózaga, when he declared in the session of 21 January 1842 that the officers had rebelled the previous October because 'the country gave the men; the government appointed their commanders', and preferred to listen to the arguments of the military journalists, who turned the radical theory of insurrection on its head.

We are compelled to proclaim a hard, incisive and powerful truth. Three risings, or so-called *pronunciamientos*, or revolutions, have taken

were given to the rest of the army. Rodil, who had shot Montes de Oca and disbanded the Guards, was given the highest honours—a captaincy-general of the army, and the Premiership in 1842.

[1] *Archivo Militar*, 28 Sept. 1841, 2. *Cangrejos* was a short-lived nickname for conservatives.

[2] Almost all the senior administrative posts in the army and provincial administration were held until 1843 by Generals Rodil, Linaje, Seoane, Zurbano, M. Iriarte, and Capaz.

[3] Martín Zurbano (1788–1845), a smuggler turned Liberal *guerrillero*, scoured the Rioja with his 'Partida del Muerte' 1835–9, and subjected Biscay to a reign of terror after the 1841 rising. Having extorted an indemnity of 6 million *reales*, he was moved to Catalonia, where he inflicted the death penalty for smuggling and provoked the rebellion of Nov. 1842, which Seoane then went to punish.

place in seven years, and they have given us little. The country was invoked, and where is the country? We understand by country the union of men who have no other ambition than the common good. And who have suffered in the three crises? We, who were shedding our blood for the true country, or the town councillors who were making up Juntas to get themselves jobs? You have shared out the spoils of victory? Really? We do not forbid you to entrench yourselves in the position which you have conquered. But has the army had its due share in the common division of advantages? What promotions have we got, which you gave us? None. What have we asked for? Nothing, except Justice and Good Laws for the Army. Then, where is the true country, the honest, disinterested country, which battles in silence, which triumphs and spares, which conquers but does not loot, which remains the same after victory as before? In the army. Yes, among us, the country is still to be met—the moral country, unstained by usurpation and pillage, egoism and baseness . . . . We do not find Moral Spain, one, compact, except in the Cortes and the Army. We cannot and we will not say— *We are the state*; but we do say: *We are the country*, or if you prefer it, *the purest part of the country.*[1]

Such were the words of Vallecillo, who, having been turned out of the War Office and ordered to rejoin his unit in 1841, was the more keenly disenchanted with the rule of the Left:

Can anyone credit that the army has yet to persuade itself that it is only an instrument managed by a faction which says to it constantly, 'Always make revolutions in my interests, and don't make others for anyone else? Which says to it: work continually for my uses and benefit and don't expect any rewards, because I have others to give those to.'

In vain, therefore, the government legislated; when a schedule of projected reforms was issued in May 1842,[2] there was little hope of rekindling the loyalty of 1840 because the abuses which were attacked were in some cases—

[1] *Archivo Militar*, 30 Sept. 1841.

[2] As regards rank, all promotions to that of captain were to go by strict seniority, and considerable limits were to be imposed on the freedom of government's choice for senior ranks. No *empleos* were to be conferred in peacetime unless there was a vacancy: and according to article 21, 'Every soldier acquires the property of his *empleo* or *grado* in virtue of the commission or Royal Letter by which it is conferred . . . the temporal exercise of these alone depends on the Government . . .'. As for rewards and pensions (art. 30), 'Soldiers of all ranks and degrees, by the fact of consecrating their liberty and life to the defence and security of their fellow citizens, acquire a positive right to their appreciation and a secure claim to the consideration of government', and the *fuero* was to be maintained intact (ibid., art. 10, Empleos y Ascensos).

the hundreds of generals, the huge 'passive army', the double-ranks and corps privileges—a form of compensation for irremovable economic pressures, already being felt more severely than at any time since the 1820's.

As early as July 1841 a regiment had struck for its pay at Alhucemas, and the penury of the soldiers of the Borbon, at Pamplona, led them to accept O'Donnell's offer of a bounty, full wages, and a promotion for the sergeants, in exchange for their support in the October rising. During the war, their Colonel could have commandeered money from the local authorities, but this practice had been expressly forbidden in the previous summer, and even after the rising had been quelled, Espartero could supply only a fraction of the arrears due to the men.[1] In 1842 he had to send out paper-money to the provincial garrisons, and since the insolvency of the government made this impossible to negotiate the troops had to subsist on regimental funds while their pay-masters tried to exchange their notes for specie with the receivers of public revenue at Madrid; a situation which eroded loyalty independent of subversion. In the summer of 1842, the Guadalajara foot, stationed at Barcelona, was purged of supposedly *Moderado* officers by its Colonel, but the men were kept so short of pay that they had to sell their bread ration to buy soap and blanco; as a result, when the city was taken over by *exaltado* revolutionaries in November, the regiment joined the insurgents for the sake of the free meals they were offered as a reward.[2] They had no sympathy with the rebellion itself—motivated by fears of free trade with England, and resentment at Zurbano's military govern-ment—but like the King's army in 1820, they were not will-ing to risk their lives for an authority that neglected them, and the league of anti-Esparterist newspapers that was formed in the same year exploited the mood of discontent until it became a widespread demoralization.[3]

Meanwhile, their first failure had taught the *Moderados* a lesson; it was no use expecting the army to rise in support

[1] See letter in the *Grito*, 1 Dec. 1841.

[2] *The Times*, 2 Dec. 1842, and *Archivo Militar*, 20 Aug. and 30 Nov. 1842.

[3] In Feb. 1843 the *Archivo Militar*, having proclaimed in majuscule 'THE SITUA-TION OF THE COUNTRY IS HORRIFYING, AND THE ARMY HAS NO FUTURE', began a series of articles on 'whether military subordination ought to be absolutely passive'.

of a civilian party, or an exiled Queen Mother, and consequently they reorganized themselves so as to appear merely the representatives of the army's own true interests. The politicians who had planned the 1841 rebellion were superseded by the military men, led by General Ramón María Narváez, the exile of 1839. His friend Córdova had died in 1840, and his young superior O'Donnell preferred to wait on events; but he was assisted by a talented clique of guardees and disillusioned colonels who had compromised themselves in the last coup or quarrelled with the exclusiveness of the régime in the ensuing months.[1] Their strength lay in the connexions they had left behind them,[2] whom they affiliated to a new form of secret society, the *Orden Militar Española*, ostensibly devoted to maintaining the discipline which Espartero's radical associates were undermining. Both civilians and soldiers were admitted to the order, but soldiers predominated, and kept the same ranks inside the chapters and lodges as they held in the army list. Thus, to be effective, the society had to win over units from the top downwards, and to do this in a political atmosphere that was still predominantly Left-wing, its appeal had to be non-partisan— hence the Gothic ceremonial, impressive to the unsophisticated officer, who enjoyed celebrating an abstract 'military virtue'. The paradox of subversion in the interests of order could be resolved by an appeal to principles higher than those of mere politics, and recollections of the societies of 1820–3 effaced by a fraternal spirit resembling that of an 'Old Comrades Association'.[3]

[1] Among the 4,000 refugees who left Spain in 1841 were Colonels José and Manuel Concha (later senators, ministers, and grandees), Fernando de Córdova (War Minister 1847, 1854, and 1864), Angel de Loigorri (co-founder of the *Guardia Civil*), Manuel Bretón (Captain-General of Catalonia 1845–7), and Major Lersundi (War Minister and Prime Minister, 1851–3).

[2] e.g. Brigadiers Lara (War Minister in 1852), Mazarredo (later chief of police and War Minister), and Colonel Roncali (Captain-General of Cuba 1847–50 and Prime Minister of Spain 1852); who, with the courtier Generals Castroterreño, Zarco, and Girón (Amarillas' heir), lived in discontented retirement.

[3] Fernando Córdova later claimed that the *Orden* was his idea, inspired by the authoritarian coup of Costa Cabral in Portugal at the beginning of 1842; but he admits that the society was already in existence when he reached Paris that May, and the Portuguese officers' clubs had been dedicated to the restoration of a civilian party in a way that the Spanish were not (*Memorias íntimas*, iii. 32; see also Pirala: *Guerra civil*, iii. 901–5 for a description of the organization and statutes of the Order).

However, it was not enemies to the Right that overthrew the Esparterist régime, but the Regent's failure to govern with the Progressive parties. He tried to adhere to the Constitution of 1837, by assuming emergency powers only when confronted with armed rebellion, but the fragmentation of the radicals made parliamentary rule an impossibility. The younger deputies resented the 'circle of men with old-fashioned and rancorous ideas, who by forming an alliance with a number of soldiers . . . constantly repulse the Liberal youth who are full of faith in their doctrines, capacity, and future',[1] and thus the Ayacucho cabinets found themselves lampooned in every newspaper, while their money bills were obstructed by a fractious and abusive Congress. The régime was compelled to rely more and more on an army which liked it less and less; until February 1843 Barcelona was kept under martial law while recovering from the bombardment of the previous December, and in the elections of March the government was discovered to have sent officers of foot and *Carabineros* to vote for the ministerial candidate at Badajoz. The exposure of this possibly isolated instance of military interference was sufficient to bring down Rodil's ministry on 11 April and compel the Regent to appoint a cabinet composed of his political enemies under López in May; but when he refused their demand that he dismiss his military henchmen from their posts, it was the radicals—pacifists, Benthamites, and positivists—who appealed to arms, and their champions Colonels Prim and Milans del Bosch who raised the black flag at Reus on 27 May rather than submit to free trade and an Ayacucho War Office. Espartero, faithful in his own way to the *exaltado* tradition, let the rising spread and ordered his officers not to 'antagonize the people', an instruction which planted a seed of doubt in the mind of every public official, whether he were already a member of the *Orden Militar* or not. Vacillation spread downwards until the amount of moral force that could be applied to stop the troops from following their economic interest and accepting the offers of pay and promotion which the rebel municipalities made them was negligible; thus a Left-wing rebellion, of precisely the kind from which the conservatives had most to

<hr />

[1] Nemesio de Pombo, *La situación de España á fines del año 1842* (n.d.), 11.

fear, served their purpose in overturning the superstructure of Ayacucho generals who might have preserved the loyalty of the army against the *Orden*. Whatever had been the pre-arranged plan of the exiled generals, their understanding with Prim was tenuous, and the British minister Aston believed that 'the defection of General Závala was undoubtedly the cause of the generality of the succeeding desertions by the other Generals'. This was the Captain-General of Valencia, a man of advanced Liberal opinions entirely devoted to the Regent, who kept his troops loyal in the face of the first civilian *émeute* on 10 June, but was unable to stand by his convictions when the *jefe político* was murdered in a subsequent attempt and renewed agitation brought the mob out into the streets.

'The most respectable persons beseeched Zavala not to use force, all claiming that it was only a question of changing the ministry, nothing was intended against the regent.'[1] News arrived that Barcelona would soon join, and Admiral Pinzon's steamer *Isabel II* reached the harbour with information that it had: some of his men began to fraternize: Colonel O'Lawlor assured him that 'they had all pronounced in their hearts', and Závala went over, announcing to his staff: 'Yesterday I only saw a riot to quell—today I see a unanimous manifestation of the will of the people to which we belong, and against which we cannot unsheathe our swords.'[2]

Other generals deduced that Závala 'must have entertained the conviction that either the designs of the Regent were unpatriotic or unjust, or that his prospects were hopeless', and Valencia's defection was followed by others. All over Spain regiments joined the highest bidders, and usually, as at Granada, the rebels had merely to supply the soldiery with the necessities of life; the superior force of government troops led there by the captain-general began to dwindle and had to be withdrawn when the men discovered how their disloyal comrades were being paid and fed. At Oviedo, on the other hand, the *jefe político* paid up the garrison from his

---

[1] F.O. to Aberdeen, 6 Aug. 1843. Juan de Závala (1804–79) was a Creole aristocrat whose Liberalism kept him unemployed 1843–9 and got him deported by Cheste in 1868; he held the Foreign Office under Espartero in 1855 and the Ministry of Marine in O'Donnell's cabinet of 1865; later serving the republic.

[2] See Pirala, *Guerra civil*, iii. 913–16.

own pocket and kept them from pronouncing; at Ferrol, the officers did the same by impounding the copper from the mint,[1] but even if such energy had been more general, it could scarcely have counteracted the inertia of Espartero himself, who left Madrid to pacify the south, and allowed it to fall while his back was turned.

For on 27 June the exiled generals had landed and recognized the insurgent government of López and Serrano, providing the movement with leadership and a striking force. Narváez marched on the capital, and at Torrejón de Ardoz seduced the defending army under Seoane by a *tour de force*; when the news reached Espartero, he abandoned the siege of Seville and fled south with an hourly dwindling retinue. On 30 July he was a refugee on board a British steamer.

The rapidity of this descent is perhaps less remarkable than the way in which it elevated him once more to the leadership of the Progressives. The events of the previous year had seemed to cut him off from the Left for ever, but the politicians who so eagerly encompassed his defeat—Olózaga and López—were not to know that before the end of 1843 they and their followers also would be crowding the cafés of Paris, Lisbon, and London, with no better hope of returning than by means of a military revolt. Beneath 'the pelting of this pitiless storm' the 'naked wretches' found their way to the same hut, and five years later a group of Progressives could claim that they 'had taken ESPARTERO as the symbol of our political beliefs just as the Christians took the cross as symbol of our religious beliefs'.[2] He could only work miracles, however, by virtue of the murmur of 'Uncle's coming back' still not altogether extinguished in the barracks and streets, and his adherence to the one political principle 'Let the People's will be done!' made him a force to be reckoned with only in times of popular insurrection when the niceties of constitutional government were forgotten. But in periods of stability a figurehead was not enough; and Espartero's departure left his enemies—the generals round Narváez—to ensure, by acting less like military heroes and more like politicians, that such periods should become normal.

---

1 S. E. Widdrington, *Spain and the Spaniards in 1843* (1844), ii. 21, 119, and 240.
2 *Espartero. Su Pasado, su Presente, su Porvenir* (1848), 76.

V

NARVÁEZ AND THE ARMY
1843–1848

I. THE EXPLOITATION OF DISORDER, 1843–1844

THE British Ambassador wrote of the 1843 rising that he could not decide 'whether it really ought to be considered the expression of the National Will, or merely the work of a few ambitious men supported by a corrupted soldiery'.[1] This was because Espartero was overthrown by two competing rebellions, one of the Left, aimed at bringing the López ministry and the independent Progressives back to power and eliminating the influence of the army in government, and one of the Right, directed against the rule of Left-wing soldiers in the army. At first (in June and July) they co-operated; radical civilians bribed the soldiers to pronounce, and the soldiers set up revolutionary juntas where the civilians were ineffective. But after Narváez had captured Madrid and disarmed the National Guard, the alliance weakened; the victors were left face to face, uncertain who would make the first move to oust the other.

Their first problem was the demoralization of the army, 'running down and running riot'[2] as a result of the bounties and remissions which had been used to engineer the rebellion. Narváez in particular had risked disarming himself, as well as Espartero, by exploiting the discontent of the *quinto* with the length of his service and offering Seoane's men their immediate discharge on the field of Torrejón; but he quickly changed his tune. Once he had been appointed Captain-General of Madrid he deferred the discharge, and both by withholding back-pay[3] and handing out gratuities kept the

---

[1] F.O., Aston to Aberdeen, 6 Aug. 1843.

[2] *The Times*, 31 July 1843.

[3] A group of *licenciados* who had been 'turned off in their shirts' begged *The Times* correspondent to put an account of their plight in his paper; see *The Times*, 3 Oct. 1843.

men with their colours; when desertion continued, he began to make arrests. At the same time the War Minister Serrano was confirming not only all the promotions bestowed by the local juntas and the invading generals, but also those by which the Esparterists had hoped to rally their forces; this was going further than Narváez and Manuel Concha liked (hence their protest of 25 August),[1] but probably it was only the fact that the rewards of the López government 'were the greatest ever known in Spain and even in Europe'[2] which kept the bulk of the officers behind the revolutionary coalition in its most critical moments. For the first group to break away, the purist *exaltados*, who wanted to set up a Central Junta composed of delegates from the provincial committees, attempted almost immediately to involve the more radical officers in a counter-revolution against their new masters; in August they had formed a secret society among the Madrid garrison,[3] and when the government finally summoned a new Cortes—instead of convening a junta—they rose up in protest. At Barcelona, Ameller's forces went over to the insurgents on 9 September, but elsewhere the military stood firm, apart from isolated instances of mutiny;[4] as *The Times* concluded, the sedition had been under-financed, and since the *exaltados* had been 'impolitic enough to haggle with Colonels'[5] they were left to man their own barricades.

At Barcelona they held out until 19 November, at Figueras until 10 January 1844; long enough to show that their colours were those of the 'Jacobin' Democrats who had disgusted military opinion under Espartero. They had still hoped to enlist the support of the army and the conventional Progressives, but the reaction of the 'respectable' classes—the flight of ten thousand Barcelona *bourgeois* from the city—imparted itself to the generals also. The radical Prim co-operated with the mild conservative Sanz and the high Tory de Meer in bombarding the Centralists, and although their defence was conducted by two idealistic army men, Colonel

[1] F.O., Aston to Aberdeen, 26 Aug. 1843.
[2] Pirala, *Historia contemporánea* (1876), i. 14.
[3] See F.O., Aston to Aberdeen, 6 Aug. 1843.
[4] At Badajoz, Cordova, Egea de los Caballeros, Saragossa, and Pamplona: see *The Times*, and Pirala, op. cit., i. 30-67.   [5] *The Times*, 9 Oct.

Baiges and Brigadier Ameller, they depended for their man-power on the *Jamancia*—militiamen and irregulars who expressed their feelings for the army in the catcalls and lampoons which drove Prim to fury. They promised to discharge all conscripts as soon as the Central Junta met, defiled the cathedral, and armed the convicts:[1] suspicions of the Left which had been allayed by the revolutionary coalition of the summer reawoke among the regulars, and made them the more attentive to the men and ideas of the Right.

This Narváez understood and exploited; he became anxious to dissociate himself from the politicians and generals with whom he had conspired and rebelled a few months earlier, and to placate the steelier professionals for whom the era of revolutions had lasted long enough: who, in 1844, would rejoice when 'those soldiers who took up arms against the government were called Traitors and punished like Traitors'.[2] At a party he gave to the officers of the Madrid garrison in November, he denounced the López cabinet as 'filthy mutineers',[3] although he was still ostensibly their servant; but by this time he was a notorious Man of Order. He had already taken hold of the demoralized soldiery of Madrid by ceremonially shooting eight men of the mutinous Príncipe regiment; he had then set the military to hounding the revolutionaries of the clubs and cafés with the help of police agents controlled by the civil and military Governor, his friend Manuel Mazarredo. This kept the capital in a state of alarm, and placed the ministers at the mercy of their Captain-General: he terrified them with warnings that 'we shall all be dragged through the streets before the week is over' while compiling lists of untrustworthy officers at the Post Office and getting his own rather than Serrano's friends appointed to key commands; with the result that he attracted a following among the officers large enough to

---

[1] See for these events the contemporary *Revolución de Barcelona proclamada la Junta Central* (Barcelona, 1844), and *Diario de los sucesos de Barcelona en setiembre, octubre y noviembre de 1843* (ibid., 1843), both anonymous; also Pirala's *Historia contemporánea*, i. 67, and R. Olivar Bertrand, *El caballero Prim* (Barcelona, 1952), ii. 17.

[2] See Ferrer's *La moral del ejército* and M. del Busto: *El ejército considerado*, both 1844, for an expression of this point of view.

[3] *The Times*, 22 Nov. 1843.

make him leader of 'the military party'. He had rivals for this position, but not close ones; O'Donnell was bought off with the finest political plum, the governorship of Cuba, and Prim was busy fighting the Centralists, having been persuaded to serve the coalition by the title of Count and the never fulfilled promise of the Captaincy-General of Catalonia; which left the War Minister Serrano, young, Liberal, and still the favourite of the dominant *Progresista* party.

But Narváez was in search of his own political connexion. He could intimidate the López coalition, but this was to be dissolved when the Queen came of age in November; unless he could ingratiate himself with the next Prime Minister his career would be at least interrupted. He therefore opened negotiations with Cortina,[1] the most influential Progressive leader next to Olózaga, offering his support for theirs; and when the serpentine Cortina demurred, he turned to the less numerous *Moderados*. They had been his fellow exiles and fellow conspirators, and they were still the party of *gobierno fuerte*; but their alliance with the Man of Order was not a foregone conclusion. They were only forty strong in the Cortes, and Narváez needed a party with a majority; they were involved with the exiled Queen Mother, who might prefer her daughter to be guided by other generals than him, and they were pledged to enforce the unpopular Municipalities Bill, which might provoke yet another rising. Thus although their politics were attractive to the disciplinarians of the army, Narváez bypassed their official leaders and adopted an ex-radical, González Bravo, as his colleague; hoping through him to attract a wide following in the Chamber that would include the conservatives and unman the Progressive leaders at the same time.

It was they, however, who forced the pace. López left Serrano to recommend his successor to the Queen, and Olózaga was the chosen man; he took office on 24 November and attacked the military party at once by deciding to rearm the National Militia and summon a new Cortes in which he could expect a triumphant majority of his own partisans. This would demote Narváez from his undisputed control of Madrid, and demolish his ambitions by establishing a

[1] A. Fernández de los Ríos, *Luchas políticas*, ii. 101.

government consisting of a strong, independent civilian party; he understood the danger, and began urgently to entice Serrano over by appealing to him as a fellow rebel of June, and a fellow officer of the army.

Since Serrano's Progressivism never allowed him to take up a stand against the organized opinion of the army, and since he was incapable of supporting his ambition to make a leading figure by a fraction of the organization, planning, and work which was to lie behind the supremacy of Narváez, he was easily swayed. He was a decorative general, with a blond moustache, and the Prime Minister forgot to treat him with respect; it only needed the scandal of 28 November, when Olózaga's haste in getting the Queen to authorize the dissolution of Cortes was misrepresented by the palace officials (in collusion with Narváez) as an act of treasonable personal violence, to convince Serrano that the politicians were not to be trusted. He signed the decree by which Olózaga was dismissed, and then discovered that in the new ministry formed under González Bravo there was no place for him.[1]

While the ministerialist deputies hounded the Progressive politicians first out of Cortes and then out of Spain, in a frenzy of loyalty, the military party took over the army. Narváez retained the Captaincy-General of Madrid, but made Mazarredo War Minister and gave six of the War Office departments to his friends; two of whom, Colonel Calonge and Brigadier Loigorri, had got him the support of the rising young editor Sartorius.[2] Thus the centre of military authority was won over to the Narváez interest as firmly as the inspectorates, and on 13 December he secured himself further by rescinding all the promotions which Espartero had awarded during the rising, and using the vacancies to reward safe men.

---

[1] He resigned on 1 December and retired from political life until 1847, when, as Isabella's lover, he recommenced a career that was to end in the presidency of the first republic (1874-5).

[2] Whose paper, the *Heraldo*, did much to reconcile conservative opinion to the rule of generals; its 23-year-old editor was later to become Count of San Luis and Prime Minister. See *Historia periodística, parlamentaria y ministerial, completa y detallada del Excmo. Sr. D. Luis José Sartorius, primer conde de San Luis* (anon., Madrid, 1850), 20.

However, he was not yet ready to assume responsibility for the whole government. Through González Bravo he hoped to get control of the *Moderados*, and, having driven the Right-wing Progressive leaders into exile for putative treason, to expel the Left-wing of the movement from its traditional resorts—the National Guard and civic rebellion. But Bravo, a *rusé* turncoat, meant to use him, as he meant to use Bravo; and it was perhaps only the fact that a fresh wave of provincial risings in January and February 1844 put the safety of ministers in the hands of their general which gave Narváez the advantage. At first, he played the Man of Order, punishing even the privates of the regiment which had joined the Cartagena rebels with two years' extra service, and ordering General Roncali[1] to shoot seven officers who had fought for the insurgents at the battle of Alcoy (January 29); but once the rebellions had been suppressed, he became the champion of legality and constitutional methods of government, anxious that the country should put the Iron Age of González Bravo behind it. For this he had only to wait until the component parts of his new régime were assembled. On 30 December 1843 the Municipalities Law had been promulgated by decree, and in February 1844 the *nacionales* were everywhere disarmed: the municipal elections went well for the *Moderados*. In March the Queen Mother returned, and on 1 April the formation of a Civil Guard, to take over the police duties of the militia, was decreed. There was no further need for martial law, and on 24 April Narváez informed the new British Ambassador, Sir Henry Bulwer, that he would follow 'a policy of peace with the same promptitude and energy when the peril was over that had been shown in combating it when it existed'.

2. NARVÁEZ AND THE *MODERADOS*, 1844–1848

On 4 May 1844 Narváez ditched Bravo and appointed a new cabinet. The Home Office he gave to Pidal, who had helped him queer Olózaga's pitch at the palace the year

---

[1] Federico Roncali, Count of Alcoy (1800–57), an ex-guardee promoted to lieutenant-general for joining the 1843 rising; he had also been active in the Aravacas mutiny of 1837, and tended to side with the Court against Narváez.

before; the Finance Department went to Pidal's kinsman Mon, and the Foreign Office to the Marquess of Viluma, elder brother of General Pezuela, the Inspector of Cavalry. But the Premiership and the War Office he kept to himself.

Why did he do this? Espartero's attempt at wielding supreme power directly had been a failure even when he enjoyed an extraordinary popularity: if Narváez had left the civilians to manage their own affairs, might he not have done better?

There are several answers to this. In the first place, he was ambitious, and if a peasant's son could become Regent of Spain, the son of an Andalusian squire need look no lower. He enjoyed power, and the public vices and private benefits which he exhibited and reaped were not an unrequited charge on the State; even Bulwer had to admit that 'as a debater and the leader of his party in the Chambers he has shewn at once tact and readiness: as an administrator his office [the Foreign Department, which he held from July to September 1844] is conducted with a regularity and despatch of which there is no example . . . '.[1] He was an abler politician than Espartero, and his contempt for the civilian 'lawyers' who depended on him was not unjustified by their performance in the periods 1846–7 and 1851–4 when they governed without him.

Equally important was the fact that his alliance with the *Moderados* was one of convenience only; he was not committed to the conservative politicians. His early Liberalism[2] had ranged him, as a Guards cadet, against the Royalist mutineers of 1822, and cost him captivity and relegation after the Restoration of 1823. To regain this loss of seniority he had become involved in the political struggles of 1836–8 which have been described in Chapter III; the ultimate object of his ambition was changed from the Postmastership of Bilbao to the chief command of the army, but even after the crash of 1838 he pledged himself to no party. The radicals could still look to him for a Marius to Espartero's Sulla,[3] and although the events of 1840 made him

---

[1] F.O., Bulwer to Aberdeen, 28 Dec. 1844.
[2] See A. Révesz, *Un Dictador Liberal: Narváez* (1953), for the best modern study of his career.   [3] See Torrija y Carrese, *Milicianos Nacionales ¡alerta!* (1839).

a partner in conspiracy of the *Moderados*, he had no sooner landed at Valencia than he joined the Progressives in public, and privately engendered the 'military party' of sympathetic generals. The cause of order realigned him with the *Moderados*, but only because 'his daring and domineering character required a subject band that could not be recruited among Liberals'[1]—Progressives, that is; and Borrego saw his influence as fatal to the conservative cause. In a world where past association was accepted as a key to actual political sympathies, his were unpredictable.

Therefore only as Prime Minister could he control the patronage by which the alliance could be made to work in his favour. The political chiefs with whom he co-operated would have got rid of him if he had not been able to dispense with them, and when, in 1846 and 1851, he lost the confidence of the Court, they did so.

For ministerialists both of the Right and the Left resented his supremacy and tried to diminish it. In 1844 the Marquess of Viluma and his followers attempted to convert the conservative trend into an aristocratic and monarchical restoration, with an hereditary upper chamber and a revival of the entail system abolished by Mendizábal; the Church was to be re-endowed with its unsold property, and the stability of government guaranteed no longer by the army, but by a régime of bishops and grandees. Such hopes were dashed by the new Constitution of 1845, which, although less democratic than its predecessor, was subservient to the post- rather than the pre-revolutionary vested interests—to the generals, capitalists, and *bourgeois*; but the authoritarian Right remained hostile, and enlisted the support of the Queen's husband to combat the Great Ministry of 1847–51, which it eventually overthrew. On the Left were the *puritano* Moderates who disliked exchanging 'a permanent, constitutional and secure influence for the sword of a man whose energy and brilliance did not make up for their losing . . . the principles which had constituted the strength of the party and given it its triumph'[2]—the rule of law, that is, in a free but orderly society, and a parliamentary rather than a

---

[1] Marliani, quoted by Borrego in *De la organización de los partidos*.
[2] A. Borrego, *Los partidarios del poder y los hombres de principios* (1874), 19.

military supremacy for themselves. These were the reputable Liberals—Pacheco, Istúriz, Miraflores—who believed that a properly organized party could govern without recourse to the army, and although their only remedy was to confide in other generals, their stand was a considerable embarrassment to the government of 1844–6.

Given these antagonisms, why did so many *Moderados* continue to agree that 'General NARVÁEZ . . . is still a necessity for all those who love monarchy and order'?[1]

The answer lies in their monopoly of power; under what was virtually a one-party system of government, 'disorder' was the only form which opposition could take, and this meant calling in the army. While the niceties of a constitutional régime could be maintained at Madrid, the Carlist and *exaltado* protest of the provinces had to be silenced by repression. 'The *Jefe Políticos* are not *Jefe Políticos* there, nor the intendants, intendants, nor the *alcaldes* presidents of their *ayuntamientos*. The distribution of public funds is altered by the will of the Captain-General: another military chief takes over the police . . . ';[2] this was in 1844, when Bulwer described the administration of Aragon and Catalonia in particular as 'little less than a system of persecution and terror'.[3] In that year, 1846, and 1848 the government assumed emergency powers to deal with its domestic enemies, but throughout this period the role of the soldier-administrator remained vital to the survival of the régime; he alone could 'tranquillize opinion' before elections, enforce unpopular legislation—the new tax system on the tradesmen of Madrid, the *quinta* on the Basques and Catalans—and manage the *haute police* of the provinces.[4] In Catalonia, for example, the government was confronted in the years 1847 and 1848 by widespread Carlist brigandage, industrial unemployment, and 'republican' agitation; it was the Captain-General, Manuel Pavía,[5] who provided jobs by encouraging railway

---

[1] *Heraldo*, 9 May 1844.   [2] *El Pensamiento de la Nación*, i. 349, 3 July 1844.
[3] To Aberdeen, 28 Dec. 1844.
[4] Note also the occasions on which civilian administrative posts were held by soldiers: Generals Shelley and Pavía were *jefes políticos* of Barcelona in 1843–4, and General Loigorri of Madrid in 1847–8.
[5] See the anonymous *Biografía del excmo. señor D. Manuel Pavía y Lacy* (1868), for an informative eulogy; and Carrera Pujal, *Historia política de Cataluña*, iv., Ch. 2.

construction (he was himself a founder-director of the Barcelona–Mataró line) and summoned a conference of bankers
and industrialists to discuss other ways of stimulating the
economy—for he had also founded a rural savings bank of
his own. He supported the business interests of the principality against the free-trade legislation of the Salamanca
government at the same time as he conducted military operations against the Carlists; and in 1848 he resigned rather
than imperil the *Moderado* supremacy. Narváez wanted him
to arm a force of rural vigilantes, to keep the ungarrisoned
areas free of brigandage, but he declined to revive even a
ghost of the National Militia; and his successor, Fernando
Córdova, was able to forestall the threat of a more immediate
restoration of the Left by setting up a military commission
on his own authority which arrested, tried, and executed the
leaders of a Democratic conspiracy among his own troops.
In both cases it seemed as if the prophecy of the *Eco del
Comercio* was being fulfilled: 'you seek to create a new
aristocracy, a hideous amalgam of wealth and sabres, a
hotch-potch of a feudal superiority composed of bankers and
Generals over-riding the Law . . . '.[1]

Thus it was his control of the army that made Narváez indispensable, and it is this aspect of his policy which deserves
particular attention. For it was here that Espartero had
failed; and the revolution had provided no solution to his
problem—how to reconcile the claims of the military class
with the expenses of the political system.

3. THE IMPOSITION OF DISCIPLINE

Although contemporary writers refer to his military reforms, Narváez was not a reformer of the San Miguel
variety; he was not the man to liberalize or modernize, and
throughout the forties the old abuses continued—the interference of politics in matters of promotion, the over-staffed
War Office, the too numerous generals, the corps privileges,
the honorary ranks, and the otiose appointments. In order to
retain the loyalty of his officers as a class, he had to subordinate questions of this nature to more pressing requirements:

[1] *Eco del Comercio*, 6 Oct. 1843.

the satisfaction of economic grievances, and the imposition of political surveillance.

In 1844 the army numbered about 100,000 men and cost 386 million *reales*, 10 per cent. more, proportionally, than in time of war.[1] It had to be reduced, and it should have cost less: its extravagances provided hostile deputies with ammunition against the régime, and its usefulness was limited to the pursuit of bandits and the intimidation of Left-wing civilians—functions of police. At the same time, its officers had made the revolution of 1843 and expected to be rewarded for their services with solider benefits than a universal promotion; unless a high level of employment were maintained they would rebel once more, and the agents of Espartero held out inducements for them to do so.

Narváez's answer was to make a feint of economizing—he announced that the next year's estimates[2] would be kept below 300 million *reales*, equipped the new recruits on the cheap, and talked of abolishing the inspectorates—while in fact securing the vital subalterns' pay-rise[3] and spending almost as much as he had the year before. He was able to do this because Mon's reform of the tax system in the same year increased the total income of the government to a level at which war estimates could remain at between three and a half and four million while occupying a decreasing proportion of the whole revenue. This was still too much, considered as a wage for services actually performed, and after 1848 his enemies chose the issue as a main opposition cry; but, as Narváez reminded them in the estimates debate of 1850, ' . . . if I had been in the Minister of War's place when he made up the estimates for 1842 I would have been obliged to present the figures he presented, just as if he had been in my place in 1845 he would have done what I did, for men are led by circumstances . . . '[4]—the circumstance, that is, that whatever the expense, the officer corps must be reconciled to the régime.

For the money was spent in purchasing loyalty rather than

[1] See F.O., Bulwer to Aberdeen, 14 May 1844.

[2] *The Times*, 25 Oct. 1844.

[3] Of 20 per cent., by the law of 20 May 1845; the last increase had been voted in 1820, and abolished in 1824.

[4] *Diario*, Congreso, 29 Jan. 1850.

efficiency. Although the War Ministers Mazarredo[1] and Fernando Córdova[2] were capable administrators, and were assisted by Generals Pezuela, Zarco del Valle, and the Duke of Ahumada (in command of cavalry, engineers, and Civil Guards) in effecting improvements within the limits imposed by the political situation, these were strict. On the one hand they had to maintain a giant active-list in the depth of peace, on the other they could do little for the 'passive' army, which was increased by hundreds of Esparterists and, in 1846, by the officers of the disbanded provincial militia; there was a rumour of war with Morocco in 1844, but after that they could only hold out the hope of active-list vacancies or civil service clerkships. Their plan for reorganizing the line into more easily manœvrable one-battalion regiments[3] had to be abandoned when the politically influential inspectors took umbrage; their powers of supervision would have been invaded. But since cavalry was expensive, horse-regiments were kept few and ill mounted; the protests of the experts under José Concha notwithstanding. When the old provincial militia system (see p. 2), which had been swamped in the general mobilization of the war, was finally discontinued, the new reserve, made up of conscripts in their last year of service, was organized so parsimoniously as to be almost a fiction. And there was no amelioration of arms or tactics in the regular army: the Spanish soldier continued to carry the flintlock musket and manœuvre according to uncoordinated manuals of exercise, and if he lost the green coat which Espartero had given him, it was because blue cloth was cheaper. It is significant that the one effective and expensive innovation which the War Office did make—the Civil Guard —was one which served a political, not a military purpose, and provided employment for redundant officers at the same time.

Its aim was to concentrate the police duties of the army in one exceptionally dependable body, which would not, like the National Militia and the Royalist Volunteers of the

[1] In office 1843-4 and 1847.
[2] Inspector of Infantry 1844-7, and 1847-8, with three months at the War Office in between.
[3] F.O., Bulwer to Aberdeen, 28 Mar. 1844. The system had been tried in 1815 and 1822-3, and had been contemplated by Espartero in 1843.

twenties and thirties, have its sympathies engaged in the party struggles which lay behind public disorder. To achieve it, the second Duke of Ahumada, son of the Marquess of Amarillas who had put forward a similar plan in 1820, and his assistant, Brigadier Loigorri, took over the organizing of the force from the Minister of the Interior and manned it with time-expired conscripts under the command of regular officers, giving the men better wages and equipment than the troops of the line (though not, at this date, tricornes) and a separate War Office inspectorate to look after their interests.[1] They remained at the disposal of the Ministry of the Interior, and were used indiscriminately in the capital, the towns, and the countryside, in street-fighting and open warfare against the Carlists; and although, during the crisis of 1848, their peculiar position aroused 'ill-feeling and jealousy' among other corps,[2] the experiment was generally successful.

As for the rest of the army, Narváez simply ensured the loyalty of his officers by regular pay and a selective use of patronage. In 1844, after the extensive promotions and purges which brought him to power, the *Heraldo* advised him to postpone more constructive reforms, because 'the reorganization of personnel has conveniently satisfied the needs of the moment',[3] and although his object was to de-politicize the army his only method of securing the military class proper was by keeping his own friends, and those of his *Moderado* allies, in control of it. At first he tried to win over the unpartisan professional by a policy of 'attraction', retaining three of Espartero's colonels and promoting the *Pro-gresista* officers Boiguez and Turon to regimental commands, but on the whole it was the conservatives who got the jobs and the others who lost them. It was safer to re-employ Carlists than Esparterists, and after 1848 the attraction was all to the Right.

Even within the *Moderado* fold, there was no keeping out of politics. When Narváez resigned in 1846, General

---

[1] The officers were granted the *escala cerrada*, that is, promotion by strict seniority as in the artillery and engineers.

[2] F.O., Otway to Palmerston, 17 June 1848.

[3] *Heraldo*, 8 May 1844.

Fulgosio and Colonel Ortega of the San Fernando conspired against the Miraflores government to bring him back; the year before, Colonel Soler of the same regiment had assisted the attempts of the Queen Mother to turn him out. Some generals were always more conservative than he: de Meer, for example, and Pezuela (who interrupted a debate in Cortes on the March crisis of 1846, protesting that it was an 'attack on the Royal Prerogative'), and the Count of Clonard, his *bête noire* of 1838; while the junior ranks had an equally dangerous tendency to the Left which could be checked only by the vigilance of their commanding officers. As Inspector of Infantry, General Córdova got up files on all his subordinates 'in which their antecedents were written down with a special mark, known only to myself, so that I could tell at a glance whether the man concerned was one on whom the government could rely'[1]—a form of security which may have tamed but certainly depressed the officers. They became to this extent the victims of the party which they had brought to power, and their resentment was expressed in the distrust and coldness which, as the military journalists complained, grew up during the forties between senior officers and their subalterns.

With the men, Narváez pursued an even more thorough policy. Half Espartero's army was discharged in 1844 and replaced by a new *quinta*; and the recruits were subjected to a severer discipline than had been usual since the reign of Ferdinand. There was no attempt to revive the Guards, but the old régime of incessant parades and punishment was extended to all units, and subordination became a matter of life and death. Three men who had been involved in the assassination of a Carlist general in 1838 were sentenced to death at Saragossa in 1844, and when the Queen Mother tried to reprieve them, Narváez threatened to resign;[2] in September of the next year, General Bretón had twelve escaped conscripts shot at Barcelona for desertion, and in 1848 the mutiny of the España regiment was expiated at Madrid by the execution of nine N.C.O.s and men. 'Mother of God, they're beating us to death', remarked one of the new

[1] F. Córdova, *Memorias íntimas*, ii. 141.
[2] F.O., Bulwer to Palmerston, 16 July, 1844.

quintas in earshot of *The Times* correspondent, and 'an officer of the line' writing in the *Revista Militar* on the morale of the private asked:

Why do you insult their self-respect when you show them in public, why do you oblige them to live like galley-slaves, always tied to the oar, never letting them speak to other men, leave their barracks, or breathe for a moment outside their confinement? . . . the laws of mechanics and the precepts of harmony are applied to the most natural and spontaneous actions of man . . . dressed off and practically at attention when they sleep, eat, work, when by chance they are allowed to go out for a walk—that is the way to make soldiers who would privately prefer to serve in the forces of the Grand Turk.[1]

Blind obedience was inculcated to an unintelligent and self-defeating excess, so that in the emergency of 1848 it was the weariness of the Madrid garrison with interminable patrols, parades, and sentry duties which threatened the safety of the government rather than revolutionary subversion. And at the same time the danger of discontent among the N.C.O.s was met by an equally unimaginative repression: it was assumed that sergeants were a security risk, despite the fact that whenever they had rebelled in the past, except at La Granja, it had been at the instigation of their superiors. Perhaps those who had lived through a revolutionary period, imbibing its morality and language, found themselves at odds with a self-conscious restoration of discipline, perhaps they resented the peacetime rates of promotion that retarded their hopes of commissioned rank; at all events, the reigning generals, particularly Mata y Alós, secretary to the Inspector of Infantry, were opposed to their existence and actually did away with sergeant-majors. They were unable to dissolve the rank entirely into corporals and subalterns (though this remained Mata's ideal),[2] but endeavoured, by banning the use of the officer-like frock-coat, frogging, lanyards, and riding-boots, to 'diminish their prestige by regulating their dress'.

However, the ordinary soldier did get some benefit from

---

[1] *Revista Militar*, iv. 545 (10 May 1849).

[2] Ibid., ii. 714, for his article 'Sergeants—considerations on their suppression in the Army', and the reply of 'A Veteran Commander' in the next issue. The subject is also mentioned in *The Times* reports of 19 Feb. 1844 and 30 Oct. 1845.

the swollen war estimates. His pay, his ration, and his kit were distributed regularly and in full, and the War Office made a determined effort to improve the amenities of his service. He was issued for the first time with soap, towels, handkerchiefs, underwear, and blankets; he was vaccinated, and from 1847 preventive rather than punitive measures were taken against venereal infections.¹ As Lord Howden put it, 'without any illustration of arms and hold upon the pride of the soldier, [Narváez] has taken sedulous care of his person and is endeared by those every day comforts which keep him fresh before the troops'.² He also attempted to re-kindle their Royalism, now they had a maiden Queen; in the summer of 1844 the Court visited Barcelona, and while the Captain-General, de Meer, turned out the garrison with an unusual brilliance, the Royal family made a thorough inspection of all his eight fortresses, tasting the soldiers' *rancho*—the Queen Mother said it was exquisite, the Infanta Luisa that 'she should be very sorry to have nothing else for dinner'³—viewing their quarters, and distributing bounties and promotions. After her return to Madrid, each barracks was visited by the Royal entourage, and before long reviews had become a diversion of good society; like her mother, Isabella became a soldiers' Queen.

4. THE DECLINE OF THE *PRONUNCIAMIENTO*

By these methods Narváez became the arbiter of military opinion, and by his control of the army he retained control of the State longer than any other Isabelline politician. His enemies realized this, and acted accordingly, so that the history of his supremacy is largely taken up with his defeat of the traditional menace of military subversion. For the *Progresistas* and other groups to the Left were unable to acquiesce in their exclusion from power, and the *Moderado* monopoly deprived them of the weapons of parliamentary opposition;

---

¹ See *Colección de Reales Decretos, Órdenes y Circulares anteriores á la publicación del boletín oficial de Sanidad Militar* (1855), and F. Córdova's *Memorias íntimas*, iii. Vaccination was first enjoined in 1832, but interrupted by the civil war.

² F.O. to Clarendon, 1 Jan. 1854.

³ *The Times*, 11 June 1844.

only by violence could the verdict of 1843 be reversed, unless, as in 1846–7, they got in through the back door of a palace intrigue. At the head of their exiled leaders stood Espartero, and in the ranks of the army there remained a fund of Esparterist loyalty[1]—in Left-wing officers and men who could remember the victorious years of 1839 and 1840; it seemed only to require a concerted effort to produce the counter-revolution which would end the régime as it had begun.

It never came; when Narváez fell from power in 1851 it was the work of enemies to the Right, and the generals who were responsible for the military rebellion of 1854 had been his own associates. The fact that most officers accepted his régime as favourable to their interests meant that Progressivism remained as suspect in their eyes as in his; only the more desperate subalterns and a small group of *jefes* disagreed, but they were never allowed an opportunity of carrying opinion with them. In 1844, before the fresh recruits had made up a new army, or the resentments of the old had been appeased, they were able to form a society—the *Ayacucho*—which eluded the vigilance of the police, but they lost their best chance of a general rising through the vacillation of their chief. Narváez opened secret negotiations once more with the exiled Cortina, and Espartero, seeing the way to a peaceful restoration, refused to support an attempt at insurrection; after a series of false alarms, which involved the arrest of General Prim, the movement fizzled out in a forlorn gesture by the wolfish General Zurbano. He took to the hills of Navarre with a small *partida*, but neither his slogans nor his promises enticed the regulars from their duty; he was too much the *guerrillero*, and too obvious a party man for military opinion to be sympathetic. Instead, Narváez was able to exploit the emergency by exiling some hundreds of political suspects from Madrid, and by the end of the year Zurbano was a hunted fugitive and the most experienced

---

[1] 'I myself have seen in the barracks of several regiments the portrait of Espartero suspended over the beds of the soldiers; and I have heard these same soldiers singing popular songs composed in Madrid, breathing aspirations for the return of the *Gitano* . . . the small envelopes in which are folded the paper cigars used by the soldiers are ornamented with the portrait of their favourite . . .' (*The Times*, 6 Nov. 1844).

military conspirators had made haste to escape with their lives.[1]

This initial failure left the *Progresista* juntas demoralized and poor; their only hope was Mendizábal, and he was too much a prey of his Parisian entourage, and too bitter an enemy of the military class, to afford them any help.[2] He would lend them no money until they had reconstructed the edifice of conspiracy; consequently, their efforts to seize control of the capital in 1845 were as uncoordinated and unsuccessful as before. It was not until the following year that Narváez's own difficulties altered their chances for the better; but the failure of their Galician *pronunciamiento* emphasized how far they were from appearing an acceptable alternative to the *Moderados* in the eyes of the influential officers. Through Miguel Solís, a gentlemanly major, they had won over the greater part of the provincial garrison, and among civilian *gallegos* there existed a traditional loyalty to the Left which rekindled at the imposition of Mon's new taxes. At Madrid, they were seconded by a group of *Moderado* politicians, including General Manuel Concha, who resented the continued supremacy of Narváez and feared that he might overcome their opposition by setting up an unvarnished military dictatorship; especially when, having been dismissed in February 1846, he regained power in March after threatening the deputies of Cortes through his mouthpiece Pezuela and assuming the new title of commander-in-chief. These malcontents undertook to raise the south and the capital, if the Progressives would begin the rebellion in Galicia; but no sooner had Narváez agreed to resign of his own accord (3 April) than the *Moderados* discarded the methods of subversion and left the Galicians to try them on their own.[3] Solís came out with his regiment, the Zamora, and got control of Santiago and a few other towns for a week; no help arrived other than a raid from Portugal under Iriarte and a band of exiles who sailed into Vigo too late, and it was Concha's brother José who routed the insurgents for the new

---

[1] See Pirala, *Historia contemporánea*, i. 280–9, and *The Times*, 26 and 28 Nov. and 2 Dec. 1844.

[2] A. de los Ríos, *Luchas políticas*, ii. 107.

[3] For this, see F.O., Bulwer to Aberdeen, 24 Apr. and 8 July 1846.

government of Istúriz.[1] On 26 April the twelve officers at
the head of the movement underwent a belated and futile
martyrdom, and for the next eighteen months their party
was to seek power through the pacific medium of General
Serrano's influence at the palace.

The more conciliatory politics of this period brought
several generals with Progressive sympathies back into
regular employment and parliamentary opposition; and
when in 1848 Narváez returned to the exclusive system of
his first ministry, only the Democrats—successors to the
Centralists of 1843—attempted to unseat him by a military
coup. They engineered conspiracies at Madrid and Barcelona, which resulted in the isolated mutiny of the N.C.O.s
and men of the España regiment; but the inferiority of their
weapons to his was so obvious as to preclude further efforts.
In fact, the events of the forties had made clear for the first
time the incompatibility of the interests of the 'military class'
with a genuinely radical movement; but it was only these
political outcasts who were prepared to exploit the resentment of other ranks against this class. In 1845 the imposition of the *quinta* on Catalonia drove the peasantry of
Igualada to open revolt[2] and suggested the most obvious
rallying cry against the military system on which the
Moderados depended: 'No Quinta' was embodied in the
Democratic programme for 1848, and the Barcelona garrison
was promised, 'once the infamous government of Madrid is
overthrown, you will receive your final discharges . . . until
that day comes, and it will not be long, you will receive six
reales a day and be looked after like Men; with us you will
not suffer the maltreatment you receive from your officers...'.[3]
The *Progresistas*, on the other hand, remained wedded to
their generals; even though some agitated for a more egalitarian kind of conscription, they stuck to the rules of
military politics, a field in which all the advantages lay with

---

[1] The best account of the rising is F. Tettamancy Gastón's *La revolución Gallega
de 1846* (Corunna, 1909), written from the Progressive point of view, as is J. Do-
Porto, *Reseña histórica de los últimos acontecimientos políticos de Galicia* (1846).

[2] See *The Times*, 29 July 1845.

[3] Quoted in F. Córdova: *Memorias íntimas*, iii. 184. Six *reales* a day was also
the wage paid by a Captain Sendra in the exiguous *pronunciamiento* which he
staged at Pego in May 1848 (F.O., Otway to Palmerston, 17 May 1848).

Narváez. He had the money—he could offer two gold *onzas* each to men who informed him of subversive activities—and he controlled the patronage; as a result he achieved a position more secure than that of any of his predecessors.

His weakness lay in his relations with the generals and politicians on his own side, in the details of the military system of government. His masterpiece was the reconciliation of the army with the Liberal State; but a notice of it, since it is intimately connected with the collapse of the *Moderados* in the fifties, may be left to the last chapter.

VI

THE MILITARY OPPOSITION
1848–1854

1. THE ROLE OF THE GENERALS IN CORTES, 1844–1850

OFFICERS had sat in every Spanish parliament since 1810, and at the end of the Carlist war their number and influence were considerable. Local heroes could sweep the polls, and once elected either spoke for the interests of the army in particular, like Seoane and his friends, or used their position to promote other causes. Prim, for example, who was chosen deputy for Tarragona in 1841, defended the industries of Catalonia against the reduction of import duties which was part of Espartero's commercial treaty with England, and in August 1842 he was serenaded at Barcelona by an enthusiastic chorus of protectionist free-corps officers:

> Diputado independiente,
> Con tesón defenderas
> Contra estranjeros astutos
> Nuestra industria nacional.[1]

And Narciso López, the radical Brigadier, elected senator in 1838, spoke on behalf of the Cuba trade until the oppressiveness of the Narváez régime drove him to attempt the liberation of the island by force of arms. After the war, fewer soldiers became deputies, but in 1843 there were over forty generals in the upper House, and when the *Moderados* reviewed the Constitution Narváez took the opportunity of establishing a permanent military contingent there. He made himself, and the other captains-general of the army, *ex officio* senators along with the Royal family, the archbishops, and richer grandees; he wished to qualify all other generals for nominated seats, and although his opponents were able to confine the honour to lieutenant-generals alone,

---

[1] *Archivo Militar*, 20 Aug. 1842.

forty-five of these were put in at once and more followed, including Esparterists after 1846—until in the House of 1853
the generals numbered 93 out of 314 members. The more
favoured sported a roll of Carlist war battles in their newly
acquired titles, and sat promiscuously with members of a less
recent nobility, who had themselves been awarded high military rank in greater numbers after the rebellion of 1843; it
was an attempt at once to create and embody the solid upper-
class support to which the *Moderados* considered their
doctrines entitled them, and to secure, for public authority,
the same legislative preponderance as, for property, was
made up by the peers of England. And what was more
germane to Spanish affairs, the army was thus so well represented in Cortes that it could never be neglected; and its
generals so lavishly rewarded that they could scarcely fail in
their duty towards the party and the chief who had elevated
them.

But this theory was partly fallacious, as many of the
generals were fellow promoters of the rebellion of 1843 who
had only accepted the leadership of Narváez in emergency
and with reservations, so that their claims to power could not
effectually be mediatized with titles, crosses, and seats. Even
before González Bravo's ministry General Manuel Concha
was competing with Narváez for the support of the politicians, and during the iron régime of January and February
1844 he made a public attack on the policy of the day in
which he was supported by General Roncali and his own
brother José. He was appeased by the Captaincy-General of
Catalonia, but this type of opposition could never be eradi-
cated; only when their interests were openly threatened—in
1845 by the economy cry of the *Puritanos*, in 1846 by the
likelihood of the Queen marrying the Carlist Pretender and
amalgamating a diaspora of legitimist officers with the
Liberal army,[1] in 1847 by Serrano's intention of restoring
the Progressives, and in 1848 by the 'Revolution'—did the
generals rally behind Narváez and reinforce his position. At
other times they were attracted to other politicians who
would treat them better, as when it became clear that Isabella
would marry her cousin Francis, and not the son of Don

[1] The Carlist exiles included 63 generals and 5,087 other officers.

Carlos; they let the Queen Mother procure the dismissal of the cabinet, and accepted the government of Istúriz, while Narváez left for the Paris embassy. The civilians who succeeded him rewarded the other generals with an effusion of promotions—1,165 to celebrate the Royal marriage alone —and under Pacheco (March–August 1847), the most anti-military of the *Moderados*, they were indulged with the luxury of a campaign of intervention in Portugal, where Manuel Concha won his Marquisate of the Douro. Only the appointment of the Progressive Escosura to the Ministry of the Interior in September 1847, and the publication of his plan for the demilitarization of the administrative system, put them once more behind Narváez and enabled him to form the 'Great Ministry' of 1847–51.

Discontent was therefore inevitable, and the granting of senatorial immunity to a proportion of the more ambitious officers was bound to increase the means by which it could be expressed. Before 1848 their political influence was usually exerted in private—they had warned General Serrano not to carry the Queen's sympathies further to the Left by sending José Concha to interview him at Aranjuez[1]—but during the atmosphere of emergency which prevailed in a year of European revolution, an apprehensive conservatism called them into the limelight. No Cortes sat, but the *Revista Militar* ran a series of articles on 'The lamentable indifference of our generals towards public affairs', exhorting them to retrieve their proper share of political responsibility from the hands of the discredited lawyers; the day of the professional persuaders was over.[2]

While the danger of revolution lasted this exhortation implied only that the generals should rally more enthusiastically to Narváez, whose assumption of dictatorial powers was regarded by the intellectual Donoso Cortes as a philosophical, and by other conservatives as a political, necessity; but when the dictatorship was ended, old jealousies revived. How could they be expressed? The prestige of the government was undiminished; it had vanquished all shades of organized opposition to the Left and could regulate newspapers and

[1] F.O., Bulwer to Palmerston, 26 May 1847.
[2] *Revista Militar*, iv. 593, 737, and v. 24 (1849).

elections with equal ease. The old *Moderado* party was pulverized into an amorphous following of ministerialists; politics had almost been swallowed up by administration. Narváez was secure enough to demobilize a portion of the 140,000 men whom he had employed in 1848, and when Cortes reassembled at the end of the following year he announced the creation of a 'Reserve Army' to which the superfluous military could be relegated. At this point he was met by a fusillade of criticism from an unexpected quarter.

For his management of the army had hitherto aroused vocal opposition from the Left only—from constitutionally minded *Moderados* and *Progresistas*: civilians who condemned the military establishment as too big, too expensive, and too menacing, and whom he could dismiss as ill informed, or unpractical. 'If, Gentlemen, there is anyone . . . who believes that the armies [of Europe] should be disbanded, let him get up and say so. If there is no one, Gentlemen, I laugh at all your economies, because all your economies are Utopias.'[1] Now, however, General Pavía got to his feet in the Senate and suggested that it was better to have no reserve at all than one as militarily indefensible as this, and in Congress, on 13 December 1849, Brigadier Fernández de San Román went as far as to censure the entire military policy of the government as chaotic and amateur. These were not Utopians, but highly conservative professionals who had quarrelled with the régime. Pavía had been dismissed from command of Catalonia, he thought unfairly (see p. 125), and San Román, editor of the *Military Review*, had been court martialled for using his magazine to criticize the management of the expedition sent against the Roman Republic.[2] Narváez was present at the session and refused to accept this type of opposition as legitimate; he ignored the personal compliments which San Román had been careful to include in his speech, and gave him a choleric reprimand. 'He has said that he learnt much while he served by my side; I wish he had learnt how to express his ideas and pursue his object

[1] *Diario*, Congreso, 29 Jan. 1850.

[2] In the summer of 1849 a division under General Fernando Córdova was sent to help reinstate the fugitive Pius IX; the Spaniards saw little action but were able to pay cash for their provisions (see Córdova's *Memorias íntimas*, iii. 274 et seq. and his *La revolución de Roma y la expedición española á Italia en 1849* (1882)).

when speaking to a lieutenant-general'—the lieutenant-general being the aged War Minister, Francisco Figueras, Marquess 'of Constancy', who had presented the Reserve Bill. Other deputies immediately protested that San Román was free to say what he liked, being protected by parliamentary privilege, but Narváez disagreed: in all places 'certain tokens of respect should be shown by an inferior to a superior in the military hierarchy'.[1]

2. THE NEW ABSOLUTISM AND SENATORIAL INDISCIPLINE, 1850–1852

This exchange marked the beginning of a new idiosyncrasy of Spanish politics. Hitherto the constitutional system and the organization of the army had been distinct in form, even if politicians had used soldiers and soldiers had meddled in public affairs; but now that the *Moderados* had accepted a permanent military influence in the legislature, the internal rivalries of the generals could be fought out according to the rules of the political, rather than the military, code. Their hegemony had been built up not in a climate of militarism but rather in response to the demoralization of the bureaucrats, unable to keep the monarchy solvent, popularize their own variety of Liberalism, or win wars; it is not surprising that the result should have been a political army rather than a disciplined State. Nevertheless, only by virtue of its discipline, 'the spirit of the *Ordenanzas*', had the army come to be regarded by conservatives as the indispensable agent of government, and if the chain of command was to be permanently unreliable the régime of the generals would be impossible. If, as senators, they claimed immunity from War Office instructions, they were bartering power for privilege: if they did not, they were renouncing the constitutional liberties for which they had fought the Carlist war, and the prizes for which they had accepted the supremacy of Narváez.

For this reason the apparently esoteric dispute between the Senate and the government which lasted intermittently for five years and culminated in the revolution of 1854 was

[1] *Diario*, Congreso, 1849–50.

one which concerned not so much the issues debated—the reserve, the estimates, parliamentary privilege, constitutional revision and railway contracts—as the future of the conservative–military alliance. And since the lack of other forms of protest in a period of 'tranquillity' concentrated public attention on the one discordant note which the system permitted, generals who were concerned chiefly with the exploitation of a *Moderado* régime which the government seemed to be betraying discovered that their cause was interesting to all who found the régime itself intolerable. When in 1850 Narváez reacted to further criticism by exiling Pavía to Cadiz, other senators rallied to his defence; not only the *Progresistas*, Generals Infante and Méndez Vigo, but two more dissatisfied conservatives, General Córdova, whose Italian campaign had been too sparingly appreciated, and the under-employed poet, General Ros de Olano.[1] They proposed a Bill to establish the 'inviolability' of senators and deputies, both in session and out; and although there was no division over this, the spirit of opposition grew, until the first week of 1851 saw the Prime Minister harangued and questioned by a phalanx of enemies. Pavía resumed his seat and his friends were joined by Generals Roncali (dismissed from the Captaincy-General of Cuba after defeating the López raid), O'Donnell, and Lersundi. The *Progresistas* were represented by Generals Alaix and Serrano, and in the Congress, from which the elections of 1850 had removed almost every trace of opposition, including General San Miguel, and the civilian Progressives, the ministers found themselves baited by the isolated but irritating voices of Generals Prim and Ortega.[2] A new Recruitment Bill was obstructed, and Narváez was compelled to defend himself from the charge of having acted seditiously in 1838; he wearied of the struggle and on 10 January resigned,

---

[1] 1808–86, a literary guardee, who had served in Salamanca's government as Minister of Commerce (Sept. 1847), and from Narváez got only the Captaincy-General of Old Castille: O'Donnell later made him Marquess of Guad-el-Jelu.

[2] Prim had returned from Puerto Rico after dealing with social unrest by authorizing planters to execute their own slaves, a measure which led to his being re-called; he resentfully took up with the Progressives again. Jaime Ortega (1816–60) had been arrested for plotting against Narváez in 1847, and was to die for the Carlists in the *pronunciamiento* of San Carlos de Rápita (see also p. 41).

complaining that 'he was born to fight his enemies face to face, not to get shot in the back'.

This was a surprising and delusive victory. When the senatorial opposition had actually put forward a motion censuring the arbitrary arrest of parliamentary officers, they had been defeated by fifty-seven votes to twenty; if the government had enjoyed the confidence of the Queen, it could have ignored what was little more than an oratorical display. But Narváez had discovered before this that the monarchical revival which he had exploited in 1843 could be used against him. His quarrel with the Queen Mother had led to his being dismissed in 1846, and though he returned to favour the following year as the only politician capable of managing a parliamentary system that excluded the radicals and satisfied the army, his very success encouraged the Royal family to think of his usefulness as past. Like Sir Robert Walpole's, his régime was proving less dependent on its leader than on its manipulator, the Count of San Luis, his parvenu Newcastle; and when the placemen on whom he depended for his majorities became aware of a *rapprochement* between San Luis and the palace behind Narváez's back, their loyalty was compromised. Rather than watch his system disintegrate, he decided to let the Queen attempt to run it without him, confident that the experiment would fail: 'if I get rid of the job before they dish me there will be a chain of short-lived ministries, and my enemies will end up by calling for me again'.[1] Thus the real trial of strength in January 1851 was between Narváez and the Crown; the opposition of the generals was for the time being ancillary to that of the Queen.

She had never liked Narváez, who had barked at her and dismissed her lover Serrano from the palace, but she had accepted him on the advice of the Queen Mother and of the entourage of courtiers whom he cultivated. After her marriage to the impotent King Francis her affairs and her piety inclined her to side against him with the clique of 'absolutists' who could offer her a complaisant husband, an approving mother, and a sympathetic confessor

---

[1] See Bermejo, *La estafeta de palacio*, iii. 314. Bermejo gives the current political gossip with a *Moderado* slant.

in return for political influence. They were not a school of doctrinaire conservatives, nor a clerical conspiracy, nor a spawn of pure administrators on the Napoleonic model; they were generals, bureaucrats, and lawyers of the usual *Moderado* stamp whom the exclusiveness of Narváez's régime had driven up the backstairs of the palace in the hope of getting office. In October 1849 General Clonard came to power for three days on the strength of the King Consort's reconciliation with the Queen,[1] but Narváez's placemen refused to accept him and he retired to compose military history; however, when in 1850 his Finance Minister Bravo Murillo went over to the lawyers Egana, Benavides, and Llorente in the Royalist camp, it was time for Narváez to retire. Thus the politicians of the Court came to power by the usual means: an exercise of the Royal Prerogative designed to anticipate the shift in public opinion that would give the new ministers their majority in parliament; but the events of the forties had wedged the party establishment of the *Moderados* too firmly into the administrative system for such a change to be negotiated without the assistance of the more important conservative figures. To avoid this, and to establish his independence of party ties, Bravo Murillo, the new Premier, was compelled to adopt the stratagem of the *Moderados* in 1845 and attempt to alter the Constitution so as to suit his own preponderance—that of the civilian bureaucrats.

For the generals, this was putting back the clock to the reign of Ferdinand VII; for Bravo it was the only hope of modernizing the country. Thus the two oppositions which had overthrown Narváez were placed in a rather misleading antagonism, the government determined to cut out the jobbery and speech-making of politics as a parasite on the economy, while the military senators took their stand on the rights of the citizen and the law of the Constitution. Over such issues, with the Senate as battlefield and Narváez leader of the opposition, the absolutists were almost bound to suffer

[1] For this see G. Hubbard, *Histoire contemporaine de l'Espagne*, 128-32, and Bermejo, *La estafeta*, iii. 239-40. The contemporary *Extracto de la causa seguida a Sor Patrocinio por el juzgado de Barquillo, precedida de la relación de todo lo acaecido en la subida al poder y caida del Ministerio Clonard-Manresa-Balboa* gives a bald narrative. General Balboa was to be Minister of the Interior (see p. 94).

defeat: and it was in fact after one day's trial of strength in
the upper chamber that Bravo Murillo handed in his resignation on 13 December 1852: but the real conflict—whether
the Court could win over enough military support to make
the army accept the Prime Minister as its chief, rather than
Narváez and the generals—had been decided elsewhere. For
Bravo Murillo was no more an 'anti-militarist' than his predecessors; neither in theory nor in practice did he oppose
the interests of the military class. His financial policy was to
reduce the 'unproductive expenditure' of the State, and
under this heading he included the wages of the rank and
file, not the salaries of the officers; to cut down on these
would be to reduce the consumption of excisable articles and
discourage the manufacture of middle-class amenities.[1] As
Narváez's Finance Minister he had sought to reduce the
military estimates by twenty million *reales* and when Narváez had refused to go lower than twelve, he had resigned;
but this was a quarrel over 7 per cent. and 5 per cent.
within the estimates, not about the proportion of the whole
budget which ought to be devoted to the army. Bravo wanted
cuts in all departments, while Narváez and San Luis preferred to spend lavishly on public works; here lay the basic
difference. In 1851 the new cabinet's first approaches were
to the opposition of the generals,[2] and only when they remained unimpressed by Bravo's offers did he turn to his project of constitutional amendment—the Senate to be turned
into an assembly of hereditary noblemen and senior officials,
the sessions of Cortes to be secret, and the right to initiate
legislation confined to ministers. To counter the opposition,
he laid plans for a *coup d'état*, seeking a Louis Napoleon in
Pezuela,[3] now Captain-General of Madrid, and sending the
Queen herself to enthuse the garrison in despite of the other
generals.[4] For once he had antagonized these, the great
bureaucrat's only resource was to use their own weapons

---

[1] See J. Bravo Murillo, *Opúsculos* (1863), ii. 252-68 for a résumé of his ideas.

[2] He offered to restore Prim to the Governorship of Puerto Rico, and gave jobs
to Lersundi, Pavía, Infante, and Córdova; but this antagonized O'Donnell, who
wanted the War Office.

[3] While Narváez helped finance Louis Napoleon's actual coup by a loan of half
a million francs at 5 per cent. (Hubbard, op. cit., v. 140).

[4] See F.O., Howden to Granville, 9 and 12 Jan. 1852; also 9 June.

against them, and it was Isabella who pointed out the inconsistency of his attitude by asking him: 'Do you believe that a constitutional Queen ought to give you an unlimited support in a matter of coercion? Powers which are insufficient to prevent insurrections ought not to seek the support of material force from a Queen who does not wish to shed blood.'[1]

3. THE REVIVAL OF THE *PRONUNCIAMIENTO*

Bravo Murillo had failed because his contempt for representative government prevented his appealing to public opinion against the generals, whereas they, by contrast, were able to get the support of the press and the parties; to defy these was to court 'insurrection'. It was obviously in the interests of the Court to narrow the field of conflict to dimensions at which the class interests of the opposition could be their only *raison d'être*; once isolated from the currents of public enthusiasm, they could be more easily controlled. Bravo's last act of power had been to prevent Narváez from bringing the Progressives back into politics—so he thought —by ordering him to 'study tactics' at Vienna; General Roncali, the next Premier, while shelving the project for constitutional reform, repeated the order and diverted the Senate once more to the defence of their own privileges. Narváez retired over the frontier and published an open protest: the War Minister General Lara[2] smugly informed him that the Queen was displeased 'by a document in which there is not only a want of respect towards her August Person from the excess of self-praise and improper comparisons in it, but also manifest contraventions of . . . the Royal *Ordenanzas* for the army'.

With the *Ordenanzas* in one hand and the promise of employment in the other, the governments of this phase (January 1853–January 1854) then began to dismantle the united opposition which had defeated Bravo Murillo, and

---

[1] Bermejo, *La estafeta*, iii. 396.
[2] Juan de Lara, an ex-guardee and *pronunciado* of 1843, became a Gentleman of the Bedchamber to King Francis and stood by the Court until frightened off by the rising of 1854.

met with considerable success. Córdova and Ros de Olano were won over by the abandonment of the constitutional reform, Lersundi by the Premiership, which he assumed from April to September 1853, Prim and San Román by posts on the military mission to the Crimea: San Luis accepted the Premiership after Lersundi, and bought off his old colleague Narváez's hostility by allowing him to return home. A certain type of soldier was bound to prefer the simple doctrine of Royalism to the more complicated fractiousness which was kept alive by O'Donnell and the Conchas—Mirasol, for example (see p. 74), Bláser,[1] and Genaro, son of the General Quesada who had been murdered by the *exaltados* in 1836; but it was more important that so many political generals now began to see the service of the Court as more profitable than that of the parties. It was this fatal erosion that drove the surviving opponents of the ministry of San Luis into a headlong assault on his innocuous Railway Bill. Before 1853 the practice of conceding railway contracts by Royal decree, to which the Senate objected, had been allowed to go unchallenged, and the ministry was prepared to abandon it for the future if past concessions were allowed to stand; if, however, the opposition could engineer a public inquiry into the details of the question, they would be able to blackmail the Queen into throwing over the Court party. For the financier Salamanca had been able to procure a grant of the *Norte* line only through the good offices of her current lover Major Araña; the Major claimed two million *reales* as his commission, and when neither Salamanca nor the government of Lersundi would pay him, San Luis had been brought to power to settle the matter.[2] He paid, but he was not anxious to have this revealed, especially as he came in with the slogan of *Moralidad*: when the debates of November to December 1853 showed him that O'Donnell and his friends were determined to get to the bottom of the affair, and when, on 13 January, they replied to his suspension of Cortes by asking the Queen to dismiss him, he decided that they had gone far enough. Confident that he had most of the

---

[1] 1807–72, son of an aristocratic Swiss mercenary, refused all employment after 1854 and declined to recognize King Amadeus in 1870.

[2] F.O., Howden to Clarendon, 29 Sept. 1853.

army on his side, he exiled O'Donnell, Infante, and the Conchas, and recalled all officers to their units.

He miscalculated. Not that his hold on the army was weaker than O'Donnell's—when the rebels actually came out in June, they were supported by less than half the Madrid garrison and had to call the civilian revolutionaries of the Left to their assistance—but that by an open challenge to the *status quo* of 1845 he called into play once more the elements of violence on which the hegemony of *Moderados* and generals had been based; and this was a kind of politics in which the most insignificant subaltern could, with luck, overthrow governments. Narváez's careful management had directed the ambition of generals into constitutional paths, and the whole history of the military opposition from 1849 indicated their preference for his system, even if shorn of its asperities. They wished only for their strength in the legislature to entitle them to govern as ministers, or serve governments that respected it; but when he was compelled to avoid arrest by hiding behind a false wall at the back of a printing office O'Donnell decided to bring down the régime by an appeal to the troops.

For a decade of 'passive obedience' had not closed their ears to such an appeal. When the military party had come to power in 1843 it had been to the accompaniment of mass promotions conceded to all officers who had come out against Espartero, and those who had not—whether deliberately or by accident—found their advancement blocked by a congestion in the rank next above them. The only other general promotions, at the Royal marriage in 1846, and at the birth of an Infanta in 1852, did not include subalterns, so that a lieutenant who missed his *grado* in 1843 was still a lieutenant in 1854.[1] The motive and the raw material of sedition therefore still existed, and after the fall of Narváez military opinion waited closely and vocally on public events. Not only was the opposition of the generals the concern of every officer, but the new governments also affected his interests by authorizing a series of military reforms which were discussed

[1] See *Revista Militar*, xi. 305, 'Some Reflexions on the Promotions Granted to the Army in 1843', and Baron Inés, *El ejército y los partidos* (1855), a pamphlet intended to show how the *Moderados* had ruined the army.

with more or less freedom in the several army periodicals which circulated during the period. The reforms were the work of San Román, the trouble-maker of 1849–50, Under-Secretary at the War Office from 1852 to 1854, of his friend the military *Wunderkind* of the Court party, Francisco Lersundi,[1] and of the older work-horse Fernando Córdova, Director-General of Infantry in 1851 and 1853 with a phase of opposition in between. In an effort to prune the Service of its anomalies they set up a committee to investigate the multifarious promotion system, tackled the basic problem of redundancy by providing gratuities for officers who resigned their commissions, reformed the commissariat, allowed sergeants to marry, sent conscripts home on long leaves, and increased the wages of N.C.O.s, majors, and infantry privates; the only 'absolutist' measures which they approved being the revival of an attenuated Royal Horse Guard in 1852, and the enforcement of the War Minister's authority over all members of the army—a provision which Narváez had first been able to extract in writing from the Queen in 1850.[2] All these measures aroused discontent among the various sections of the military whom change could only injure. To unify the promotion system was to insult the artillery and engineers, privileged with the *escala cerrada*, and the scheme had to be dropped; modernizing the commissariat involved frustrating those corps commanders who believed they could supply their men on their own; to indemnify retiring officers was bribery, and to insist on War Office control was flying in the face of the *Ordenanzas*, which emphasized the personal supremacy of the Sovereign.[3] In

---

[1] Both Lersundi and San Román were in their thirties (like San Luis; the opposition generals being all over forty), and had risen through acts of rebellion—Lersundi in 1841 and 1843, San Román as president of the junta of Valencia in 1843 —to important desk jobs and loyalist convictions. Lersundi was recommended to Bravo Murillo as a War Minister by King Francis, as fond of handsome soldiers as his wife, and held office again in 1856–7 and 1864, refusing to serve the Republic; San Román attained the highest military honours under Alfonso XII. For an inflated biography see F. Vargas Machuca, *Vida política, militar y pública del Excmo. Sr. Don Francisco Lersundi, Actual Ministro de la Guerra* (1851).

[2] See Appendix I.

[3] For these reforms see *Revista Militar*, x. 48 (a summary of Lersundi's work), xii. 249 (the pay rises), xiii. 177 (the Guard), and 466, 572, 761 (the problems of the commissariat): also F. Córdova, *Memorias íntimas*, iii. 335, and the MS. 'Reflexiones sobre la actual organización del ejército: Memoria', by R. Madina y Orbeita

particular, the new Horse Guard offended the cavalry officers who were not included in it, and the infantry pay rise was considered unfair by the troopers; which was, in the event, unfortunate, since the Director of Cavalry, Manuel Concha, was one of the leaders of the opposition in the Senate. How far he was able to exploit these technical grievances it is impossible to say; in April 1853 the British Ambassador remarked on 'the happy and contented state of the Army', in December Concha was dismissed from his post, and in January his brother informed Lord Howden 'that if there was a revolutionary movement the whole of the cavalry would go over in a body to the insurgents'[1]—as, on 28 June 1854, most regiments did.

But the decision to rebel might not have been taken even after San Luis had declared open war on the opposition. His high-handedness was largely bluff, for he was unsure of the Queen's support (she was negotiating for a new cabinet under either Bravo Murillo or General Córdova), and the economic prosperity which had favoured the activities of the Court party since 1850 was coming to an end. In Galicia there was famine, in Barcelona, unemployment, and while in April 1854 officials had to borrow from town councils to make up their tax quotas, in May the government was compelled to raise a forced loan in order to avert a stoppage at the Treasury. It had become apparent before this that without a Cortes to pass money bills, San Luis would either have to impose a new Constitution by force (which would turn Isabella and the whole army against him, as in 1852) or resign; and if he resigned, O'Donnell and his friends might succeed him in the ordinary way. Neither side could claim the undivided sympathy of army opinion which alone could guarantee the success of rebellion and repression alike. When O'Donnell approached the garrison commanders of Madrid they reported the fact to the War Office without revealing his hiding-place, because 'they had served with the General and therefore desired that no harm should happen to him, but they thought it their duty to put the Government on its

(S.H.M. 4-2-2-21), which analyses the results of this régime. The *escala* dispute occupies columns in all military periodicals from 1847 onwards.

[1] F.O., Howden to Clarendon, 18 Jan. 1854.

guard',[1] and shortly afterwards Concha's directorate of the cavalry was given to General Dulce, who made no secret of his complicity with O'Donnell and the conspirators; even the police agents, many of them ex-regular sergeants, were playing a double game. No one wanted blood but San Luis himself.

There was no liaison between these military Frondeurs and the forces of discontent outside the *Moderado* establishment; the generals made plans for a movement, but meanwhile thought in terms of getting Narváez to abandon his neutrality and approach Isabella on their behalf, or of a coup by which the Queen or the dynasty might be changed,[2] but not the political infrastructure. On 18 February Howden reported that

the government inspires no sympathy anywhere, the opposition no sympathy, and the throne no sympathy. Out of these three negations arises a political existence which can hardly be said to possess vital action. . . . It will go on in this way until something strikes the interest, imagination, or caprice of the people, or until some individual happens to electrify the army by one of those words or actions which . . . it is impossible for spectators to foresee.

Two days later the unforeseen action occurred, at Saragossa. Brigadier Hore pronounced against the government with the Cordova regiment, was attacked by loyal troops, and died under the impact of seventeen balls, shouting 'Don't shoot, we are brothers'. He was a conservative ex-guardee who had got himself involved in O'Donnell's conspiracy possibly to escape from financial difficulties, but had come out in accordance with a plan for a general rising which had been called off; a gaffe owing not so much to his infatuation with the Riego tradition—he refused to allow his band to play Riego's March—as to the hesitation of the chief conspirators and the double-dealing of General Dulce, who seems to have acted both as instigator and informer. His

[1] F.O., Howden to Clarendon, 25 Jan. 1854.
[2] The idea had been mooted by the generals since the previous year: both the Conchas and Narváez had declared to Howden that 'it was absolutely necessary for the tranquillity and prosperity of Spain, to do away completely with the Bourbon dynasty' (F.O. to Clarendon, 4 Jan. 1854).

death was uninteresting to 'the people',[1] but it compelled the generals to go through with their rebellion or incur the blame of having suffered a fellow officer to sacrifice himself in vain.[2]

Even so, O'Donnell was anxious to keep the insurrection 'clean', both because he was a political conservative, envisaging his actions as the defence of a violated constitution,[3] not as revolution, and because he knew that a popular movement would involve both the restoration of Espartero and the cry of 'No Quinta'. Until he had failed to capture Madrid, and was forced to call the Progressives to his assistance by the programme of Manzanares, he agreed in matters of political principle with loyalists such as Córdova, who told his officers on 28 June:

If the honour of the Infantry were not a powerful motive to make you act like soldiers, if the fate . . . of these poor privates, who know nothing of our dissensions and will gain nothing by them, did not interest you, at least do not forget that the triumph of the revolution is perhaps the extinction of the army and that without your commissions you will not get bread to feed your children, nor the right to expect your just and merited promotions.

Córdova admitted that he was trying to keep his forces together 'not for a ministry which I saw travelling into a bottomless abyss, but for the good of the army itself', and the attitude was common to both sides.[4] When Dulce and O'Donnell led out the cavalry on 28 June 1854 they gave

1 In Madrid the *Progresistas* ignored Hore, and at Saragossa they 'denounced the movement as not being theirs, and had done all they could to prevent the people joining in it' (F.O., Howden to Clarendon, 25 Feb. 1854).

2 This is the conclusion of C. Martos in his *La revolución de julio en 1854*, 57; Bermejo insinuates (*La estafeta*, iii. 411–412) that Dulce deliberately betrayed Hore in order to remove suspicion from himself; see J. Buxó de Abaigar, Marqués de Castell-Florite, *Domingo Dulce, general Isabelino. Vida y época;* (Barcelona, 1962), 291–3 for the lame excuses of an encomiast.

3 'The Revolution does not spring from the masses nor emanate from the people: it has come from the governing power which has placed itself outside the law' (O'Donnell's first proclamation). This was of course a conventional attitude: the army's first duty to the law, not the government. The Marquess of Castell-Florite inflates it into Dulce's own 'theory of the ethics and legality of military insurrections' (*Dulce*, 295–300).

4 See F. Córdova: *Memoria del Teniente Gral. D. Fernando Fernández de Córdova sobre los sucesos políticos ocurridos en Madrid en los días 17, 18 y 19 de julio de 1854* (1855).

all their officers the chance of returning to serve the government, and when the two armies engaged at Vicálvaro the fighting was hardly serious; some units may have used blank, or wild trajectories. It was not incongruous that the régime of the *Moderados* should, in the end, have counted less with the officers of the army than the spirit of military solidarity which in 1843 had led to its establishment.

Thus although the *pronunciamiento* became a revolution, and the revolution led to the return of Espartero and the reoccupation of the civil service and the Cortes by the Progressives, the conditions for a demilitarized administration and an army confined to executive rather than deliberative functions were still unrealized. When the spontaneous proletarian risings of Madrid, which overthrew General Córdova's last-minute cabinet, appeared likely to adopt the programme of the Democrats, it was the doyen of military politicians, Evaristo San Miguel, who persuaded[1] them to accept the leadership of those orthodox *Progresistas* who had contributed nothing to the insurrection; when Isabella was threatened with deposition, and her mother with a public trial, the Royalism of Espartero saved them; and when O'Donnell was appointed War Minister the army was saved from its radical enemies and its autonomous position within the State secured. There was no significant reduction in the number of officers or the size of the estimates, the *quinta* system was retained, and whenever the provinces were disturbed the government imposed martial law; even though Espartero himself was in favour of voluntary enlistment, his wishes could be disregarded because, as Howden discovered in August 1854, 'the Army is not Esparterista'. The old military establishment, pruned of a few loyalists and richer by a promotion of returned exiles, was allowed to exist side by side with a Constituent Cortes of Left-wing civilians empowered to reconstruct the State on the most Liberal plan possible.

[1] Through the mob-leader Pucheta; according to Howden he told Pucheta ' "you are a Republican, and I am for Constitutional Monarchy . . . therefore as we represent two incompatibilities, you must either shoot me or I must shoot you." Pucheta answered, "I never thought much about these diplomatick puzzles but you are a fine fellow, and I'll soon settle the business"—upon which he turned round to his followers and said—"the first who cries for a Republic, I'll shoot him," after which nothing more was heard of the Republic.'

From the first embrace of Espartero and O'Donnell on 29 July 1854 the relationship was an uneasy one, and it was exacerbated by the revival of the National Militia and the incidence of bad harvests and unemployment; the reign of liberty was confronted by the problem of maintaining order before it could achieve the reconciliation of social interests. Espartero was unable to dispense with O'Donnell, but O'Donnell and the Queen, alarmed by the persistence of a radical threat to the *status quo* in both the army and the Church, were able to engineer the retirement of Espartero. Her recovery of the prerogative of choosing her ministers enabled the forces of conservatism to rally, and the Constituent Cortes was replaced by Narváez's *Moderado* chamber in 1857; the generals were more durable than the revolutionaries. 1854 and 1856 marked the limits of interference by the Right and Left beyond which the loyalty of the army to itself ran counter to its loyalty towards the State; only within these limits was compromise possible, but they were broad enough to include the régimes both of soldiers such as O'Donnell and of the civilian Cánovas.

Thus the military incubus of Spanish politics had survived the transition from an absolute to a constitutional monarchy, and it remained for the generals and deputies to work out between them whether the army was to exert its pressure legally, through the parties and the Cortes, or violently—in antagonism to an uncontrolled prerogative power as in 1868, in defence of social order as in 1873–4. This was not so much the failure of Spanish Liberalism as the condition of its reconcilement with the unitary State. Only through the development of economic interests could the experiment of a freer society engage the sympathy of even the diminutive political class which the Constitutions of 1834–68 had established; and while the privileges of the military ensured their own allegiance to the new system, the hegemony of the other classes depended ultimately on their ability to command force—either that of the populace, in the militia, or that of the army. To the peasants and labourers who made up the passive population of the country the politics of interest could mean little but extortion by the employees of the State and exploitation by the 'comfortable' classes: protest was their only weapon, and as long as this situation lasted, so would the rule of the military.

Yet the army was more than a militant trade union for the more unproductive half of the middle classes. It was the one political institution in which all sections of society could participate towards a common aim, hence the popularity it enjoyed in periods of actual warfare—the 1830's and 1860. The conscript was in many ways the victim of his employer's —the officer's—hold on the State, but he was not, as in civilian life, irretrievably fixed in his station at the bottom of the social structure; and in the army, as in no other instruments of exploitation, the pay and living conditions of the men improved considerably from 1800 to 1850. Although they lived under the day-to-day severity of the *Ordenanzas*, they were activated by the rhetoric of liberty, and in the *trabajos* of the sergeants which preceded movements of military support or dissent, they experienced a primitive form of electioneering that gave them a share, however minute, in the decisions of the 'nation'.

And the idle multitude of officers were able to pursue their class interests only in terms of the 1820 tradition, as a further conquest for that nation. The limited freedoms secured for the individual in the 1830's could never be abandoned for long with their consent, and if, in styling themselves champions of liberty, they exaggerated, they were at least a receptive audience to the civilization of the nineteenth century: to the liberating opera-choruses of Bellini and Verdi which they included in the repertoire of their bands, to the romantic prose in which they composed their letters home,[1] to the journalism, morals, and aspirations of the French *bourgeoisie*. In the disintegration of the Thomist front with which official and Royalist Spain had reacted to the French Revolution, the literary officer played a not inconspicuous part; uniforms are prominent in contemporary pictures of the meetings at the *Ateneo* and *Liceo* where the intellectual life of Madrid was reborn, and the less fortunate exiles of 1840–3 were able

---

[1] Typified by Galdós in *Los ayacuchos*. The illiteracy of the generals seems to have been deduced too hastily from their spelling; it was a difficult period for Spanish orthography. Narváez's allusion to the battle fought between Cicero and Hannibal at Cannae I have been unable to trace in the *Diario*.

to support themselves by translating Dumas for serialization at home.

They were in fact neither Junkers nor Janissaries, nor unworthy participants in political life. The civilians who wanted to exclude them, who considered, like Martínez de la Rosa, that under a representative system the army must never act against government since in the government the nation is embodied,[1] made the mistake of assuming that Spain enjoyed a Liberal government, rather than a government run by Liberal politicians.[2]

[1] See *Espíritu del siglo* (1835), i. 99–104.

[2] Since I wrote the above chapter, the history of the period 1854 to 1856 has been lucidly expounded in V. G. Kiernan's *The Revolution of 1854 in Spanish History* (Oxford 1966).

APPENDIX I

THE MINISTRY OF WAR AND THE PROMOTION SYSTEM

UNDER the absolute monarchy the King controlled the army and the War Secretary assisted him in his transactions with the regiments of the line; the Ministry of War developed out of this situation, but it was not until 1850 that the Minister was acknowledged as supreme by the whole army. Until 1835 the Guards were administered according to their own regulations directly by the monarch through two commandants, and after this the Captain-General of Madrid (more correctly of New Castille) took his orders from the palace, not the ministry; a privilege which Narváez exploited and then abolished. Even under constitutional régimes the fact that the War Minister was always a general meant that he was more responsible to the King, by virtue of his military oath, than to the Cortes; and he had no powers over his own subordinates except through the order, decree, or circular, all of which required the Royal signature. Like the other ministers he worked on the ground floor of the palace,[1] and Ferdinand VII would spend several hours a day there; his sub-secretary and heads of departments were all serving officers, and even the clerks enjoyed the *fuero militar*.

The department was organized into sections or *mesas* by Generals Amarillas and Zarco in 1820, and these took care of routine administration—each giving formal audience to suitors and job-hunters once a week[2]—while the Minister decided on policy and troop movements with the King; but his competence was seriously limited from below by the right of each branch of the army to administer most of its own affairs. In theory, the inspectors-general[3] were dependants of the War Office; in practice, their appointment was a cabinet decision and their role was to ensure that no measures could be enforced by Madrid which would conflict with the political and economic interests of the arm they represented. Thus the leading generals of the artillery, engineers, infantry, cavalry, provincial militia, Royalist Volunteers, *Carabineros*, National Militia, and Civil Guard were invested with their own establishments of aides, officials, and clerks to organize the

[1] Until the end of Ferdinand's reign, when the office was moved with the other ministries, except that of foreign affairs, to Godoy's old palace, and later to the Calle de Alcalá.

[2] For a good account of such an audience, see *Madrid in 1835, by a Resident Officer*, 2 vols. (1836), ii. 49.   [3] Called Directors after 1847.

annual inspections and intervene in all communications between the troops and the government; they shared in the distribution of patronage and filed the service sheets (*hojas de servicio*) on which every officer's career depended.

But they were not the only autonomous subordinates of the Minister. To the provincial captains-general was delegated authority over local troop movements, leaves, and N.C.O. promotions; the military lawyers were answerable to a permanent 'Supreme Tribunal of War and Marine', and the commissariat—*administración militar*—was run by the Intendant-General's office through his own network of some 500 auditors, intendants, and paymasters. The *administración* was transferred from the Ministry of Finance to that of War in 1828, but despite its breakdown in the Carlist war retained a life of its own, and was reinvigorated by the School of Military Administration in the fifties.

A War Minister had thus to be a diplomat as well as a bureaucrat and a politician; and the sphere in which most finesse was demanded was that of promotion, for here the economic interests of the State and the officer were most apt to differ.

There were two kinds of rank; the *empleo*, effective, with full pay and insignia, and the *grado*, which was titular, a reward for conduct rather than seniority, and held concurrently with an *empleo* by those awarded it. Before 1836 it was possible, but not usual, to advance from one *empleo* to the next; thenceforward honorary status intervened. It was never possible to advance from one honorary rank to the next; thus, although there were only seven ranks from ensign to colonel inclusive, twelve promotions were required to make the ascent.[1]

At the same time, an officer could hold a rank in more than one promotion ladder. As the engineers and artillery were only allowed to rise in strict order of seniority within their corps, they were given complimentary promotions in the ordinary scale by way of signalling particular achievements.[2] As the Guards were supposed to be the pick of the line regiments, their ranks were equivalent to the next highest in the ordinary scale, and both could be held at once. As a result the same man could be an effective captain of artillery, an effective captain of infantry, and an honorary major of infantry; or an effective lieutenant of

---

[1] The ranks were, after 1835: ensign (*alférez, subteniente*), lieutenant (*teniente*), captain (*capitán*), junior major (*segundo comandante*), senior major (*primer comandante*), lieutenant-colonel (*teniente coronel*), and Colonel. Honorary ranks had been abolished from 1820 to 1823: the value of the promotion had gone up and favouritism and corruption had consequently increased: the period from 1824 to 1835, on the other hand, was distinguished for 'regularity of promotion' (see *Revista Militar*, 1848, 19).

[2] See Luján's speech in Cortes, 24 Feb. 1838: *Diario*, 1837–8, iii. 483–5.

Guards, an effective captain of infantry, and (before 1835, when the *comandante* promotion was finally enforced) an honorary lieutenant-colonel of infantry. However, an officer could only enjoy the pay of the one effective rank he held in his own corps.[1] As there were too many officers needing promotion, and advancement could not, in peace time, be accelerated, so milestones were multiplied.

Ways of securing promotion were also various. To the rank of captain it was by 'selection', that is recommendation to the War Office by the regimental commander through the Inspector-General, or by any other influence. Above that rank it was usually by seniority in peacetime, although the War Office reserved the right to select whom it pleased. Colonels were chosen by the King: the same was true of brigadiers and generals.[2] The advantage of securing the favour of the War Minister or of the Inspector-General was obvious—'hardly any one ever dreams of getting forward by his deeds—no, he has a surer card, a good friend . . .',[3] but since the seniority lists were not made public until the 1840's, irregularity in both advancement and relegation were hard to prove. Thus it became an *idée fixe* of military opinion that the only fair promotion was the promotion by strict seniority enjoyed by the artillery and engineers; this led to Narváez's decree of 1866 by which the *grado* was abolished and all *empleos* up to colonel made attainable by *rigurosa antigüedad* alone.

(See also: A. López de Letona, *Estudios críticos sobre el estado militar de España* (1866); and E. Fernández San Roman, *Statistique, organisation et institutions militaires de l'armée espagnole* (1852), 59 et seq. The *Guías de Forasteros* give annual lists of War Office personnel.)

---

[1] For an example of the innumerable debates on the promotion system, see Perrotte's article in *Revista Militar*, i. 481 (1847) and reply by Riquelme in ii. 19 (1848).

[2] See ibid., 1848, 21.   [3] Bacon, *Six Years in Biscay*, 218.

APPENDIX II

THE MUTINY OF LA GRANJA

THE best account of the rising was written by one of its leaders, Sergeant Alejandro Gómez, some four years later, with the express purpose of vindicating his companions from the charges of venality, drunkenness, and prearrangement with which their enemies accused them.[1] His narrative seems to be that of a truthful if an interested man. He shows that the discontent of the first provincial grenadier guards, to which he belonged, dated from their return to palace duty in June 1836 from a campaign in the north in which two-thirds of the regiment had been killed, wounded, or captured. On 21 June they were given a welcome feast at the Pardo palace by the Queen Regent, which was reported at length by the *Eco del Comercio* of 25 June, a paper to which the sergeants were already subscribing in the north. The *Eco* does not add that this 'abundant and delicate luncheon' was broken up the instant one of the chaplains gave a toast to liberty which offended the courtiers present. In the ensuing weeks the rigid discipline insisted upon by the Marquess of San Román, their commandant, proved unendurable to men who had been used to the rough and ready soldiering of Navarre. Their pay was short—Villiers wrote to Palmerston that it was three months in arrears by 13 August, but that may be an exaggeration[2]—and the constitutional songs and tunes they were used to were forbidden. Gómez insists that they were not *worked* by radical agents: but after the regiment had accompanied the Court to La Granja, the sergeants could meet in the Theatre Café and read the *Eco* and the *Jorobado*, 'so that in the end the liberal spirit was predominant in all that we did'.[3] The articles they read were frankly inflammatory. The *Eco*'s leader on 5 July declared 'grave, most grave is the responsibility which weighs on the immediate commanders of the army, for the smallest fault or omission they may commit in the critical state in which we are now; but even more terrible are the charges to which the government must answer if, for whatever motives, they fail to employ for the conclusion of the civil war the great resources which a magnanimous nation has given them'. On 28 and 29 July the leaders discussed the merits of a just revolution. 'It is impossible to avoid the

---

[1] *Los sucesos de La Granja en 1836. Apuntes para la historia*: first published Madrid, 1864.
[2] F.O., Villiers to Palmerston, 13 Aug. 1836.   [3] Gómez, 12.

overthrow of a vitiated society in which the law, which is only the expression of the common interest, yields every moment to private calculations or passions.' On the 28th also the *Eco* mentioned the news that a roving Carlist band was threatening La Granja, and added tendentiously 'we do not pay much attention to what is being said, nor do we see that sensible persons believe it, either—despite that on the other hand all appearances seem to confirm it'. This referred to a rumour that the courtiers were planning to betray the Queen to the Carlists and end the war by arranging a marriage between her and a son of Don Carlos. From 3 August the *Eco*'s articles were subject to censorship: by then the sergeants had been 'worked' as effectively as by a real agent.

When an arbitrary confinement to barracks made the men amenable, and the officers happened to be absent in the theatre, the sergeants took over and the mutiny was achieved: the Regent had a talk with Gómez, Sergeant Juan Lúcas, and a private, and agreed to promise a plan of constitutional reform when Cortes opened. Here the mutiny might have ended, had not the Queen's decision been read out by the unpopular San Román: the soldiers grew noisy, and the sergeants pacified them by getting her to promise the Constitution of 1812.

After this the direction of the movement fell into the hands of Sergeant Higinio García, San Román's clerk, who organized the distribution of money and wine to the men, the setting up of the *lápida*, and the blockade of the entire Royal entourage, including the ambassadors, at La Granja until they were assured that the cabinet no longer controlled Madrid and they were secure from punishment. Gómez insists that the officers joined the movement promptly in the beginning[1] and denies that the constitutional fiesta on the 14th was tumultuary, two points at variance with other sources. Villiers' dispatches were written on the spot, but in fear and vexation: in the end, he claims, 'the exasperation of the soldiers was even beginning to exhibit itself against the Non Commissioned Officers who endeavoured to keep them within some bounds of moderation'.[2]

As the apologists of the sergeants were to point out, the country had already declared for the Constitution of 1812, and it was only the heroic steadiness of Quesada that maintained the government in power at Madrid . The enemies of the *Exaltados* were anxious to discredit their rise to power, and so emphasized the tumultuary aspects of the mutiny and invested it with an importance it had not possessed.[3] Foreign observers saw it as the beginning of a period of praetorian politics: Cánovas later interpreted it as the last idealistic *pronunciamiento*, before the species became debased by prostitution to the private interests of

---

[1] Gómez, op cit.   [2] F.O., Villiers to Palmerston, 14 Aug.
[3] Fernández de los Ríos, *Luchas políticas*, i. 239.

military politicians. Clearly it was neither of these things, since soldiers had bullied governments since the beginning of the war and before, and it was on the strength of their popularity with the mutineers that three *exaltado* generals, Méndez Vigo, Seoane, and Rodil, took over the government and handed it to their party.

APPENDIX III

THE SEVILLE *PRONUNCIAMIENTO* OF 1838

THE Seville *pronunciamiento* has remained a mystery largely because the behaviour of the protagonists was an embarrassment to the political parties they subsequently joined. Luis Córdova became one of the eponymous heroes of the *Moderado* party: his brother Fernando, who was probably not informed of all Luis's activities at the time, was an aristocrat by temperament and, until the abdication of Isabella, an active conservative in politics. Cortina rose from the presidency of a regional revolutionary junta to a leading position in the parliamentary Progressive party: Narváez became Córdova's successor as the military champion of the *Moderados*: Clonard was to join the same party, and in it move further to the right than Narváez. Most contemporary authorities accepted Córdova's explanation—that he had been virtually captured by an inexplicable rising of the *Nacionales* of Seville, that he had taken command to save the city from disorder, that he had summoned Narváez to help him, and been the victim of a mistrustful and over-hasty exercise of his authority by his old friend Clonard, who, by declaring their actions seditious, handed over Córdova and Narváez to the vengeance of Espartero. This is the account given with copious detail and documentation in Fernando Córdova's *Memorias íntimas*.[1] Cánovas in '*El Solitario*' *y su tiempo* pointed out some of the inconsistencies and improbabilities in this version: he was able to infer that Córdova was involved with the *Exaltado* conspirators, since his main concern was to explain the desertion of his post by Córdova's friend, the *jefe político* Estébanez. In a letter to Pascual Gayangos, Estébanez wrote that 'neither Córdova who was in Seville nor Narváez who came from Loja played any part in the *pronunciamiento* but that once it was made, Córdova saw a probability of making himself master of the movement . . . '.[2] From the Clonard papers it appears that before the *pronunciamiento* Córdova was involved with the revolutionaries: however, it is likely that the commotion which broke out in Seville on 10 November was not part of a concerted plan but simply a local response to the news of disturbances in Madrid and a rumour that Clonard was

---

[1] ii. 295–385: see also *Diario de las sesiones del Senado*, 1851, ii. 62–65, and 95 for Narváez's own public statement in Cortes made 7 Jan. 1851. See also Pirala, *Guerra civil*, iii. 200–6 for a reasonable summary.

[2] '*El Solitario*', ii. 62–64, Estébanez to Gayangos, 5 Feb. 1839.

going to disarm the National Guard.[1] When the civil authorities handed over to a provisional junta on the night of the 12th, Córdova was probably, as he claimed, entirely ignorant of the fact: but once it was accomplished, and the *pronunciados* asked him to join them, he had either to do so or give up all hope of leading a general Andalusian rebellion. Alaix was in Madrid: the Esparterists had the Regent's confidence. On the 15th the elderly General Fontecilla, who had been elected their military commander by the junta, decided to retire, as he had been unable to elicit any coherent demands from the National Militia and found them still disposed to casual rioting. The regular garrison had already declined to join the movement: the *jefe político* Estébanez had disappeared. A meeting was called which Córdova attended: when the commander of the garrison had left the meeting, Córdova accepted the presidency of the junta and the military command of the province. The regular artillery asked for their passports: the rest of the garrison recognized his military but not his civil authority.[2] The National Guard were enthusiastic and orderly.

The news written by his agents to Clonard was alarming. On 13 November he was told that the real aim of the *pronunciados* was to set up a Junta of Reprisals, and thus inaugurate a radical reign of terror: and that Córdova, if not already involved, meant to turn it to his own advantage, with the assistance of Narváez.[3] On 16 November Córdova wrote confidentially to Clonard that he was the victim of circumstances: 'my reputation, my faith and my honour apparently destroyed and the remainder of my life poisoned'. At the same time he sent Cortina to fetch Narváez with an equally pathetic appeal. He seems to have expected that Narváez and he together would have sufficient prestige to turn 'the most ridiculous farce of all the movements that have ever taken place in Spain' into a successful rebellion.[4] Clonard had remained at Cadiz, the centre of the revolutionary network, apparently accepting Cordova's explanation and confiding in his good intentions. He had sent his second-in-command General Sanjuanena, a Peruvian veteran, to resume control of the city: Sanjuanena waited for Córdova to resign. On 18 November an agent wrote to Clonard from Seville: 'yesterday at five General Nárvaez having accepted the post of

[1] Pirala, who had access to recondite sources, alleged that the movement was started by 'an agent hostile to Córdova' who was sent from Madrid to stir up trouble: by whom, is uncertain (*Guerra civil*, iii. 200).

[2] *Exposición de los sucesos de Sevilla* (Seville, 1839), 9. Córdova was the senior officer in the city.

[3] Clonard MSS., Legajo 29: from C. Yriarte, 13 Nov., and an unsigned letter of the same date.

[4] Córdova, *Memorias íntimas*, ii. 295 et seq.: Córdova's own words to his brother.

Vice-President of the Junta entered amid *vivas* and bell ringing, and resolved by this the question of his adhesion or separation from General Córdova's cause'.

Clonard's response was electric: on the 20th he issued a proclamation from Cadiz stating that 'Generals Córdova and Narváez failing in their duties as soldiers, in their oaths as deputies, abusing the confidence of their fellow citizens, blinded by their unmeasured ambition and eager to satisfy personal resentments, have torn aside the hypocritical mask which veiled them, raised the standard of rebellion in Seville and disturbed the peace in these fortunate provinces, attempting to plunge them into a fresh civil war with all the calamities which accompany it. ANDALUSIANS:—Do not give ear to their deceitful words: know that they only try to make you victims of a terrible dictatorship.' At the same time he sent four hundred regulars to Sanjuanena with instructions to put the rising down.

This was too much for Narváez, whose style can be detected in the counter-proclamation issued at Seville on the 22nd, in which Clonard is accused of lying and treachery: Córdova wrote to his brother on the 23rd that 'Clonard is seeking how to associate himself with Espartero' by discrediting the generals at Seville. On that day Sanjuanena entered the city and received the command in exemplary order from Córdova and Nárvaez at a parade of *Nacionales* and regulars in the main square. On the 24th he wrote to Clonard: 'The thing was done as well as could be, nevertheless we were very near to an outburst. For me it was very painful, very painful indeed. Narváez was the one who did most to calm people's minds and make sure there was no opposition in handing over the command. . . .'

The agent Iriarte also wrote: 'Córdova has taken his passport to-day for Madrid, those two are breathing fire against you and shouting that you won't last another eight days in the Captaincy-General. You must take very good care they don't surprise the government.' Both Córdova and Narváez had the right to defend themselves in Cortes, and on 27 November they left Seville: but their prospects in Madrid were not fair. Borrego wrote to Narváez that 'Majority, minority, whites and blacks, all condemn you and our best friends say that you have done wrong, even if there is no crime in it. The common people, and those whose interest lies that way, say unanimously, "*Just you see, Espartero is right, they are wanting a Dictatorship.*" Clonard's proclamation is approved, the reply reviled; the worst of it is, that neither *Moderados* nor *Exaltados* will believe that the revolution you say you have stifled amounted to nothing: on the contrary they say that Serafin [Estébanez] prepared it, Córdova gave it form and you took advantage of it.' He warned Narváez that they would be handed over to a Council of War under Clonard, 'not a judge but a hangman'.[1] Córdova had reached Valdepeñas when he was interrupted by two cabinet couriers who ordered him to return south and place himself at Clonard's disposal; Narváez was confined to Osuña. They awaited trial until it became apparent that their processes were to be separated from those against the other Seville *pronunciados*, and that Narváez's was to be conducted at Valladolid under Espartero's immediate supervision: both fled to Portugal, and Espartero's supremacy was assured.

Clonard's behaviour was rational: it is true that he was anxious to win the approval of the new Esparterist government, and on 25 November he appealed to Espartero through the War Office for two battalions as a reinforcement; but there is no evidence of previous collusion in the Clonard papers—on the contrary, letters from Madrid in December suggest that he was still uncertain of Alaix's approval. The severity of his *Bando* on the 20th is accounted for by his leniency towards Córdova beforehand: he already suspected Córdova of complicity with a revolutionary movement and of duplicity towards himself, but he trusted his good sense if not his good faith. The summons to Narváez was unnecessary for the restoration of order in Seville:[2] Córdova had clearly been deceiving him, and the proclamation exposed his annoyance. He had no ties with Córdova that could have interfered with his loyalty to government. His chief interest was the suppression of radical discontent in the south, and when he entered Seville in December he made this clear by disarming the *nacionales* and imprisoning Cortina. This sympathy with the *Moderado* party at Madrid was based on his feeling for order: his conduct in the Seville affair was also consistent with this.

Fernando Córdova wrote to his brother from Madrid that among the *Moderados* themselves 'there is great interest in you two, and keen sympathy and wishes for seeing end for the common good by this business the compromises in which two of their most principal members are involved; but for the reasons I showed you in the last part when I indicated the principles of this party which you yourself know better than I do—Clonar [sic] is the legal authority, although not the authority *de facto*, and they have to support Clonar as far as they can in this prevalent question because otherwise the principles established and proclaimed by Alaix will be compromised.'[3]

---

1 Clonard MSS., Legajo 29, Borrego to Narváez, 27 Nov.
2 See Clonard to Narváez, 2 Feb. 1841, quoted in *Diario*, Senado, 1851, ii. 64. 'I had to believe that you went with the object of making common cause with the already established Revolutionary junta which from the first attacked the Government of the Queen and the authorities which emanated from it.'
3 Clonard MSS., Legajo 29, Fernando to Luis, Nov. 1838.

APPENDIX IV

THE MILITARY PRESS

AMONG the 330 newspapers issued during the War of Independence (see M. Gómez Imaz: *Los periódicos durante la guerre de la independencia*, 1910) few were issued for specifically military consumption; among these the *Memorial militar y patriótico del Ejército de la Izquierda* (1810–11) and the *Periódico del Estado Mayor General* (1812) were published by the corps concerned, and the *Declaración contra el despotismo militar y contra la criminal interpretarción de las ordenanzas del exército* (Aug. 1811) was anti-military in tone. The true ancestor of this genre was the *Diario Militar* which came out at Madrid during the allied occupation of autumn 1812, and was designed to keep up morale and avoid politics; it lasted for two months.

During the Carlist War the idea was revived with the publication of a purely technical journal, the *Boletín Militar*, which was apparently still being issued in January 1836 but ceased to appear soon afterwards; while the *Guerrero* and the *Compilador Militar de Vizcaya* were defunct before the end of 1835. In April 1838 a more ambitious magazine began the true line of army periodicals; this was the *Revista Militar*, edited by Evaristo San Miguel, the patriarch of military politicians, who wrote in the prospectus—'the nature of this periodical production necessarily excludes from it political matters. There will be no mention in it of Cortes, of government, of administration, no mention of anything or anybody who might be the object of controversy or polemic.' It came out monthly until 1840, and although the general tone remained didactic and formal, essays on military affairs were included which had political implications. In June 1838 there was an article on 'The Relations of an Army with the Executive and Legislative Power of a State': in April 1838 another on 'Military Despotism'; and a number of writers published demands for administrative reform that coincided with some of the complaints of radicals in Cortes. The *Revista* appears to have been the organ of the Seoane group, in that it ventilated grievances and kept up a decidedly Liberal tone without committing itself to a political party: but the controversial articles were sandwiched between heavily instructive material that subsequent journalists found ridiculous. The *Revista* ended with the war: with the anxieties of peace two successor journals were started simultaneously. In March 1841 Captain Eduardo Perotte informed prospective readers of his *El Grito del Ejército* that 'today more than ever before the army has great need of an organ to transmit the faithful expression of its wants and to serve as a tribune from which its lawful demands may be clearly and loudly voiced', and nine monthly issues followed, each bearing the motto 'The Spanish Army has done more for its country than any other army past or present—it has thrice given it Liberty!!! Justice requires that the country do something for the army.' Perotte sneered at the academic tone of the old *Revista*, and promised that he would not be concerned with 'whether the Greeks were formed in close order or open order inside the belly of the Trojan horse'. The second distinguished military journalist produced by the regency of Espartero was Antonio Vallecillo, an official at the War Office, who later became an authority on military law.[1] His *Archivo Militar* appeared in April 1841, disclaiming all scientific pretensions but hoping to provide elementary military education for subalterns, and 'favour the material interests' of soldiers generally; but it soon rivalled the *Grito* in its attacks on the government, and the didactic tradition was carried on in Colonel Busto's *Ejida* of 1842. The *Grito* barely survived the hostility of its chief target, Evaristo San Miguel, now Minister of War: but Perotte was able to continue the publication of the *España Militar* for another year, and from the whole canon of military journalism under Espartero's regency an authentic picture of the views and attitudes of the more articulate officers may be obtained. Just before the rising of 1843 several ephemeral papers seem to have been issued for the use of the men, deliberately inciting them against Espartero;[2] I have found no copies or titles of these. After the rising the *Archivo Militar* became the *Boletin del Ejército*: Vallecillo was replaced by José Marcá Gómez Colón as editor, and in 1846 this title was changed to the *Militar Español*, which lasted until April 1848. Pedro Echevarría's *Observador Militar* ran from then until August 1848.

Meanwhile a superior type of magazine had been started by Colonel Eduardo Fernández San Roman under the old title of *Revista Militar*: this ran from 1847 to the middle fifties: the bound editions usually end in 1853. This periodical came out twice a month and contained articles by leading soldiers on subjects of technical and topical interest. In 1851 it was joined by the more polemical *Gaceta Militar*, the illustrated *Mundo Militar*, and the *Veterano*, designed for subalterns and men: none of which lasted two years. Excluding *Guardia Civil*, colonial, and naval publications, forty-four military papers of various kinds seem to have been issued in the reign of Isabella: the majority technical and very ephemeral.[3]

[1] See Barado, op. cit. 133.   [2] Widdrington, *Spain in 1843*, 266.
[3] The leading corps and technical journals were the *Memoriales* of engineers (1846), artillery (1847), and infantry (1852): the *Academia Militar* (1850), the *Estandarte* (1845), and the *Asamblea del Ejército* (1846, 1856).

A LIST OF PRIME MINISTERS AND MINISTERS OF WAR
1834–1854

The Premiers are printed in capitals: where gaps occur in the succession of War Ministers, the War Office was usually taken by the Prime Minister. Not all provisional War Ministers are included: some were too ephemeral.

MARTÍNEZ DE LA ROSA	15 Jan. 1834–9 June 1835
Zarco del Valle	to 2 Nov. 1834
Manuel Llauder	2 Nov. 1834–24 Jan. 1835
Jeronimo Valdés	17 Feb.–18 Apr. 1835
Valentín Ferraz	18 Apr.–13 June 1835
THE COUNT OF TORENO	4 June–14 Sept. 1835
The Marquess de Las Amarillas	13 June–28 Aug. 1835
The Duke of Castroterreño	28 Aug.–14 Sept. 1835
MENDIZÁBAL	14 Sept. 1835–15 May 1836
Mariano Quirós	14–27 Sept. 1835
The Count of Almodóvar	27 Sept. 1835–27 Apr. 1836
José Ramón Rodil	15 May 1836
ISTÚRIZ	15 May–15 Aug. 1836
Manuel Soria	17 May–8 July 1836
Santiago Méndez Vigo	8 July–14 Aug. 1836
CALATRAVA	15 Aug. 1836–17 Aug. 1837
Andrés García Camba	14–20 Aug. 1836 and 15–26 Nov. 1836
José Ramón Rodil	20 Aug.–15 Nov. 1836
Francisco Javier Rodriguez Vera	26 Nov. 1836–27 Feb. 1837
Facundo Infante	22 Mar.–16 June 1837
Almodóvar	16 June–29 July 1837
Baldomero Espartero, Count of Luchana	29 July 1837
BARDAJI	18 Aug.–16 Dec. 1837
Pedro Chacón vice Espartero	to 21 Aug. 1837
Evaristo San Miguel	21 Aug.–1 Oct. 1837
Ignacio Balanzat	1–4 Oct. 1837

Francisco Ramonet	4 Oct.–8 Dec. 1837
Jacobo de Espinosa	8–14 Dec. 1837
Espartero	14 Dec. 1837

OFALÍA 16 Dec. 1837–6 Sept. 1838

Espinosa vice Espartero	to 17 Jan. 1838
José Carratalá	17 Jan.–20 Mar. 1838
Manuel de Latre	20 Mar.–20 May 1838
Juan Aldama	26 Aug. 1838

THE DUKE OF FRÍAS 6 Sept.–27 Nov. 1838

Juan Aldama	to 9 Oct. 1838
Isidro Alaix appointed	9 Oct. 1838:
provisionally Valentín Ferraz	9–11 Oct. 1838
Francisco Hubert	11–31 Oct. 1838

THE DUKE OF GOR 27 Nov.–10 Dec. 1838
Isidro Alaix

PÉREZ DE CASTRO 10 Dec. 1838–20 July 1840

Alaix	to 30 Oct. 1839
Francisco Narváez	30 Oct. 1839–8 Apr. 1840
Fernando Norzagaray	8–14 Apr. 1840 and 27 Apr.–25 May 1840 (int.)
The Count of Clonard	14 Apr.–18 July 1840

GONZÁLEZ 20 July–12 Aug. 1840
Ferraz

FERRAZ 12–28 Aug. 1840 (with W.O.)

CORTÁZAR 28 Aug.–12 Sept. 1840
Javier de Azpiroz

SANCHO 12 Sept.–3 Oct. 1840
Facundo Infante

ESPARTERO, THE DUKE OF THE VICTORY 3 Oct. 1840–22 May 1841

Chacón	to 10 Jan. 1841
Joaquín de Frías	10 Jan.–21 May 1841

GONZÁLEZ 22 May 1841–29 May 1842
Evaristo San Miguel 21 May 1841–17 June 1842

THE MARQUESS OF RODIL   29 May 1842–9 May 1843
                                                        (with W.O.)
   García Camba   20 Oct.–20 Nov. 1842
   Dionisio Capaz   20 Nov. 1842–9 May   } (int.)
                                                        1843

LÓPEZ   10–20 May 1843
   Francisco Serrano

GÓMEZ BECERRA   20 May–29 June 1843
   Isidro de Hoyos   19–24 May 1843
   Agustín Nogueras   24 May–20 June 1843

LÓPEZ   29 June–24 Nov. 1843
   Serrano

OLÓZAGA   24–28 Nov. 1843
   Serrano

GONZÁLEZ BRAVO   29 Nov. 1843–3 May 1844
   Serrano   to 1 Dec. 1843
   Mazarredo   5 Dec. 1843–3 May 1844

NARVÁEZ, THE DUKE OF   3 May 1844–11 Feb. 1846
VALENCIA   (with W.O.)

THE MARQUESS OF   13 Feb.–16 Mar. 1846
MIRAFLORES
   Federico Roncali   11 Feb.–16 Mar. 1846

NARVÁEZ   16 Mar.–3 Apr. 1846
                                                        (with W.O.)

ISTÚRIZ   12 Apr. 1846–28 Jan. 1847
   Laureano Sanz

THE COUNT OF   28 Jan.–28 Mar. 1847
SOTOMAYOR
   Manuel Pavía   28 Jan.–15 Feb. 1847
   Marcelino Oráa   15 Feb.–28 Mar. 1847

PACHECO   28 Mar.–1 Sept. 1847
   Mazarredo

GARCÍA GOYENA   1 Sept.–4 Oct. 1847
   Fernando Fernández de Córdova

NARVÁEZ   4 Oct. 1847–10 Jan. 1851
   Córdova   to 3 Nov. 1847
   Francisco de Paul Figueras   24 Dec. 1847–10 Jan. 1851

THE COUNT OF CLONARD	18–19 Oct. 1849 (with W.O.)
BRAVO MURILLO	14 Jan. 1851–13 Dec. 1852
The Count of Mirasol	14 Jan.–6 Feb. 1851
Francisco Lersundi	6 Feb. 1851–16 Jan. 1852
Joaquín de Ezpeleta	16 Jan.–13 June 1852
Juan de Lara	13 June–16 Aug. 1852
Ezpeleta	16–31 Aug. 1852
Lara	31 Aug.–27 Nov. 1852
Cayetano Urbina	27 Nov.–14 Dec. 1852
RONCALI (THE COUNT OF ALCOY)	14 Dec. 1852–11 Apr. 1853
Lara	14 Dec. 1852–14 Apr. 1853
LERSUNDI	11 Apr.–19 Sept. 1853 (with W.O.)
THE COUNT OF SAN LUIS	19 Sept. 1853–17 July 1854
Anselmo Blaser	19 Sept. 1853–7 July 1854

BIBLIOGRAPHICAL ESSAY

(1) UNPUBLISHED SOURCES

F.O. Foreign Office records in the Public Record Office, consisting of Ambassadors' Reports in the series F.O. 72 (vols. 367 to 847). These provide a commentary on Spanish affairs in the period from 1830 to 1854, as well as miscellaneous information about the army and finances.

Clonard MSS. The Colección del Conde de Clonard at the library of the Servicio Histórico Militar in Madrid; this contains correspondence between the Count and his friends relating to war and politics from 1835 to 1840, and includes pamphlets and other documents connected with military history.

Papers in the Sección de Estado of the Archivo Nacional (Madrid) relating to army estimates under Ferdinand VII; in particular Legajo 217. 46.

Vaughan MSS. The Spanish sections of the Vaughan Papers in the Library of All Souls, Oxford, which provide miscellaneous and diplomatic correspondence for 1808 to 1824.

Clarendon MSS. The Clarendon Papers on loan to the Bodleian Library, Oxford, for Lord Clarendon's correspondence, etc., from 1833 to 1839.

(2) NEWSPAPERS

The *Gaceta de Madrid* gave official announcements throughout this period, but true newspapers came into being only after 1833. From then until 1854 the *Eco del Comercio* gives the Left-wing view of events, and is joined in 1837 by the more conservative *Correo Nacional*; both are overshadowed in the forties by the Moderado *Heraldo*. Files of these papers may be found in Madrid libraries, but they do not compare for their coverage and reportage with the Spanish news in *The Times*; from 1833 to 1848 (when *The Times* was banned) this was composed by Messrs. Moberly and Irving in a Gallophobe and Whiggish vein. William Turnbull of the *Morning Chronicle* sent back accounts more favourable to the Carlists.

(3) PUBLISHED SOURCES

(The Biblioteca de Autores Españoles is abbreviated BAE. The place of publication for Spanish books is always Madrid unless otherwise stated; for English books, London, and for French, Paris.)

The two indispensable bibliographies are:

J. DEL BURGO, *Bibliografía de las guerras carlistas y de las luchas políticas del siglo XIX*, 3 vols. (Pamplona, 1953–5);

B. Sánchez Alonso, *Fuentes de la historia española e hispanoamericana*, iii (3rd ed., 1952);

and much biographical detail may be extracted from:

A. Carrasco y Sayz, *Icono-biografía del generalato español* (1901);

P. Chamorro y Baquerizo, *Estado Mayor General del Ejército Español. História del ilustre buerpo [sic] de oficiales generales formada con las biografías de las que mas se han distinguido é ilustrada con los retratos de cuerpo entero*, 3 vols. (1851);

N. Pastor Díaz and F. Cárdenas, *Galería de españoles celebres contemporáneos* (1842–6);

Estadística del personal y vicisitudes de las Córtes y de los Ministerios de España desde 29 setiembre de 1833 . . . hasta el 11 de setiembre de 1858 (1858);

Galéria Militar Contemporánea, colección de biografías y de retratos de los generales que mas celebridad han conseguido en los ejércitos liberal y carlista, 2 vols. (1846).

For laws and army regulations:

Novísima recopilación de las leyes de España, 6 vols. (1805–29);

Decretos del Rey Nuestro Señor Don Fernando VII, 18 vols. (edited successively by F. M. de Balmaseda and S. M. de Nieva, 1818–34);

Real Ordenanza en que S. M. establece las reglas que enviolablemente debeu observarse para el reemplazo del exército (1800);

Ordenanzas de S. M. para el régimen, disciplina, subordinación y servicio de sus ejércitos, 3 vols. (ed. A. Vallecillo, 1850–2);

Instrucción para los ayuntamientos constitucionales, juntas provinciales y gefes políticos superiores. Decretada por las Córtes generales y extraordinarios en 23 de junio de 1813 (Mexico, 1820);

Noticia de las órdenes de caballería de España, cruces y medallas de distinción, con estampas (1815);

Colección de Reales Decretos, Ordenes y Circulares anteriores á la publicación del boletín oficial de Sanidad Militar (1855);

J. Vicente y Caravantes, *Tratado de los procedimientos en los juzgados militares* (1853).

(i) 1800–30

For the army of the *ancien régime*, and for all details of military organization, the Count of Clonard's

Historia orgánica de las armas de infantería y caballería españolas desde la creación del ejército permanente hasta el día, 16 vols. (1851–62)

is invaluable; and for the artillery, J. Vigon:

Un personaje español del siglo XIX (*El Cuerpo de Artillería*) (1930);
Historia de la artillería española, 3 vols. (1947).

Details of the status of the military in society and government will be found in:

A. Alcalá Galiano, *Recuerdos de un anciano* (BAE, 1878);
—— *Memorias de D. publicadas por su hijo*, 2 vols. (BAE, 1886);

J. F. DE BOURGOING, *Nouveau voyage en Espagne, ou Tableau de l'état actue, de cette monarchie* . . . , 3 vols. (1789);

CONDE DE CABARRÚS, *Cartas* (BAE ii, 1870);

Campañas en los Pirineos a finales del siglo XVIII 1793–1795 (published by the Servicio Histórico Militar in 3 vols., 1949);

A. DOMÍNGUEZ ORTIZ, *La sociedad española en el siglo XVIII* (1955);

G. N. DESDEVISES DU DÉZERT, *L'Espagne de l'ancien régime*, 3 vols. (1897–1904);

J. MERCADER, *Els Capitans Generals* (Barcelona, 1957);

S. DE MI~ANO Y BEDOYA, *Cartas del Doctor Don* ——— ———, *publicadas en el año 1820, bajo el título de Lamentos Políticos de un Pobrecito Holgazon que estaba acostumbrado á vivir á costa ajena* (in BAE ii, 1870);

H. SWINBURNE, *Travels through Spain, in the years 1775 and 1776* (1779);

J. TOWNSEND, *A Journey through Spain in the years 1786 and 1787*, 3 vols. (1792).

The fullest general history of the War of Independence is J. Gómez de Arteche y Moro, *Guerra de la Independencia*, 14 vols. (1868–1903), while the best account in English is still R. Southey, *History of the Peninsular War*, 3 vols. (1823–32). W. Napier's *History of the War in the Peninsula* . . . , 6 vols. (1828–40) and C. Oman, *A History of the Peninsular War*, 7 vols. (Oxford, 1902) both distort or neglect the political history of the war, unlike the Count of Toreno's classic *Historia del levantamiento, guerra y revolución de España* (BAE lxiv, 1953).

Two pedestrian but sometimes informative accounts are:

J. MUÑOZ MALDONADO, *Historia política y militar de la guerra de Independencia de España contra Napoleon Bonaparte desde 1808 á 1814*, 3 vols. (1833);

B. SCHEPELER, *Geschichte der Revolution Spaniens und Portugals und besonders des daraus entstandenden Krieges*, 2 vols. (Berlin, 1826–7).

M. Artola's *Los orígenes de la España contemporánea* (1959) is an interesting study of the social implications of the war, and the role of the Duke of Wellington in Spanish politics is described in the useful P. de Azcárate, *Wellington y España* (1960) and the Duke's own *Dispatches* and *Supplementary Dispatches*.

Other aspects of politico-military history are illustrated by:

THE MARQUÉS DE AYERBE, *Memorias* (BAE xcvii, 1957);

G. N. DESDEVISES DU DÉZERT, 'Le Conseil de Castille en 1808', *Revue Hispanique* (1907), 66–378;

F. ESPOZ Y MINA, *Memorias del general* ——, 2 vols. (BAE cxlvi, 1962);

A. FUGIER, *La Junte supérieure des Asturies et l'invasion française* (1810–1811) (1930);

F. J. MOYA AND C. REY JOLY, *El Ejército y la Marina en las Cortes de Cádiz* (Cadiz, 1912);

F. PITA EZPELOSÍN, *El Marqués de la Romana. Su influencia en los sucesos de Galicia 1808–10* (1917);

THE MARQUÉS DE SAN ROMÁN, 'El Duque de Bailen. El Ejército español en 1808', in *España en el siglo XIX*, i, 41–79;

J. L. Villanueva, 'Mi viaje á Cortes' (in BAE xcvii, *Memorias de tiempos de Fernando VII*, ii (1957)).

The pamphlets

Apología de los palos dados al Excmo. Sr. D. Lorenzo Calvo por el Teniente Coronel D. Joaquín de Osma, por el licenciado Palomeque (n.d.);

El Exército español destruido por las leyes (Cadiz, 1812, and Majorca, 1813: in fact by M. F. Capabon);

Exposición que hace un oficial subalterno (D. Tomas Fenestra) á sus compañeros de armas sobre la decadencia de los exércitos españoles (La Palma, 1813: also by M. F. Capabon)

illustrate the exasperation of the military with the press and the Liberals, and the Liberal view of the army is expressed in:

A. Flórez Estrada, *Constitución para la nación española. Presentada a S. M. la Junta Suprema Gubernativa de España é Indias en 1° de noviembre de 1809* (Birmingham, 1810);

—— *Constitución política de la nación española por lo tocante á la parte militar* (Cadiz, 1813);

El Duende de nuestros Exércitos, descubierta por un buen patriota (Mexico and Cadiz, 1810);

Mi asistente y yo (Cadiz, 1822).

The only good modern study of the post-war period is J. L. Comellas, *Las primeros pronunciamientos en España 1814–20* (1958), but some account of the leading generals is given in A. Rodriguez Villa, *El teniente general Don Pablo Morillo, primer conde de Cartagena, marqués de la Puerta 1778–1837*, 4 vols. (1908–10), and, more summarily:

J. Rúa de Estasin, *El general Elío* (1940);

J. Sarrailh, 'Un défenseur du trône de Ferdinand VII. Le général Eguia, premier comte du Real Aprecio', *Bulletin Hispanique* (1925), 18–35.

M. J. Quin's *Memoir of Ferdinand VII King of the Spains by Don —— Advocate* (1824) is a slight, but interesting, essay.

The Constitutional Triennium 1820–3 is better treated, but again there is no adequate modern survey; one aspect is covered in J. L. Comellas, *Las realistas en el trienio constitucional*, although from a traditionalist point of view, and the older general histories are equally biased. M. de Quintana, *Cartas á Lord Holland* in *Obras completas* (BAE xix, 1946) gives the view of a Spanish Liberal, and S. de Miñano y Bedoya, *Examen crítico de las revoluciones de España de 1820 á 1823 y de 1836*, 2 vols. (anon., Paris, 1837) that of an afrancesado. E. Blaquière's *An Historical View of the Spanish Revolution* (1822) is the effusion of an English radical, and W. Walton gives the Tory version in *The Revolutions of Spain, from 1808 to the end of 1836*, 2 vols. (1837). Some interesting miscellaneous detail is to be found in Abbé de Pradt, *De la révolution actuelle de l'Espagne, et de ses suites* (1820) and in the disappointing Marqués de Miraflores, *Apuntes histórico-críticos para escribir la historia de la revolución de España, desde el año 1820 hasta 1823*, with 2 vols. of documents (London, 1834), but the best general account of events is probably still contained in H. Baumgarten, *Geschichte Spaniens vom Ausbruch der Französischen Revolution bis auf unsere Tage*, 3 vols. (Leipzig, 1865). Otherwise the course of military politics can best be traced in pamphlets and occasional literature.

For Riego and his rising:

L. FERNÁNDEZ DE CÓRDOVA, *Breve exposición del capitan D. Luis de Córdova* (Cadiz, 1821);

M. FREYRE, *Manifiesto que da al público el teniente general Don Manuel Freyre, para hacer conocer su conducta en el tiempo que tuvo el mando del Egército reunido de Andalucia* (Seville, 1820);

Manifiesto que la Junta de Gobierno de Galicia creada por el pueblo en 21 de febrero de 1820 . . . hace á la nación (Corunna, 1820);

Memoirs of the life of Don Rafael del Riego: by a Spanish Officer (1823);

F. NARD AND A. PIRALA, *Vida militar y político de D. Rafael del Riego* (1844);

R. DEL RIEGO, *Memoria de las operaciones de la columna móvil de las tropas nacionales* (1820);

—— *Carta del Gral D. Rafael del Riego á sus compañeros de armas los generales Lopez-Baños y Arco Agüero* (1820);

—— *Representación al soberano Congreso por el ciudadano Riego* (Cadiz, 1822);

E. SAN MIGUEL Y F. MIRANDA DE GRAO, *Memoria sucincta de las operaciones del ejército nacional de San Fernando* (1820).

For military grievances and the army law of 1821:

Clamores de un militar subalterno (Mexico, 1820);

Declamación de un militar (Mexico, 1820);

Exposición dirijida a S. M. por los oficiales que la firman en Pamplona (1820);

Invitación al ejército americano, by Capt. M. D. B. (Mexico, 1820);

Observaciones que la junta de oficiales del quinto departamiento de artillería nacional . . . hace al proyecto de ley constitutional del egército (Segovia, 1821);

Opinión de la junta auxiliar del arma de infantería, sobre el proyecto de ley constitutiva del egército permanente (1821);

Reflexiones sobre el proyecto de ley constitutiva del ejército presentadas al gobierno por la junta auxiliar de milicias (1821);

L. BALANZAT, *Exposición del estado actual del ejército español, leida en las Cortes ordinarios de 1822 el 4 de mayo* (n.d.).

Among foreign observers, the Italian radical Count J. Pecchio in *Anecdotes of the Spanish and Portuguese Revolutions* (1823) and *Journal of the Military and Political Events in Spain during the last 12 months* (1824) describes the quarrels of masons and *Comuneros*, and M. J. Quin: *A Visit to Spain . . . 1824*, gives a detached view of the clubs and crowd-manipulation of the capital.

For the various Guards mutinies, see:

G. AGUILERA, *Conducta observada por los guardias de la persona del rey arrestados en la mañana del 10 de julio* (1820);

THE MARQUESS DE VILLADARIAS: *Representación dirigida al Congreso Nacional* ... (1821);
Exposición sencilla de los sentimientos y conducta del cuerpo de guardias de la persona del rey ... (1821).

For radical influence in the army, see:

J. MORENO DE GUERRA, *Manifiesto a la nación española y particularmente a las futuras Cortes de 22 y 23 sobre las causas que han paralizado la revolución* (n.d.);

J. ROMERO ALPUENTE, *Discurso sobre el ministerio actual* (Cadiz, 1822);

S. ROTALDE, *La revolución ó hechos sin máscaras, sobre el origen de las turbulencias y discordia de los españoles* (1823).

M. Fernández Alvárez, *Las sociedades secretas y los orígenes de la España contemporánea* (1961) is the only recent study of this subject.

For the final débâcle in 1823, see F. Galli, *Mémoires sur la dernière guerre en Catalogne* (1828)—a disillusioned account of the military collapse of the Liberals: Mina's own memoirs are wholly unrealistic: and G. Mathewes, *The Last Military Operations of General Riego* (1824)—eye-witness hagiography.

For the enlightened despotism of 1824–33, see (E. de Koska Bayo): *Historia de la vida y reinado de Fernando VII de España* ... (1842), which gives a summary of events, and J. Arzadún: *Fernando VII y su tiempo* (1942), for some illuminating material on the King's own policy. See also N. Rívas Santiago, *Luis López Ballesteros. Gran Ministro de Fernando VII* (1945)— a sketch of the career of his leading minister; the chief Liberal martyr of the period is commemorated in L. Saenz de Viniegra (Countess Torrijos), *Vida de general D. José María de Torrijos y Uriarte* (1860). A typical protest against the régime is *La España bajo el poder arbitrario de la Congregación Apostólica* (Paris, 1833), while the Liberal and Carlist views of the events of 1827 are exemplified in:

Les agraviados d'Espagne suivi des notices sur les hommes qui ont joué un rôle dans les affaires d'Espagne, depuis l'abolition de la constitution des cortès en 1823, par F. C. (Paris and Leipzig, 1827);

(A. DURFORT), *Révélations d'un militaire français sur les agraviados d'Espagne* (Paris, 1829).

No study of Zambrano's military reforms exists, but references to army life are to be found in books by foreign observers: viz.:

THE EARL OF CARNARVON, *Portugal and Galicia, with a review of the social and political state of the Basque Provinces* (3rd ed., 1848);

S. S. COOK, *Sketches in Spain during the years 1829, 30, 31, and 32*, 2 vols. (1834);

H. D. INGLIS, *Spain in 1830*, 2 vols. (1831);

(A. S. MACKENZIE), *A year in Spain, by a young American*, 2 vols. (1831);

THE MARQUIS DE CUSTINE, *L'Espagne sous Ferdinand VII*, 4 vols. (1838).

The events of 1832 are examined in detail in F. Suárez Verdeguer, *Los sucesos de La Granja* (1953). For the Carlist view, see the Baron de los

Valles, *The career of Don Carlos since the death of Ferdinand the Seventh: being a chapter in the History of Charles the Fifth* (London, 1835); and for a useful chronology, *Fastos españoles o ephemerides de la guerra civil desde octubre de 1832* (1839).

(ii) 1833–43

The most detailed general histories for this period are: F. J. de Burgos, *Anales del reinado de D.ª Isabel II*, 6 vols. (1850–1)—a conservative view; A. Fernández de los Rios: *Estudio histórico de las luchas políticas en la España del siglo XIX*, 2 vols. (2nd ed., 1879)—a radical view. See also the Marquess of Miraflores: *Memorias para escribir la historia contemporánea de los siete primeros años del reinado de Isabel II*, 4 vols. (1843–73), and two invaluable local histories:

V. Boix, *Historia de la ciudad y reino de Valencia*, 3 vols. (1845–7);
J. Carrera Pujal, *Historia política de Cataluña en el siglo XIX*, 7 vols. (Barcelona, 1957–8).

The *Mis memorias íntimas*, 3 vols. (1886) of General F. Fernández de Córdova are indispensable as a guide to military and political affairs from 1833 onwards, and I. Bermejo's gossipy *La estafeta de palacio*, 3 vols. (1872) is sometimes useful. See also:

V. de la Fuente, *Historia de las sociedades secretas antiguas y modernas en España y especialmente de la Franc-Masoneria*, 3 vols. (Lugo, 1870);
J. F. Pacheco, *Historia de la regencia de la reina Cristina* (1841).

The first Carlist war has been industriously chronicled in A. Pirala, *Historia de la guerra civil y de los partidos liberal y carlista*, 3 vols. (1889), and may also be studied as a whole in F. J. de Burgos, *Anales* (*v. supra*) and in W. Bollaert, *The Wars of Succession of Portugal and Spain from 1826 to 1840* (1870). The following are the most informative works by contemporary foreign observers:

J. F. Bacon, *Six years in Biscay* (1838) (a tendentious account of the fighting round Bilbao by an English radical);
L. Badcock, *Rough Leaves from a Journal kept in Spain and Portugal during the years 1832, 1833, and 1834* (1835) (on the state of the army in 1833);
G. Borrow, *The Bible in Spain* (Everyman ed.);
C. Dembowski, *Deux ans en Espagne et en Portugal pendant la guerre civile 1838–40* (1840);
C. Didier, *Une année en Espagne*, 2 vols. (Brussels, 1837);
A. S. Mackenzie, *Spain revisited*, 2 vols. (1836);

and the anonymous:

Poco Mas, *Scenes and Adventures in Spain 1835–40*, 2 vols. (1845);
Madrid in 1835 . . . by a resident officer, 2 vols. (1836)
(all useful for the state of the country behind the lines).

C. F. Henningsen, *The most striking events of a twelve month's campaign with Zumalacarregui*, 2 vols. (1836);
M. B. Honan, *The Court and Camp of Don Carlos* (1836);
F. Lichnowsky, *Souvenirs de la guerre civile*, 2 vols. (1844);

G. d'Ortasini, *L'Espagne constitutionelle* (1840);

E. B. Stephens, *The Basque Provinces* (1837)

(for Right-wing accounts of the theatre of operations; of which Henningsen's is outstanding).

F. Duncan, *The English in Spain* (1877);

T. Farr, *A Traveller's Rambling Reminiscences* (1838);

C. Shaw, *Personal memoirs and correspondence*, 2 vols. (1837);

F. W. Vaux, *Rambles in the Pyrenees* (1838)

(for the role of the British Legion, of which Shaw witnessed the formation and Vaux the dissolution).

The following is a selection from the large pamphlet literature which was occasioned by the war and the generals:

B. Espartero, *Esposición . . . con motivo del Real Decreto* (1838).

—— *Esposición . . . sobre los sucesos de Sevilla* (1838).

G. de L. Evans, *Memoranda of the contest in Spain* (1840).

Exposición de los sucesos de Sevilla . . . y manifiesto de la conducta observada . . . por los Géfes . . . de Artillería (Seville, 1838).

L. Fernández de Córdova, *Memoria justificativa* (1837).

La Milicia por de dentro, y las militares de las partidas (Cadiz, 1836).

R. M. Narváez, *Al congreso nacional y al público* (1837).

—— *Manifiesto . . . en contestación a las acusaciónes del . . . Conde de Luchana* (1839).

Reflexiones políticas sobre el estado actual de España, por D. Guillermo A. . . . (1834).

Reflexiones sobre la situación de España, y medios para terminar con prontitud la guerra civil, por un ciudadano español (1837).

R. Rodil, *Manifiesto . . . a la nación española* (1838).

—— *Sumaria en averiguación de la conducta militar observada . . . desde 20 de setiembre de 1836 (1838).*

E. San Miguel, *Breves observaciones sobre los sucesos de agosto de 1836 y sus resultados* (1838).

(A. Torrija y Carrese), *Milicianos nacionales ¡alerta! Que la libertad peligra* (1839).

—— *El Guiriguay, los ministros, y Espartero* (1839).

Three contemporary biographies provide much interesting detail: the unfinished *Historia militar y política* of Narváez (1849), the 4-volume *Espartero* by J. Flórez Segundo (1844), and the *Historia científica, política y ministerial* of Arrazola (1850, anon.). The *Memorias documentadas* published by General Llauder in 1844 are worth consulting for his tenure of office in Catalonia, and the appendixes of *Espartero, el General del Pueblo* by the Conde de Romanones include some valuable letters. A. Cánovas del Castillo wrote a study of the political intrigues surrounding General Córdova in '*El Solitario*' *y su tiempo*, 2 vols. (1883), a biography of Estébanez Calderón, and Pio Baroja's books on Aviraneta illuminate the history of the conspiracies. Ex-Sergeant A. Gómez published his account of the La Granja mutiny in *Los sucesos de La Granja en*

1836 (1864), and the anonymous *Las bullangas de Barcelona* (Paris, 1837) provides a highly Jacobin chronicle of urban insurrections.

The revolution of 1840 is itemized in the two pamphlets:

Detalles históricos del celebre pronunciamiento de Madrid, el 1° de setiembre de 1840 por Don M. B. A. (1840);
Reseña histórica del glorioso alzamiento de 1840 (1840);

and the regency of Espartero described as a whole in M. Marliani, *La regencia de D. Baldomero Espartero* (1870).

For the *pronunciamiento* of 1841 see two studies of the political background:

J. M. DE AREILZA, *Historia de un conspiración romántica* (1950);
J. MÚGICA, *Carlistas, Moderados y Progresistas* (*Claudio Anton de Luzuriaga*) (San Sebastian, 1950).

See also Massa y Sanguinetti's *Vida militar y política de Diego León* (1843) and E. Chao's *Historia de la vida militar y política de Martin Zurbano* (1846) for hagiographies of the opponent and champion of the régime.

Further details may be gathered from Córdova's *Memorias íntimas*, Pirala's *Historia de la guerra civil*, and the *Espartero* of Flórez Segundo; see also:

Spain, Tangier, etc., visited in 1840 and 1841, by X. Y. Z. (1845);
NEMESIO DE POMBO, *La situación de España á fines del año 1842* (n.d.).

(iii) 1843–54

The best, and only detailed, political history of this period is A. Pirala's mildly Progresista *Historia contemporánea: anales desde 1843 hasta la conclusión de la actual guerra civil* (1876), which may be supplemented by the disgruntled A. Fernández de los Ríos, *Luchas políticas* for details of opposition activity. E. Vera y González, *Pi y Margall y la política contemporánea*, 2 vols. (Barcelona, 1886), and J. Ordás de Avecilla, *La política en España: pasado, presente, porvenir* (1853), provide radical surveys of events, and A. Borrego, *De la organización de los partidos en España* (1855), gives a *Moderado* survey. The most informative foreign history is G. Hubbard, *Histoire contemporaine de l'Espagne*, 6 vols. (1882); and for local government consult the invaluable M. Fernández Almagro, *Orígenes del régimen constitucional en España* (1928).

For the revolution of 1843–4, see:

Sucesos de Barcelona, desde 13 de noviembre de 1842, hasta 19 de febrero de 1843, en que se levanto el estado de sitio. por Adriano (Barcelona, 1843);
Diario de los sucesos de Barcelona en setiembre, octubre y noviembre de 1843, por unos testigos presenciales (Barcelona, 1843);
Revolución de Barcelona proclamada la Junta Central (Barcelona, 1844);
E. SAN MIGUEL, *Sobre las ocurencias de Madrid desde principios hasta el 23 de julio del presente año* (1843).

S. E. Widdrington's *Spain and the Spaniards in 1843*, 2 vols. (1844) is the best eye-witness account, and for the parliamentary coup of November 1843, see E. Quinet, *Mes vacances en Espagne* (1846).

For the life of the army in this period, see:

F. Barado, *Literatura militar española en el siglo XIX* (1889);

M. del Busto, *El ejército considerado bajo el aspecto político, moral y religioso* (1844);

A. Carrasco y Sayz, *Reseña de la prensa periódica militar* (Barcelona, 1898);

E. Fernández San Roman, *Statistique, organization et institutions militaires de l'armée espagnole* (1852);

J. Ferrer, *La Moral del Ejército* (1844);

Baron de Inés, *El Ejército y los partidos* (1855);

A. López de Letona, *Estudios críticos sobre el estado militar de España* (1866);

J. M. Paniagua, *Elocuencia militar, ó arte de entusiasmar y escitar á las tropas* . . . (2nd ed., 1844);

J. Rodríguez Perea, *Instrucción General Militar para el Régimen, Disciplina y Subordinación del Ejército* (1856);

and for an interesting analysis of contemporary military politics in Portugal:

Autopsia dos Partidos e Guardo-Quedas dos Governos: ou Ensaio sobhe as continuas revolucões de Portugal (Lisbon, 1847).

There is only one good account of life under the *Moderado* régime, T. H. Hughes's *Revelations of Spain in 1845, by an English Resident,* 2 vols. (1845), but there exist the following biographies of its chief men:

Count Adhémar d'Antioche, *Deux diplomates: le comte Raczynski et Donoso Cortes Marquis de Valdegamas, dépêches et correspondance politique 1848–1853* (1880);

A. Borrego, *Historia de la vida militar y política de Don Francisco Serrano* (1892) (a very meagre sketch);

A. Bullón de Mendoza, *Bravo Murillo y su significación en la política española* (1950);

The Marqués de Castell-Florite, *Domingo Dulce, General Isabelino vida y época* (Barcelona, 1962) (full, but trite and over-written);

C. Navarro y Rodríguez, *O'Donnell y su tiempo* (1869) (pious and perfunctory);

Anon., *Biografía del Excmo. Señor D. Manuel Pavía y Lacy, Marqués de Novaliches* (1868);

R. Olivar Bertrand, *El caballero Prim,* 2 vols. (Barcelona, 1952) (despite its curious structure, the only good full-length study of an Isabelline general).

A. Révész, *Un dictador liberal: Narváez* (1953), is an interesting summary of a career that needs a much fuller treatment. The anonymous *Historia periodística, parlamentaria y ministerial, completa y detallada del Excmo. Sr. D. Luis José Sartorius, Primer Conde de San Luis* (1850) is an informative contemporary account of Narváez's henchman, and the rather absurd F. Vargas Machuca, *Vida política, militar y pública del Excmo. Sr. Don Francisco Lersundi, Actual Ministro de la Guerra* (1851), eulogizes one of his protégés. L. Taxonera has written a slight study of *Gonzáles Bravo,* and A. de Urbina, the Marqués de Rozalejo, a more valuable work on Pezuela: *Cheste, ó todo un siglo (1809–1906)* (1939).

For the rising of 1846, see F. Tettamancy Gastón, *La revolución Gallega de 1846* (2nd ed., Corunna, 1909), and the contemporary account by J. Do-Porto, *Reseña histórica de los últimas acontecimientos políticos de Galicia* (1846). For the Progresista view of their leader, see *Espartero: Su pasado, su presente, su porvenir. Por la redacción de El Espectador y El Tío Camorra* (2nd ed., 1848).

For the revolution of 1854, V. G. Kiernan has provided a highly readable narrative in *The Revolution of 1854 in Spanish History* (Oxford, 1966).

For further details, see:

The attaché in Madrid; or Sketches of the Court of Isabella II (New York, 1856);

I. BERMEJO, *Alzamiento popular de 1854* (1854);

F. FERNÁNDEZ DE CÓRDOVA, *Memoria del Teniente Gral. D. Fernando Fernández de Córdova sobre los sucesos políticos ocurridos en Madrid en los días 17, 18 y 19 de julio de 1854* (1855);

J. DE LA GÁNDARA, *Manifiesto de Don ―――― al Pueblo Español, sobre los sucesos de los días 17, 18 y 19 de julio de 1854* (1854);

F. GARRIDO, *Espartero y la revolución* (1854);

J. DE LARA, *Aclaraciones que hace el teniente general D. Juan de Lara, sobre los acontecimientos militares de Madrid en los días 17 y 18 de julio de 1854* (1855).

Since going to press, the whole period covered by this book has been examined and re-assessed in A. R. Carr's *Spain 1808–1939* (Oxford, 1966).

INDEX

Administración militar, see Commissariat.

Afrancesados in 1813, 12 n.

Ahumada, Duke of (Francisco Javier Girón), General (1803–69), 112 n., 127; founds Civil Guard, 128.

Alaix, Isidro, Count of Vergara, General (1790–1853), 37 n., 71, 73; deposed, 74; gazetted War Minister, 82, 163; as War Minister, 85–92; biog., 85, 92 n.; embraces Olózaga, 90; in Senate, 141.

Alava, Miguel de, General (1771–1843), 25 n.

Alcalá, engineers of, 12.

Alcalá Galiano, Antonio, politician (1789–1865), 7, 26 n.; opposes Mendizábal, 62.

Alcaldes, 9, 49; in 1844, 124.

Aldama, Juan, General (1786–1863), 97.

Alfonso XII, King of Spain (1875–85), 148 n.

Alhucemas, mutiny at, 111.

Almeria, volunteers of, 47.

Almodóvar, Count of (Ildefonso Diéz de Rivera), General (1777–1846), 63.

Alojamientos, 4 n., 9.

Amadeus, King of Spain (1830–73), 146 n.

Amarillas, Marquess de las, later Duke of Ahumada (Pedro Agustín Girón), General (1778–1842), 25 n, 48; on Council of Regency, 49; father of Ahumada, 128; as reformer, 156.

Ameller (Ametller), Victoriano, General (b. 1818), 117, 118.

America, 10; reconquest of, 20, 292 n.; reluctance to reconquer, 21, 41.

Angel, Exterminating, Society of the, 29 n.

Anglona, Prince of, General (Pedro Alcántara Tellez Girón y Pimentel) (1776–1851), 19, 48.

Angoulême, Duke of, invades Spain, 27.

Anti-clericalism, 45; in army, 56.

Apostólicos, 42.

Araña, José, Major, 146.

Aranda, Count of, statesman (1719–98),

protects military, 9; introduces freemasonry, 19.

Aránzazu, burnt, 56.

Aravacas, *see* Guards, Meeting of 1837.

Archivo Militar, 108; (quoted) 109–10, 111 n., 167.

Arco Agüero, Felipe, General, 23 n.

Argüelles, Agustín, politician (1776–1844), insults army, 15, 73; minister of interior, 23; as patriarch, 67 n.

Arizábalo, Colonel, 39.

Arquijas, defeat of, 53.

Arrazola, Lorenzo, politician (1797–1873), takes office, 88; his aims, 93.

Arteta, Fermín, Officer, 87.

Artillery, privileges, 2, 26, 35 n., 106; in 1808, 10; liberalism, 26, 35; education, 35 n.; in Carlist War, 91; insulted, 148; journal, 167 n.

Aston, Arthur, Minister Plenipotentiary from 1839 to 1843, 114, 116.

Ateneo, the, 154.

Audiences, 8, 49; suspended by de Meer, 79.

Aviraneta, Eugenio, Conspirator (1792–1872), 73 n., 75 n.

Ayacucho, defeat of, 33 and n.

Ayacucho society, 132.

Ayacuchos, 85 n., 106.

Ayacuchos, Los (novel), 154 n.

Ayerbe, Marquess of, General, 11, 13.

Aymerich, José, General (1774–1841), War Minister, 31.

Bacon, J. F., 57.

Bagajes, see *Alojamientos*.

Baiges, Antonio, Colonel (1797–1843), 118.

Balanzat, family of, 51 n.

Balboa, Trinidad, General, 94, 143 n.

Ballesteros, López, Francisco, General (1770–1833), War Minister, 19 and n; a *Comunero*, 26.

Ballesteros, López, Luis, Finance Minister, 32, 33.

Barcelona, in 18th century, 8; guilds, 50; riots in 1835, 59; under de Meer, 79–80; rising of 1840, 93, 97; of 1842,

PRINTED IN GREAT BRITAIN
AT THE UNIVERSITY PRESS, OXFORD
BY VIVIAN RIDLER
PRINTER TO THE UNIVERSITY